Casebook of Organizational Behavior

By

Andrew J. DuBrin
Rochester Institute of Technology

PERGAMON PRESS
New York / Toronto / Oxford / Sydney / Frankfurt / Paris

Pergamon Press Offices:

U.S.A.	Pergamon Press Inc., Maxwell House, Fairview Park, Elmsford, New York 10523, U.S.A.
U.K.	Pergamon Press Ltd., Headington Hill Hall, Oxford OX3, OBW, England
CANADA	Pergamon of Canada, Ltd., 207 Queen's Quay West, Toronto 1, Canada
AUSTRALIA	Pergamon Press (Aust) Pty. Ltd., 19a Boundary Street, Rushcutters Bay, N.S.W. 2011, Australia
FRANCE	Pergamon Press SARL, 24 rue des Ecoles, 75240 Paris, Cedex 05, France
WEST GERMANY	Pergamon Press GmbH, 6242 Kronberg/Taunus, Frankfurt-am-Main, West Germany

Library of Congress Cataloging in Publication Data

DuBrin, Andrew J
    Casebook of organizational behavior.

    Bibliography: p.
    1. Organization--Case Studies. 2. Decision-making--Case studies. 3. Leadership--Case studies. I. Title.
HM131.D8 1976   301.18'32   76-50655
ISBN 0-08-020503-8
ISBN 0-08-020502-X pbk.

Printed in the United States of America

To Douglas

Contents

Preface

The *Casebook of Organizational Behavior* aims to provide a panorama of absorbing, appropriately complex, modern cases from a diversity of work (and some volunteer) organizations. The cases chosen are designed to illustrate a wide range of organizational behavior concepts and principles — those ordinarily described and discussed in any comprehensive textbook in organizational behavior. The structure of this casebook parallels my *Fundamentals of Organizational Behavior* but also is planned as a companion volume to other current texts in the field. *Casebook* may be used independently, with a book of readings, or supplemented by appropriate journal articles.

A casebook of the nature presented here is intended for use in courses dealing with human behavior in organizations, such as organizational behavior, behavioral science in management, organizational psychology, human relations, and behaviorally oriented management. The cases presented are also for college and university undergraduate and masters level courses, and in programs of management development. Our emphasis is clearly upon knowledge workers (managers, professionals, staff specialists, technicians, and salespersons) as opposed to first-line foremen, clerical and production workers.

The case method has strong appeal to educators and students in diverse fields, including law, medicine, political science, business, and organizational behavior. People attempting to sharpen their skills in an applied discipline welcome the opportunity provided for simulated experience, personal involvement, and experimental learning. Beginners as well as experienced practitioners find pleasure in projecting themselves into a new situation — one they would not see from the inside except for the case method.

Another important advantage of the case method is its time-saving element. Few people interested to improve their skills in managing human problems in organizations, for example, have enough time (or money) to personally investigate 100 different organizational situations. A well-conceived casebook, at its best, can *almost* substitute for direct experience. Cases that fail to stimulate reader interest and involvement because of their blandness, vacuity, complexity, or obviousness, however, are poor substitutes for first hand experience.

All of the cases presented in this book are based upon true incidents in business, governmental, educational, community, and recreational organizations of the past or present. None of the cases presented is a reprint of any that have appeared in other texts or casebooks. Several are amalgams of incidents that have taken place in two or more real situations. All organization names, locations, and personnel have been disguised. When a case researcher other than I conducted most of the investigation underlying a given case, he or she is identified, and appropriate permission has been obtained to publish the case.

Acknowledgments

A number of people contributed to this project. Gerry Deegan, former Managing Editor at Pergamon, suggested that the world needed a casebook of this nature. My students in the MBA program at Rochester Institute of Technology researched and wrote several of the cases, as indicated by footnote. Many of my cases stemmed directly from interactions with clients; thus, the contributions of many anonymous people from a variety of organizations and perspectives are found in the following pages. Once again Lois Smith performed superbly as my manuscript typist. Dottie Miller and Kathy Kulp promptly and willingly executed a variety of clerical chores.

My children — Drew, Douglas, and Melanie — served as constant reminders that effective learning materials must be attention arousing. Marcia DuBrin helped by occupying two roles. A guidance counselor in a school system, she provided me with many useful anecdotes and observations. As my wife, she provided me with large doses of emotional support and evaluative reinforcement.

Lastly, thanks to the staff at Pergamon for their willingness once again to invest time and energy on my behalf.

Andrew J. DuBrin
Rochester, New York

PART I
INTRODUCTION

1
Guidelines for Case Analysis

Cases are written descriptions of human behavior based upon real-life situations. At its best, the case method allows you to simulate decision making and decision analysis in a variety of situations you would not have access to otherwise. Cases are a convenient way of condensing and encapsulating work experiences — provided that the cases are meaningful and the approach to analysis is thorough. At its worst, the case method is a platform for aimless, free floating, undisciplined and uncensored discourse (unstructured rap or bull sessions).

The case method has a high probability of adding to the managerial skills of the case analyst when he or she approaches the task of case analysis in a focused, planful manner. Even that mysterious quality called *managerial intuition* can be improved upon when the person having the intuitive hunches uses appropriate framework and concepts to investigate situations.

Common sense is similarly heightened by a systematic analysis of diverse cases. One reason common sense is so uncommon in organizations is that common sense is essentially good judgment stemming from the results of trial and error in a multitude of situations. What becomes common sense to the experienced practitioner is regarded by the neophyte in the field as admirable wisdom. The case method, when used properly, is an economical vehicle for acquiring common sense about a variety of situations in organizational life.

Realistic, absorbing cases, combined with systematic tools of

3

analysis, give the case analyst a chance to sharpen his or her managerial skills, common sense, and intuition. Such is the purpose of this casebook.

SEVEN SALIENT OBJECTIVES

Educational technology has advanced to the point where many formal learning experiences have objectives. Individual instructors and students will probably formulate some of their own objectives in a case method course, depending upon the unique properties of their individual situations. Jeffrey A. Barach, a marketing professor, has developed a set of performance objectives for case method courses that are coincident with the aims and objectives of most users of this casebook.[1] A person attaining all or most of these performance objectives would undoubtedly improve his or her managerial capability and communication skills.

Decision Making

The student must be able to make the decisions required by the case. Not every question following each case in this book requires the student to make a major decision, but every case involves at least one decision. Many knowledge workers are comfortable analyzing facts about a given decision situation, but only a few people have the courage and self-confidence to actually recommend a course of action. An important performance objective is thus to learn to "fish or cut bait." As stated by Barach, "A passion for passing the buck in favor of discussing profundities is inadequate performance."[2]

Logical Thinking

"The student must demonstrate the ability to think logically, clearly, and self-consistently." Conclusions should follow from assumptions made by the student in support of recommendations

[1] Jeffrey A. Barach, "Performance Criteria Used in the Evaluation of Case Course," *Collegiate News & Views* (Published by South-Western Publishing Co.) Winter, 1974, 75, 19-20.

[2] *Ibid.*, p. 20.

and analyses. "This statement is not dependent upon subject matter, but the definition of what is consistent, what is logical, is subject matter dependent. A student must show a knowledge of what are appropriate fact, assumptions, realities, and the determination of this is subject matter dependent."[3]

Oral Communication Skills

A vital objective of the case method is for the student to acquire skill in making oral presentations to a group of people. Case method courses lend themselves naturally to giving all class members a chance to make a case presentation during the quarter or semester. When small groups are used to analyze cases, the spokesperson or team leader for the group is assigned the task of making a class presentation. Most people contemplating careers in managerial work can benefit from additional experience in speaking before groups.

Improvement of Common Sense

The student should heighten his or her common sense (defined as the capacity to see the obvious and the relevant) as a result of the case method. If common sense were more frequently applied to organizational problems there would be fewer people in work organizations who are frustrated, bored, restless, underutilized, over-worked, or alienated. "A student should be capable of recognizing and putting appropriate weight on the fundamental issues and factors relevant to the case. This objective is so crucial, that it has been said that the total impact of the Harvard Business School education can be summed up as teaching one to apply his (or her) common sense in an administrative context."[4]

Analytic Problem Solving and Quantitative Methods

"The student must demonstrate his (or her) willingness and ability to apply analytical muscle and quantitative analysis where

[3] *Ibid.*
[4] *Ibid.*

relevant. A coherent, self-consistent, basically relevant argument which ignores the fundamental tools of managerial problem solving analysis is deficient."[5] Although the cases contained in a casebook about organizational behavior typically do not present statistical data for analysis, the student should be alert to what types of quantitative analysis might be beneficial. For instance, if a case describes the problem of turnover in middle management, the case analyst might suggest an appropriate research design to discover causal factors underlying this turnover.

A case presents raw data for analysis. In attempting to analyze the case, the student should reach into his or her armamentarium for the most appropriate methodological tool. A real danger exists in overapplying a selected few concepts and theories to almost every case about organizational behavior. For instance, the ubiquity and simplicity of Maslow's theory of human motivation has led to its overapplication in case analysis. Oft repeated is the sentiment, "This case is basically a situation of somebody whose needs for self-actualization have been frustrated. Give that person a chance to be self-actualized and the problem will be solved."

Generalizing to the Broader Context

"The student should be capable of transcending the concrete situation, adding perspective, and demonstrating competence." Most cases have implications beyond the immediate boundaries of that specific case. An important characteristic of an effective case is that it serve as a springboard to broader discussions. Not every case (nor every instructor) requires that the broader implications of a case be analyzed, but this will be a desirable objective for many cases. An important purpose served by the case method is to allow the student to develop some general principles useful in solving other cases and problems encountered in live organizational settings.

Filling in the Details

"A student should be able to make use of available data to form a fairly detailed and well-argued plan of action, or a fairly detailed and well-argued analysis of situations requested for analysis.

[5] *Ibid.*

Although like some of those above, this objective is different in the sense that simply making a decision and arguing for it without filling in the concrete details — the many little decisions which make the main decision meaningful — does not represent a fully successful case analysis. There is a quality of follow-through required."[6]

Similarly, a staff specialist or manager must consider carefully and weigh an array of facts and specific acts of behavior when making decisions involving people. Cases frustrate some people because many of the necessary facts have to be assumed or inferred. Interviewing characters in the cases in order to obtain more details is not possible.

SUGGESTIONS FOR CASE ANALYSIS

Casebooks traditionally present a series of elaborate or brief situations, each ending quite as abruptly as a picture on a screen suddenly gone dark in a movie or on a television receiver. An alternative approach, and the one presented in this book, is to ask a series of questions following each case. Reacting to these questions may seem less contrived to the student than mechanically applying the scientific method to every case. Ideally, questions should serve as probes which do not discourage the use of the scientific method, but rather add new perspectives to a systematic analysis of the case at hand. Questions do not exclude the traditional method of case analysis, but add a new dimension. Whether the traditional method of case analysis (without questions) is used or the questions at the end of each case provide the framework for case analysis, a few experience-based suggestions might prove fruitful to the case analyst.

Define and Clarify the Problem

The initial step in any problem solving situation is to properly define and then (almost simultaneously) clarify the problem. In cases about human behavior in organizations, problem definition and clarification usually involve recognizing and explaining the more prominent patterns of behavior found. For instance, in "The Decimation of Denver Printing" (presented later in the book) the case

[6] *Ibid.*

analyst will anticipate what patterns of behavior will most probably surface when a sudden, dramatic reduction in the executive work force takes place. The dominant form of behavior occurring in another case might be dysfunctional response to managerial controls. Until this major pattern of behavior is recognized, further analysis and recommendations for action are likely to deal with peripheral issues.

Clarification of the problem involves becoming specific about the major behavioral patterns. Assume that a case is primarily concerned with resistance to change. Clarification here might ask such questions as, (1) Which people will resist the change? (2) Why will some people resist the change and other welcome it? (3) What form will this resistance take? — Statements of resentment? Turnover? Sabotage? Espionage?

Apply a Wide Range of Concepts

One introductory textbook in the field of organizational behavior has 2500 items in its subject index. A dictionary of behavioral science terms runs to several hundred pages. Despite the plethora of concepts available (admittedly, some more useful than others) many students confine their case analysis to a handful of basic behavioral science concepts. All of human behavior in organizations cannot be neatly tucked under the rubric of a handful of concepts. The student is, therefore, urged to try a variety of concepts in answering the questions to cases. For instance, instead of stating that a manager in a given case appears to be "too production oriented" in his style, it might be appropriate to note that he has done little to make the path toward goal attainment easier for his subordinates (one aspect of the path-goal theory of leadership effectiveness).

Cases in this book (or any other book of cases familiar to the author) are not written to imply that only one or two variables may be used to explain the case dynamics. Even when a case is presented in a chapter dealing with small-group behavior, it does not mean that no other concepts may be used profitably. In analyzing the problems faced by a work team, for example, it might be profitable to suggest the utilization of a different type of communications network in the group — a variable more nearly relating to interpersonal communication than small-group behavior.

Respond to the Issue at Hand

The case method has the inherent disadvantage of almost inviting tangential thinking. Cases are often springboards for discussing almost anything related to the general topic of the case. One objective stated earlier was for the student to be able to generalize from a specific case to other situations — to look for the general "message" involved in each case. Springboarding of this nature should take place only after the issue at hand has been dealt with satisfactorily. Digressions in case analyses take many forms, but three concrete examples will illuminate the frequent tendency of people to neglect the issue at hand.

• A woman enrolled in a behavioral science in management course made a presentation to the class that involved primarily the problem of finding a suitable location for a franchise hamburger restaurant. The case was included in a section of the course dealing with behavioral aspects to decision making. The student presented an intriguing analysis of how management would have to perform different leaderships styles, depending upon the neighborhood in which it was decided to locate the restaurant. However intriguing this analysis, it did not deal with the issue at hand.

• A young man prepared an analysis of a case about a 45-year-old manager experiencing a mid-career crisis. One part dealt with how the manager found himself in that predicament. Another part dealt with management's attempts to handle the situation. Thé analyst used this case as a platform to discuss how "being nice to people" is a solid theoretical concept, but is an ineffectual way to practice management.

• An older student was assigned the responsibility of presenting his group's analysis of the circumstances dealing with sudden reduction in a work force. Under the pressures of declining business, a mortgage insurance company found it necessary to lay off one third of its clerical and managerial staff. The case analyst presented a lengthy discourse about the importance of tight managerial controls. His reasoning was that with proper controls in the past, the company would not have been in this predicament. Perhaps his reasoning was true, but he was still ignoring the central issue of the case: the functional and dysfunctional consequences of a company laying off one third of its work force at one time.

Make a Few Assumptions

However thoroughly written, cases are at best vignettes of experience. In frustration, a serious student often bemoans that the case writer has not provided enough information for anybody to properly answer questions about the case. Since all the information required to analyze a case (or answer questions about it) is almost never available, the student must assume that certain facts exist or that certain conditions prevail. The case analyst must simultaneously operate as a case writer to a small degree. Making assumptions to fill in for incomplete information is not unique to the case writer. Managers must often use the same process in organizational decision making. Only a limited number of facts are available to make any decision. Here is a sampling of the types of assumptions the case analyst is often forced to make.

• A case is presented about how a family business begins to degenerate after the President appoints his son-in-law Vice President of Marketing. Although the case is 15 printed pages in length, all the facts desired by the case analyst are not available. In order to prepare her analysis and respond to questions about the case, one woman made these assumptions:

1. The President and his son-in-law do not *want* the business to fail.
2. If the President confronts the Vice President with his mistakes, this will not precipitate a crisis in his (the President's) daughter's marriage.
3. Should the Vice President of Marketing have to be replaced, the company would be capable of finding a suitable replacement.
4. The President is accurate in his assessment of the problems facing the business — he is not just finding a convenient excuse to fire his son-in-law.

• Another case deals with the dilemma of a hospital administrative staff when they learn that the resident physicians and interns intend to strike unless working conditions in the hospital are improved. Bad conditions cited include excessive periods of time on duty and too few orderlies to carry the patient load. Among the assumptions the student might have to make are:

1. The doctors are not bluffing; physicians have been known to strike in other situations.
2. It would be extremely difficult to fire the residents and interns and replace them with other licensed physicians.
3. The hospital is working within the confines of a tight budget.

The simple solution of hiring more professional and paraprofessional ward personnel to reduce workloads cannot be quickly accomplished.

In both the family business and hospital cases, the case analyst could have made a different set of assumptions. Which are made is not as important as the fact that certain assumptions are made. Assumptions made should be stated in the case analysis or in response to questions about the cases. Ordinarily only one, two, or three assumptions per case are required to furnish enough information to adequately handle the case assignment.

Empathize with the Characters

An insightful case analyst intuitively empathizes — but not necessarily sympathizes — with the central characters in a case. To develop *a feel* for what is transpiring in a given case, it is important to attempt to see things as they are seen by the principal people involved. Case analysis and role playing have much in common. In order to effectively assume the role of a character in a role playing exercise, you must enter that person's phenomenological sphere ("walk a mile in his or her shoes"). Empathy is possible even if you have had no direct experience in the situation faced by a given character. Sometimes it is possible to relate similar experiences.

- A woman supervisor presented a case analysis about an aggressive young Black man who felt he was being held back in his company because top management did not want Black people in management jobs. The woman claimed one of the reasons she could present such a lucid analysis was because she has at times been the victim of anti-female prejudice.

- A student presented an in-depth analysis of how a special sales promotion failed to win new customers to the company sponsoring the promotion. He explained how he could empathize with the customers who bought the special promotional merchandise but failed to come back as repeat customers. The student mentioned that he does most of the shopping for his family. A strategy he uses to stay within the monthly budget is to shop for bargains, but he does not necessarily return to the store that had the sale once the sale has passed. He argued, "Why should industrial customers feel any strong obligation to look out for the welfare of their suppliers? Everybody shops for bargains, and few people have much concern for the welfare of the company offering the bargains."

• An accountant presented a case analysis of a group vice president (annual salary $75,000 per year) who, in frustration, quit his job to open a bicycle sales and service shop. The group vice president, in his letter of resignation to the corporation, explained that he now perceived his job as a farce. Despite an impressive sounding title, he rarely had any urgent or important problems to resolve.

A common ground of frustration for the executive and the student was that the latter also felt underutilized in his occupational role: "That high flying, high paid executive feels like he doesn't have a real job. My situation isn't too different. The kind of accounting work I'm doing could easily be handled by an intelligent high school student with decent clerical skills."

Formulate Action Decisions

However grim the predicament faced by an organization or its members in a given case, some action decision must be proffered by the student. An important purpose of the case method is to place you in the same situation that managerial workers face daily — the necessity of doing something about a problem. In some instances the decision to "leave well enough alone" may be the appropriate decision.

For many cases it is best to suggest several alternative courses of action — one, two, or three things you intend to do about the situation. The action decisions you choose should stem logically from a careful analysis of the manifest (surface) and latent (underlying) factors in the situation. Assume that a man described in a case is experiencing migraine headaches because of the stresses he faces in his credit manager position. One action proposal that deals with the manifest problem would be to transfer this man to a less stressful job. A proposal that reaches the latent factors in this case would be to suggest a reengineering of the credit manager's job. Perhaps the job is so inherently stressful that most long term occupants of that position will experience stress reactions.

A student in a case course asked "Where do I get ideas for action proposals when I've never really managed anything? How do I know if I'm not recommending something that would be preposterously naive if carried out in an actual job situation?" My answer to this student and others posing similar questions is to use common sense, logic, and direct application of principles of organizational behavior and management. Many of the ideas presented in current texts about organizational behavior or the practice of management are ready for application. Give them a try — perhaps just within the safe confines of the case method.

These same principles can be applied later to an organizational setting when situations similar to the cases present themselves. The feedback received from using these principles of management or organizational behavior (Did it work or not?) will influence whether or not they are retained in the practitioner's repertoire.

Discuss Implications of Action Decisions

Every course of action chosen to remedy a problem in an organization has implications. Some of these implications are positive while others are negative, as described by the concept of functional analysis. Just as management must recognize the calculated risks inherent in any decision, the case analyst must engage in some speculation about the positive and negative implications of each chosen course of action.

Assume you are analyzing a case about a scientist who occupies a central position in insuring that a large scale, highly technical project is completed in time to meet contract specifications. Three months before the targeted deadline, he confronts his boss with the fact that he has been offered a job with another company for $4000 more per year than his current salary. He contends that unless is present salary is matched, he will leave the company within 30 days.

Every action you take in this situation will have implications. If you grant the increase, perhaps other employees will learn that "holding a gun to management's head" is an effective way of obtaining a higher salary. If you deny his request, the project may fail or miss its targeted completion date. Your job may then be in jeopardy and your company may lose a valued customer. Perhaps another action proposal, such as offering to hire the scientist as a part time consultant until the project is completed may be the most promising solution. The implications of this action decision must also be examined. Might this action proposal result in additional scientific personnel in key positions resigning and then offering to complete projects on a consulting basis?

Discuss Implementation of Action Decisions

Implementing a decision is often more difficult than formulating one. Dates have to be set, people have to be informed, and resources have to be allocated to carry a decision through to completion. Every case cannot become a term project, yet a few thoughts about implementation should be carefully described. For instance, after reading a case about a poorly motivated sales force you might decide that a new system of motivating salespersons should be installed. Apparently inspirational talks delivered by tape cassettes and similar exhortations by sales executives have failed to stimulate sales up to the level desired by the company. Your recommendation is to use a more rigorous approach to motivating employees, such as expectancy theory or behavior modification. How you are going to implement your program is equally as important as the motivational system chosen. Are you going to unleash a task force of junior psychologists who will travel around the country administering positive reinforcers whenever your salespersons exhibit motivated behavior? Will you tailor-make an incentive system for every salesperson? Will you, instead, simply coach each sales manager on techniques of employee motivation?

Finally, would you estimate that your cost of increasing motivation will exceed the profit derive from the additional sales generated by the program? Since this question is more nearly an implication than an implementation item, it cannot be discussed until you have speculated about problems of implementation.

Develop New Insights

Aside from its entertainment value, the case method has little justification unless students develop new insights into problem solving as a consequence of working with cases. New insights can be developed in two primary ways via the case method. First, the person doing the analysis might realize that the case at hand has implications for other situations. A subordinate described in one case might rectify an unjust wage differential between himself and another individual performing comparable work by practicing gentle confrontation. According to this basic method of resolving interpersonal conflict, the person of lower organizational rank confronts the higher ranking organizational member about a mistake — in an explicit but not harsh manner. This same method of conflict resolution may be used by the case analyst in his or her work life, or as a method to recommend in similar cases.

Second, new insights develop as the student attempts to use new tools of analysis or concepts to solve cases. As described earlier in this chapter, you are urged to use a wide range of concepts in analyzing cases. Unless you try new concepts, few new insights will emerge. Many case method courses have at least one student in the class who insists, "This is all common sense. If you use your head and treat people like human beings you can solve any management problem." With this rigidity of thought, the student is unlikely to develop new insights into dealing with human problems in organizations.

Rarely will the student be able to comfortably implement all of the preceding nine suggestions for case analysis. These suggestions should be regarded as ideal standards to work toward. Other suggestions for case analysis not described here might readily be substituted for some of the items on our list. References concerning the case method are given at the end of this chapter.

FORMAT OF THE CASEBOOK

Our book rests upon a foundation of cases about human behavior in organizations drawn from a wide variety of settings. Cases in each chapter are chosen to illustrate concepts that fall under the particular chapter heading, but the classification is not rigid. Organizational behavior in practice (cases *are* a form of practice) does not fall neatly into non-overlapping categories. For example, a problem of faulty organizational climate could also be a problem of ineffective interpersonal communication or inappropriate leadership style.

Each case is accompanied by several questions designed to focus the student's attention upon some of the more important issues raised by the case. It is hoped that these questions add focus to the cases, but not all course instructors will elect to use these questions. Many professors and students prefer to provide their own structure to cases.

A list of key references is also presented after each case chapter. The references selected usually refer the reader to an original source about several of the major concepts illustrated by the cases. For instance, in a case that might profitably be analyzed by using equity theory, the reader is referred to an article which describes equity theory in considerable depth.

The Appendix is an annotated bibliography that selectively samples current (1970 and later) sources of information about the topics indicated by the chapter headings. Included in this bibliography are general texts, speciality texts, anthologies and articles. The annotations are designed to serve as guidelines for making a decision about where to invest your supplementary reading time. All of the references themselves provide additional references. Textbooks and books of readings cited in the bibliography are also a convenient source for locating major written contributions to the field of organizational behavior.

REFERENCES

Andrews, Kenneth (Ed.). *The Case Method of Teaching Human Relations and Administration.* Cambridge, Mass.: Harvard University Press, 1960.

Barach, Jeffrey, A. "Performance Criteria Used in the Evaluation of Case Course," *Collegiate News & Views* (Published by South Western Publishing Co.) Winter, 1974-75, 19-20.

Clark, James, V. *Education for the Use of Behavioral Science.* Los Angeles, Calif.: Institute of Industrial Relations, U.C.L.A., 1962.

Harlow, Dorothy, N. and Hanke, Jean, J. *Behavior in Organizations: Text, Readings, and Cases.* Boston: Little, Brown, 1975. Pp. 605-616.

Roethilisberger, F.J. *Training for Human Relations.* Cambridge, Mass.: Harvard Graduate School of Business Administration, 1954.

PART II
INDIVIDUALS

Individuals, rather than small groups or total organizations are the focus of the cases presented in this section. The cases are structured under the general topics of work motivation, the human element in decision making, stresses in managerial and professional life, and political maneuvering in organizations. Despite the apparent logic to this structure, the cases do not belong exclusively under any one topic. For instance, "The Compulsive Career Planner" fits best under the chapter on political maneuvering, but concepts of human motivation and decision making are also helpful in analyzing this case.

Another qualification about the classification of cases in this section is that the study of individual behavior does not preclude the study of group or total organizational behavior. Every individual must be understood in terms of the context in which he or she is functioning. The disgruntled sales representative described in a case in Chapter 4 would have a different problem (or no problem at all) if he worked in a different organizational climate.

2
The Motivation to Work

Case 1
Bruce, the Behavior Mod Landlord

Bruce Charter, a tennis professional teaching at the Seaview Swim and Tennis Club, reached a major business decision. He would invest the $14,000 he inherited from his father in real estate. After combing the real estate pages of the local newspapers and speaking to real estate agents for a three-month period, Bruce decided what kind of property to purchase. With the assistance of Carol Travis, his agent, Bruce took possession of a six-family, 70-year-old frame building in a low to moderate income section of the city.

Margot, Bruce's girlfriend, had some reservations about this business venture. She explained it this way:

"Bruce, friends of mine have gone into the real estate business and most of them have wound up broke. They tell me the whole thing can be a nightmare. If you don't get the right kind of tenants, they can wreck the place.

"Another problem I've heard about is collecting rent. Poor people just don't send you the rent the first of the month, right on time as though they were worrying about getting a bad credit rating. You'll probably be spending many of your evenings knocking on doors trying to collect rent money that has already been spent in the neighborhood bars."

"Margot, I'm well aware of the stories about how landlords have failed in their real estate ventures," said Bruce, "But, I'm going to take a scientific approach to dealing with tenants. I do the same things with my students on the tennis court. I was never a famous tennis player myself, but I'm very knowledgeable about teaching people the right responses. My study of the psychology of learning had made me realize that tennis coaching closely follows the principles of behavior modification."

"In what way?" asked Margot.

"I may be oversimplifying, but it works something like this," replied Bruce. "In coaching a person about tennis, we give him or her reinforcement almost every time the right response is made. Either we say 'nice shot' or the ball goes over the net in the right way, which is a reward in itself. The more I analyze Skinner's theories and apply them to tennis, the stronger the association I see between reinforcement theory and tennis.

"When a person is an absolute beginner, he is also subject to direct application of some of Skinner's ideas. For instance, we use successive approximations. Let's say a man age 40 has decided to take up tennis. We start him off with the simplest task imaginable. We throw him a ball from a few feet away and have him tap it back to us — just to get the feel of the ball on the racket. It works, the guy smiles, he's reinforced for doing something that approximates a tennis stroke. He get's a little reinforcement at every step. Usually, he learns how to stroke a tennis ball by the end of the season."

"What about punishment?" asked Margot. "Isn't that ever used in Skinner's framework?"

"As you know, behavior modification emphasizes praise and reward more than punishment, but punishment of a mild sort is sometimes used. One of my colleagues, Don, screams at people in a good-natured way when they do something awful like standing facing the net when they hit a ground stroke. Of course, seeing a ball go over the fence or dribble off the racket is punishment in itself."

"Bruce, I like your ideas, and I wish you the best of luck" said Margot. "But you're forgetting one major thing. People who take up tennis do so voluntarily. They want to learn. Some of the characters who rent apartments in a building like the one you've bought have no interest in paying the rent, protecting their credit ratings, or in pleasing you. They have no pride. Their values are warped."

"Margot, there is where you are wrong. In Skinner's system, you don't have to worry about values like pride and good citizenship. You just manipulate the environment so you get the right response from people."

"Bruce, your analysis sounds terrific. I can't argue with logic like that, but let's see what happens after you own the building for a while. I hope you do become the first Skinnerian real estate tycoon, but I'm skeptical."

Thirteen months later, Bruce Charter gave a verbal report of his experiences at applying reinforcement theory to real estate management. Margot, intrigued with her boyfriend's behavioral science experiment, suggested the case writer interview him. A full disclosure of the highlights of his experiences follows, at least to the extent that Bruce was able to present an accurate picture of the events that took place.

"After over one year of running the building, I would have to say that I'm mildly encouraged. The events that have taken place during the last year are so complex that I can't give you a categorical 'Yes, it was a success,' or 'No, it was a failure,' response. It's necessary to sort out my observations into different categories. Running a building involves much more than collecting rents and making minor repairs. It's like running an enterprise all by yourself.

"Who your tenants are is one very important consideration. I would assume that if you rent to people who are willing to pay $475 a month for housing, you have a different set of problems than if you deal with tenants on public assistance who are paying an average of about $155 per month rent. Welfare pays the rent for all my tenants, but Welfare sends them the money. They in turn cash the check or mail it directly to me if their welfare payment is the same as the rent.

"I'll begin my explanation of trying to use reinforcement theory at Watkins Street by telling you about the lawn mowing situation. Although the building is hardly a showplace, it does have a front lawn and some grass in the back yard. When I took over the building the lawn and yard were a mess. I made the classical mistake that a lot of people in the real estate business make — I tried to appeal to the pride of my tenants. I told them that they would have a much more attractive place to live in if they took it upon themselves to clean up the yard and mow the lawn. A few of them nodded in agreement, but they didn't seem committed to sprucing up the outside of the house. When no results were forthcoming from the simple approach of appealing to their pride, I made an attempt to change the natural barriers that were preventing my tenants from having a neat and trim yard.

"I invested about $100 in new garbage cans, a set of clippers, and a push lawn mower. I left the mower with the woman who lived in one of the downstairs front apartments. My assumption was that anyone who wanted to take his or her turn mowing could use the mower without having to drag it up and down stairs. Two weeks after I bought the garden equipment and the garbage cans, I made an on-site inspection of the building. The lawn and yard were in passable condition, but only one garbage can out of six was in the yard. At least some progress was being made. I had successfully arranged conditions so that tenants who wished too could do a better job of keeping the outside of the house in good shape.

"I praised the tenants for the appearance of the lawn and asked their opinion about what could be done to keep garbage cans in the yard. One tenant suggested that we use chains and a lock to keep the cans secured every day but on garbage collection day. I took care of that condition for about $12. One night Margot and I were coming home from a downtown movie. I drove by the property and saw that the yard was fairly clean and that the garbage cans were intact. The next day I wrote post cards to each of the six tenants telling them how pleased I was with the appearance of the yard. According to behaviorism, you have to tie the reward (my post card) pretty close to the response that is to be rewarded.

"After about two months of ownership of the property it dawned on me that it paid to take periodic trips to the building. Sometimes I would duck down there in the morning before I went to the club. One purpose of these trips was to give the tenants an on-the-spot reaction to the appearance of the place. It seemed a quick transfusion of praise was enough to keep everything in passable shape for a couple of weeks. Of course, I served another function at the same time, so we cannot say that what I was doing was 100 percent behavior mod. I would spend a few minutes chatting with the tenants and listening to the problems they were having with each other or with the plumbing and/or heating. It would be reasonable to assume that the tenants like the fact that I took a sincere interest in their problems.

"I developed a simple method of dispensing praise or disapproval. I would tell each tenant something like this, 'The porch is real clean. It looks great. But the grass has a lot of dog droppings. What seems to be the problem?' If I bought some paint for a tenant and she did a good job painting a room with it, I would buy her a few more cans of paint (if she wanted them). My approach was taking time and it seemed somewhat childlike. But, it was working.

"By now you must be wondering why I was turning over the supplies to the women, and also dispensing rewards to them, rather than also working with the male tenants. My reasoning is simple. In these families the women call the shots. They obtain the apartment; they pay the rent; they call when there are any problems associated with the apartment — plumbing, heating, or screaming neighbors.

"Even if you were the best applied behavioral scientist in the world, and even if you had the most sincere, trustworthy tenants imaginable, you still are left with the mechanical problems in keeping an old building running. For instance, it's inevitable that a hot water heater will blow every once in a while, or that a faucet will stop functioning, or that a furnace will shut off at three in the morning and not return to normal functioning. You also have to cope with suppliers of plumbing and heating services.

"I try a little behavior mod in this area, too. The first people I dealt with were Conkey Heating and Plumbing, an outfit recommended to me by my real estate agent. My first hot water heater cost me $225 installed. I kind of gulped, but paid the bill without voicing a complaint. Next, I called them to replace a faucet. That bill was about $85. Again I paid the bill without complaining. The next time I had a problem, though, I switched suppliers. I told the man in charge of Culver Plumbing and Heating that I was giving them a try because the people I had been using seemed to be high priced and their work wasn't anything exceptional. Culver installed their first hot water heater for me. I paid their bill of $175 in 48 hours.

"I wrote a note on the invoice, 'Thanks for your prompt and efficient work. I appreciated your fair price. Keep up the good work.' Two weeks later another faucet went out. They replaced it for $50. Again I paid the bill promptly and wrote a note of appreciation. I intend to keep up this approach of dispensing praise and paying bills promptly. Maybe that's the kind of reward suppliers need to keep their prices down.

"Rent collection, obviously, is the mainstay of the property owner's business. If you can't collect almost all of the rent due, you go under faster than a restaurant that's been declared unsafe by the Board of Health. Another consideration is that you can't spend too much time and effort collecting rent. If I have to give up a tennis lesson here and there to chase rent, owning real estate becomes very unprofitable. Also, if I have to worry about rent while I'm supposed to be coaching somebody, real estate has become a detriment to my regular work.

"My first step in collecting rent was to promise each tenant that she would be eligible for a prize if she was paid to date at the end of a six-month period. Four of the tenants qualified for the gifts — a choice of clock radio, lamp, or hanging plant. All chose the clock radios which I purchased through a friend for $13 each. One of the other professionals at the club told me that he thought offering people prizes for paying rent on time would be demeaning their character. My experience was that each of my tenants thought I was a nice guy for doing it and gladly accepted the radios. If their feelings were hurt, they sure are good actresses.

"In over a one-year period I have only hand collected rent about three times. I insist that the tenants mail the rent directly to me. When a rent check comes promptly, let's say within the first four days of the month, I call the tenant to say 'Thanks for the rent. It's very helpful to me to receive the rent on time.' I don't make the phone calls all the time; behaviorists would call this intermittent reinforcement.

"There are times when rent collection does not proceed swiftly or smoothly. I did have to ease one tenant out — my only bad experience. She finally left without my having to start formal eviction procedures, which has to be a landlord's last resort. It can easily cost up to $500 in legal fees, plus you don't get any rent for a minimum of two months. Nobody will send you rent if she knows about the eviction.

"When a tenant is more than 10 days late with the rent, I telephone her a few times to describe the gravity of the situation. When tenants are behind on their rent, they may not answer the phone or one of their children may answer and tell you 'She isn't home.' People are hard to locate when they fall behind on the rent. So I try my stern letter — a form of punishment to be used only in emergencies. My recent collection letter goes something like this:

Dear Mrs. Gray:
    You are now 15 days late in your rent. That means the bank will fine me for being late. When the tenants don't pay the rent, the cost of running this building goes up. That will mean higher rents for everybody.
    If you do not pay your rent on time you will have to leave my building. I like you and your family and I want you to stay as long as you pay the rent.
    Call me right away. This situation is very important.

                        Sincerely,

                        Bruce Charter
                        Landlord
                        244-4048

"There are times when I have to use unusual rewards to get a tenant back on track with respect to paying the rent. Audrey

Thompson, a woman in her fifties, is a hardworking person. She's on public assistance, but she also takes care of elderly people in their homes as well as raising her own three children. If she were a better organized person, she might not be in her present predicament. Her disorganization shows up in the fact that she is chronically late with her rent, despite her good intentions. It would be hard for me to live with myself if I evicted this woman and her family.

"Two months ago, Mrs. Thompson had slipped behind in her payments so that she owed me the December and her current rent — over $300. She kept telling me that she would be caught up soon, but she could never quite get up that past due rent from the month of December. I decided to offer her a substantial reward if she would get caught up with her rent. I told her that if she paid up the rent I would give her a sofa in good condition. (I was contemplating purchasing a new sofa, so I could easily afford to give her my present living room sofa.) Mrs. Thompson made arrangements with her minister who owned a car to drive her to my apartment to pick up the sofa. She arrived 24 hours late, but she did bring $300 in small bills with her. She thanked me profusely for the sofa and for having been so patient.

"When I told Margot about the incident, she said, 'Good play, Bruce, but what do you do next month when you don't have another sofa to give Mrs. Thompson? How will you collect your rent then?' I hope that Margot isn't missing the point of what I'm doing."

Questions

1. What is your reaction to the statement ". . . what do you do next month when you don't have another sofa to give Mrs. Thompson? How will you collect your rent then?"
2. What explanation can you offer other than reinforcement theory for the good results that Bruce Charter seems to be obtaining?
3. To what extent do you think Bruce is "manipulating people"?
4. What other approaches to motivating the tenants to pay rent and keep the grounds clean would you recommend that Bruce try?
5. How appropriate do you think the management approach described in this case might be for managing a large apartment complex with tenants from higher socioeconomic groups?

Case 2
The Elusive Quota *

"If you'll excuse the pun," said Kevin Graham, "I'll tell you about a sales team in the metal industry that is all bent out of shape. Since I am one of the salesman involved, I may be distorting some of the facts. Perhaps even placing too much blame on management. In any event, I will try to present a description of what happened in as objective a manner as possible.

"The packaging division of a large aluminum producer, Vital Metals, Inc., is organized into five geographical areas for sales purposes. Each of these major areas is, in turn, subdivided into smaller units called districts. Each district follows a traditional sales office arrangement. Four or five sales personnel (up until the last few years virtually all Vital Metal field sales people were male) plus an office secretary report to a sales manager. Sales service personnel, including troubleshooters and sales engineers, are located at the regional level. In general, field sales personnel receive adequate support from the region when sticky customer problems arise. Shipments are a major problem in our industry, but thanks to a sophisticated inventory control and order entry system, our customers seem to get what products they want at the time they want them.

"Let me explain about the compensation plan. Here is what my story is really about. The sales people are salaried, but each salesman

*John H. Gooch conducted the research for this case and is responsible for most of its writing.

or saleswoman can increase his or her total remuneration by means of the company incentive plan. This plan provides a bonus, payable at the end of the year, based upon how well the sales district as a whole performs against a quota. This quota is a dollar volume sales figure. For every percentage point over 85 percent of quota that the district achieves, each sales person within the district receives one percent of his average yearly salary up to a maximum of 33-1/3 percent. Therefore, in a good year, a salesman on a $20,000 annual salary might receive a $4000 bonus — a sizeable chunk of change. If the maximum were reached, this same person might gross close to $27,000 for the year, including bonus.

"Early in the year the sales manager for the Hartford, Connecticut sales district called his five salesmen together (we had no saleswomen in that district at the time) to announce what sales quota had been received from headquarters. Although slightly higher than expected, the district members enthusiastically went about formulating plans to achieve the maximum payoff. Due to some unfortunate circumstances leading to a loss of several large orders the previous year, the last payoff was rather disappointing. Two of our biggest customers had major contract cancellations, forcing them to cancel orders with us. As frequently happens with sales people, several of us had already spent the bonus that we never received. It's not unusual for a salesman to purchase a color TV he cannot afford on the way home from a customer's agreement to place a big order. Later when the customer changes his mind, the salesman may be overburdened with debt.

"Every salesman in our office was determined to make up for the previous year's mediocre performance. Target accounts that had better than average potential were singled out for special effort. Obstacles were identified and strategies developed to overcome them. Each of our salesmen left that initial meeting eager to do his part in order for the district to meet its goals. The feeling quickly developed that the result of the added effort would be the maximum allowable bonus at the end of the year for each member of the sales team. Tony, a veteran with the company, expressed it this way, 'I was beginning to wonder where I could come up with the cash to send my oldest daughter to college. Our new quota may be the answer.'

"The district jumped off to an excellent start by landing several target accounts right away. At the end of the first quarter, another sales meeting was called. According to the figures presented, the group was already ahead of forecast. The nation's economy was in one of its periodic upsurges. As the economy expanded at a rapid pace, the demand for aluminum products far exceeded the available supply.

"These prosperous conditions remained almost unchanged until late in the summer when a slackening in demand became apparent. Almost as though a spigot was turned off, early in the fourth quarter the economy seemed to come to a crunching halt. Order delays and cancellations poured in as customers frantically tried to react to the new situation. Although the fall-off in demand was having a significant effect on the Hartford district's sales, they were far enough ahead of quota at that point to coast the rest of the way.

"Suddenly, in early December, top management announced that due to the need to compensate for the extraordinary inflationary pressure experienced during the year, all of the quotas would be revised upward. Unbelievably, our targets had shifted right in the middle of the game. The quotas that everyone had been shooting for all year long were changed. Nobody on the sales force believed something like this would happen. Although the incentive plan allowed management to make such adjustments, it had never done so before.

"Unanimous reaction to this decision was astonishment, frustration, and anger. Chris, the youngest salesman in the office, lamented: 'It's as if management was looking for a good way to turn us away from the company. I've heard before that sometimes a company will make life unbearable for people in order to get them to resign. I wonder if that's what's happening here?'

"Although the Hartford District finished the year only slightly below the original quota, after the adjustment was made each man received only about half the bonus he had anticipated. It was as if somebody learned that management had been putting pollutants in the water cooler. The effect this management action had on sales force morale was drastic. It became obvious that salesmen stopped hustling as much as they had previously. Quotas for this year haven't been assigned yet, although nearly half of the year is already past.

"More surprising than the fact that quotas haven't been assigned is that nobody seems particularly disturbed about it. Quotas used to be the major topic of conversation every year. The group incentive plan seems to have completely lost its usefulness as a tool to increase sales. No longer do the salesmen feel reasonably sure that hard work will lead to the promised bonuses.

"It's my analysis that top management will have to start all over again and come up with a new incentive plan. Even then it will take a lot of selling before the salesmen will have faith in the new incentive system.

A lot of damage has already been done.

"What I find so puzzling about the changes in our incentive system is that top management doesn't believe anything is wrong. A marketing executive who visited our office told us, 'You fellows have to learn to roll with the punches. We can only stick with a plan until conditions change. Inflation has made it necessary for us to adjust our sales quotas. We're still running a business around here.' "

Questions

1. What might management have done to prevent the negative reaction to changing the sales quotas?
2. Did Vital Metals management overemphasize financial incentives in dealing with their sales personnel? Explain your answer.
3. Should management have changed quotas despite the impact of inflation?
4. Does management now need a new incentive plan for its sales personnel?
5. What should be done to get salesmen "moving again" (remotivate the sales force)?

Case 3
Why Do I Need a License to Get Ahead? *

Engineer Kurt Hayes, after many years of industrial experience, is now employed by the state government. Aged 37, he has a wife and two children. His bachelor's degree in electrical engineering was obtained from Purdue University. Although an engineering supervisor, he is also involved in some design work in his field. He is well regarded by his superiors, as reflected in his performance appraisals.

Kurt left private industry in a quest for job security. A victim of two layoffs in previous years, he felt he could not risk another layoff at this time in his career.

The company for which Kurt worked prior to his joining the governmental agency did not require a Professional Engineering License (P.E.) for job advancement. Such licensure was recognized, however, in that Professional Engineers commanded higher starting salaries than engineers who did not possess that designation. However, an individual who did not hold a P.E. could advance on the basis of his or her performance record.

Kurt worked for the State Engineering Authority for three years. The S.E.A. involves itself in all phases of engineering for a city of 400,000 population. The technical personnel employed by the agency includes engineering aides, and various technical and professional classifications. A person may rise to the highest level of the

*Peter L. Grassadonia conducted the research for this case.

technical classification without a college degree, but a bachelor's degree in engineering is required for further advancement. A "college degreed" engineer is allowed to advance one step beyond the technical level classification, but the agency requires a Professional Engineering license for promotion to the highest level. An exception to the P.E. requirement exists at the top of the organization. Several senior executives in the Agency have advanced to the top without the benefit of P.E. licensure.

Governmental agencies performing similar kinds of work to the engineering agency (and the medical departments) do not have licensing requirements for advancement beyond the technical classifications. Employees of those agencies (such as city planning and specialized administrative functions) interface with engineering on almost a daily basis.

Kurt Hayes expresses his thoughts about his compensation in this manner: "My input in terms of dreaming up successful designs, holding up my own on routine engineering work, and still running a good sized department is worth a lot more than the money I receive. My job is good, even exciting at times, but I am very discouraged about the pay I'm receiving. There are actually other engineers in this agency who hold the same job title as I do, yet they are doing less work and have less formal responsibility.

"What really gets to me though is the handful of people with P.E. certificates hanging on their walls with bigger jobs than mine, yet they are doing less important work than I do. One P.E. only supervises two people and he rates a higher job classification than I do.

"I never pursued a P.E. license because it is viewed as somewhat of a frill in a business environment. Right now I'm blocked from further advancement in S.E.A. Yet there is an urgent need for people of my abilities at higher levels in the agency. The way I see it, a qualified person should be allowed to travel as far up the organization as his talents will take him.

"My immediate superior, Gus, and I have gone round and round on this issue. I've told Gus that the agency is really using a double standard here. Some people in key positions do not have P.E. certification. Gus tells me the reasoning behind the license is to give assurance by examination and state approval that a person so licensed be qualified to certify a design and the integrity of that design. Kind of a quality control function.

"My point of contention is that it seems superfluous to have people reporting to a supervisor with the ability to certify when the supervisor himself has that ability. In fact, the supervisor has to seal each project personally anyway. Other agencies comparable to ours in professional status do not have this requirement. They don't throw roadblocks to advancement in those agencies.

"All I get is aggravation from discussions about this topic with Gus. He gives me the bureaucratic routine. Something to the effect that the certification of professionals is the criteria set up by the organization. According to Gus, certification as a Professional Engineer as a precondition for advancement is part of the system in every state governmental agency that employs engineers. He tells me that policies such as these must be strictly adhered to.

"I wonder if Gus or anybody else who outranks me in this agency really understands my point. Although I swore to myself and my family that I would never consider relocation again, I must give some serious thought to exploring the options available to me outside of the State Engineering Authority."

Questions

1. What would you advise Kurt Hayes to do next?
2. What is the essential inequity that Kurt Hayes perceives?
3. What should Gus do to recapture Kurt's enthusiasm for the job?
4. Should the State Engineering Authority change its policy about the P.E. license as a qualification for advancement? Explain your reasoning.
5. Should the State Engineering Authority provide support for obtaining the P.E. license such as offering to pay for refresher courses for the exam? Why or why not?

REFERENCES

Deci, Edward L. *Intrinsic Motivation.* New York: Plenum, 1975.

Durand, Douglas E. "Effects of Achievement Motivation and Skill Training on Entrepreneurial Behavior of Black Businessmen," *Organizational Behavior and Human Performance,*" Vol. 13, August 1975, 76-90.

Fein, Mitchell. "Job Enrichment: A Reevaluation," *Sloan Management Review,* Vol. 15, Fall 1973, 69-88.

Finn, R.H. and Lee, Sang M. "Salary Equity: Its Determination, Analysis, and Correlates," *Journal of Applied Psychology,* Vol. 56, August 1972, 283-292.

Greene, Charles N. "Causal Connections Among Managers' Merit Pay, Job Satisfaction, and Performance," *Journal of Applied Psychology,* Vol. 58, June 1973, 95-100.

Kesselman, Gerald A., Hagen, Eileen L. and Wherry, Sr., Robert J. "A Factor Analytic Test of the Porter-Lawler Expectancy Model of Work Motivation," *Personnel Psychology,* Vol. 27, Winter 1974, 569-579.

Lawler, III, Edward E. "Job Attitudes and Employee Motivation: Theory, Research, and Practice," *Personnel Psychology,* Vol. 23, Summer 1970, 223-237.

Lawler, III, Edward E. *Motivation in Work Organizations.* Monterey, California: Brooks/Cole, 1973.

Meyer, Herbert H. "The Pay-for-Performance Dilemma," *Organizational Dynamics,* Vol. 3, Winter 1974, 39-50.

Slocum, Jr., John W. "Motivation in Managerial Levels: Relationship of Need Satisfaction to Job Performance," *Journal of Applied Psychology,* Vol. 55, August 1971, 312-316.

Work in America: Report of a Special Task Force to the Secretary of Health, Education and Welfare. Cambridge, Mass.: The MIT Press, 1973.

3
Behavioral Aspects of Decision Making

Case 4
Can Backyard Gossip Condemn Me?

Olaf Scher nervously opened his awaited letter from South-western Metal Products Incorporated. Several days overdue, this letter could be the turning point in Olaf's quest for a more challenging job. He turned his back toward his wife and children in order to more carefully attend to the contents of the letter. Olaf's feelings turned from eagerness to bewilderment as he worked his way down the letter. It read:

Dear Mr. Scher:

My staff and I at Southwestern were favorably impressed with your qualifications for employment as Manager of Manufacturing Services, and we appreciate having had the opportunity to interview you for this position. However, a decision like this is not an easy one to make. We finally decided to fill this opening with an individual whose background more closely fits the job description.

We will be back in touch with you should a new position open up here that more closely fits your qualifications. Best of luck in obtaining the right position for yourself.

Cordially,

Marshall Goulden
Vice President, Manufacturing

After shaking off the initial feelings of discouragement, Olaf gave some careful thought to this latest letter of rejection. He reasoned that Marshall Goulden's letter could not be an accurate description of the reason he was turned down for Manager of Manufacturing Services. The job represented a one step jump in responsibility over his present position. In discussing the job with the President and the Manufacturing Vice President, both were pleased that he had relevant experience in every manufacturing function that would report to him. Besides, one of Goulden's initial comments was how pleased he was with Olaf's work experience — that it represented the kind of "hands on" exposure the company needed in this job.

With these thoughts in mind, Olaf telephoned Marshall Goulden the next day. To his surprise, Goulden did not seem to avoid his call. Olaf began the conversation.

"Marshall, this is Olaf Scher. I was somewhat disappointed by your letter of rejection. Somehow it doesn't satisfy me. I guess you could say I don't buy it completely."

"Gee, that's too bad," replied Marshall, "we could only fill that job with one person, as much as we liked you as a person."

"My concern is not so much that I didn't get the job," said Olaf. "What I'm worried about is the reason you rejected me. It's just hard to understand. Could I possibly make an appointment to see you about this matter?"

Marshall Goulden obliged, and Olaf and he met in Goulden's office two days later. Olaf decided he would not hold back any of his concerns since no chance remained of his obtaining the position as Manager of Manufacturing Services at Southwestern Metal Products.

"Marshall, could you please tell me, off the record, why I was turned down for this position? I promise not to pass our conversation on to anybody else."

"Olaf, you were turned down because we found somebody else with reasonably stronger qualifications than yours for the job. Isn't that what we told you in the letter?"

"Yes, that is what you told me in the letter, but it is not very convincing. I've ruminated over that one for three days now, and the reason just doesn't hold water."

"As you know from your own business experience, Olaf, there is never only one reason for giving a job to one person over another. It is possible that another thought might have passed through the minds of Jay (the President) and myself. But basically we did find somebody with experience as Manager of Manufacturing Services at a competitive company."

"Marshall, let's level with each other. It appeared that you and I got along well in the interviews and during my plant tours. Everything seemed to be all set in terms of my getting this job. It wouldn't be so disturbing to me except that this is the second fine job that has slipped through my fingers this year. I've got to know if I'm doing something wrong."

"To my knowledge, you are not doing anything wrong," responded Marshall. "You have a pretty good background; I would say there is not too much for you to worry about. Maybe you will have better luck next time."

Olaf replied, "Marshall, do me a favor. Review my file with me here and now. I know that if I wanted to get testy about it, I would have the legal right to see all the information you have collected about me. But instead of my using a legalistic method, how about your giving me the information I want on a friendly, informal basis?"

"Okay, Olaf. Let's do this systematically. I'm kind of interested in what goes into a selection decision myself. First, here is your application blank listing a lot of vital information about you. It looks pretty good, and your experience is certainly appropriate for the job."

"That's just what I thought," interrupted Olaf. "I'll bet it was the psychologist's report. She and I seemed to get along well during the interview, but maybe she came up with some unusual finding on the test results."

"No," said Marshall, "her summary report says that you are well qualified for the job and she recommended you."

"What about the impressions that you, the President, and the Personnel Manager had of me? Was there anything too deviant there?"

"On the contrary," answered Marshall, "you made a favorable impression across the board. However, a selection decision has to also consider background factors about a person. These days you have to check out everything. Any serious red flag, and we are obliged to turn down a job candidate."

"Are you getting to the truth now, Marshall? Did you uncover any 'red flags' about me. I'd sure like to know what they are. To my knowledge, I have a fine background. My military service was undistinguished, but I had no trouble. I have no criminal record. My furniture or car has never been repossessed. What are you talking about?"

"Sometimes, Olaf, we have to rely on outside information to give us a full picture about a job candidate. We are not in a position to challenge the type of sensitive information that such a report can furnish."

"What are you talking about?" Olaf anxiously asked. "What kind of sensitive information have you uncovered about me? I just can't imagine what in my background could fit the category of sensitive information."

"Your Consumer Reference Bureau report was not very favorable," replied Marshall. "There was some information there that made us think twice about hiring you. It was nothing criminal, just some indicators that perhaps we should look further for another candidate."

"Now that we've gone this far, Marshall, please let me see those reports. I'm very skeptical that Consumer Reference Bureau could have anything derogatory about me in their files."

"Let me read you exactly what they found. A field investigator prepared a fresh report about you, so we figure it's current. We use them in hiring just about every employee in this company. We have found them to be reliable."

Marshall pulled an orange-colored report from Olaf's pre-employment folder. He slowly read the derogatory findings to Olaf.

"One neighbor reports that although Mr. Scher is a good family man, he is known to date women other than his wife, somewhat on a regular basis. It has been rumored that the Schers may split because of this. It is also rumored that Mrs. Scher would want a substantial settlement from Mr. Scher, putting him in an unfavorable financial position should the divorce or legal separation come to pass.

"A former business associate reports that Scher can become argumentative if he has one drink too many. Once they were asked to leave a restaurant because of Scher's boisterous behavior.

"Jefferson Appliance Store says that they were in dispute with Scher over payments for a color T.V. He refused to make the last few payments until they replaced a major tube. They claim that this was not part of the warranty.

"Home Finance Corporation contends that he did not repay his full loan because of a dispute over the amount of interest charged."

Olaf responded with a smile that partially covered his anger. "Come now, Mr. Goulden, you don't take those reports from the Consumer Reference Bureau seriously. A cousin of mine used to work for them before she quit in disgust. She told me two very interesting facts about them. For one, the field reporters are so over-worked that they fictionalize many of their reports just to keep up with the work load. They sit at their desks and make up things about people, figuring that the person being investigated will never get to see the report.

"Even worse, they operate a little like highway state troopers are alleged to operate. They have a certain quota of negative information to turn up per week, just as the troopers have to turn in a few speeding violators. The way Consumer Reference Bureau figures, if they never turn up any negative information about people, they will lose their customers. Maybe I got zapped because the investigator was overdue to write a negative report. .

"What concerns me as much as the fact that I didn't get this job is the weight you put on these cockamamie reports. What is society coming to? Can backyard gossip condemn me?"

Questions

1. How much emphasis should the executives at Southwestern Metals have placed upon the Consumer Reference report?
2. What should Marshall Goulden have done after he listened to Olaf Scher's comments about the Consumer Reference Bureau?
3. What emphasis should be placed upon background checks in making management selection decisions?
4. What should Olaf do about the negative report about him on file at the Consumer Reference Bureau?
5. Would you consider the information obtained by the Consumer Reference Bureau to be objective or subjective information? Explain.

Case 5
Creativity Requires
the Right Atmosphere

"Mr. Farnsworth, tell me about the size of your business," said Honey Levine, business reporter for a nationally circulated trade magazine. "Actually how big is the Maxwell restaurant chain?"

"My latest estimate is that our total annual sales volume is at the rate of $890 million. That's approaching $1 billion, and the figure improves every day. We are a worldwide operation, with outlets throughout the non-communist world. But we are concentrated in the United States, Canada, and Western Europe. As of this morning we had 2300 outlets. By this afternoon we will probably have added one or two more outlets. We are a moving, pulsating, dynamic, exploding operation. It is a true figure that over seven billion Maxwell Mini-Subs have been consumed by people."

"Mr. Farnsworth, we in the business writers community cannot help but admire the success of your empire. We recognize that the failure rate is very high in the fast food franchise business. Could you speculate about the factors that underly the success of your business?"

"Honey, I do not have to speculate. I *know* the reasons for our success. It's a simple case of creativity. Our small corporate staff is very creative. You have to be creative to prosper in this field. Applied creativity is undoubtedly the number one success factor in our business. I'll give you a few examples of the creative approaches we have used to promote our Mini-Subs, Maxade, and the total concept of our restaurants.

"One simple, but effective, example is our 'Q.S.T.' campaign. Every employee of our firm, from Maxwell Farnsworth down to the minimum wage floor mopper, wears a button whose initials signify our business motto: Quality, Service, Tidiness. And let me assure you, we are tidy around Maxwell's. Our team of field inspectors makes sure that every Maxwell location and every Maxwell employee is tidy looking. Anybody with an open sore is sent home for the day, usually with pay. Our refuse cans are shiny white enamel. Our dumpsters out back are also shiny and white. We will take a franchise away from an operator who violates our Q.S.T. code. It's written into the original contract.

"Our Mini-Sub University is also a creative concept. We train potential franchise operators on every last detail of our operation. People take our course work quite seriously in their 10-day program at our university headquarters. Everybody leaving here knows the precise thickness of the slice of ham, and every other ingredient that goes into a Maxwell Mini-Sub. They also know exactly how many shakes of oil are placed on top of the open sub. It's a precision operation. We want to insure that the Kansas City school teacher who visits Honolulu will be guaranteed a Maxwell sub there as tasty as the one she gets back in Kansas City.

"Perhaps our creativity reaches its greatest heights in our special promotions. In our business you need an ever changing number of promotions and special events. A Maxwell shop should be a happening, a place to go for excitement and adventure. One very successful promotion was 'Grandparent Day.' Every grandparent, accompanied by his or her grandchild or grandchildren on a given Wednesday from opening to closing, could order a sub for 10¢. Grandparent Day was a huge success. We wound up capturing a lot of the senior citizen business. Most chain restaurants make no special attempt to attract older people.

"The wildest promotion we ever had was in Columbus, Ohio. One of our executives selected Columbus as the site for trying out a 'Mini-Sub Submariner Look-Alike Contest.' Submariner, of course, gets right at the nostalgia kick. He was a superhero of the original Batman era. The three kids our judges decided looked the most like Submariner received a $50 gift certificate at Maxwell's. We received a good deal of T.V. and newspaper publicity on the basis of that promotion. A couple of local disc jockeys and Miss Ohio State judged the contestants."

"Maxwell, it's important for me to comment here that rumor has it you use very unconventional methods to bring about creativity in your staff. Is that true?"

"Honey, that is absolutely correct. Most people are not creative. That means that you have to set up the right atmosphere to induce creativity. Suppose I just issued a corporate directive that I wanted everybody to be creative in their jobs. Predictably, the response would be zilch. You need specialized techniques. All of our approaches to bringing about creativity are not unique, but some are.

"Our corporate Think Tank is certainly unique. When an executive has a creative assignment, he or she is urged to give our Tank a try. It consists mainly of a huge waterbed, some 12 feet in diameter at the bottom of a tank. The executive is supposed to lie on the bed alone until he or she comes up with a creative solution to the problem at hand. It seems to me that our Grandparent Day promotional stunt came out of the Think Tank. Even when an executive does not get the idea that he or she is seeking right away, it tends to clear one's head for later problems. Twenty minutes in the Think Tank and you are refreshed. Something like Transcendental Meditation.

"A very popular creativity inducing technique is our head massage. We have a young woman who gives an executive a gentle head massage in the privacy of his own office. So far no woman corporate staff executive has availed herself of this service. Melinda, the woman we call in for the massages, claims that the massaging stimulates the passage of blood through the brain cells, thus energizing one's thinking capacity. I find that the experience certainly does clear the mind. It seems to erase distracting thoughts.

"Another approach to bringing about creativity similar to the Think Tank, is our No Distraction Room. Some call it solitary confinement. We have a room about 20 feet square, with pastel blue walls, and no furniture in it but a wire chair, something like what you might find in an old-fashioned candy parlor. According to the rules we have established, the executive entering this room is forced to concentrate on the problem at hand. No telephone messages, no distracting gazes at the outside world. It seems to work. Our special holiday promotion of subs in Christmas gift wrapping paper came out of the No Distraction Room."

Honey Levine, not content to base her story entirely on the perceptions of the company president, requested that she be allowed to interview a few executives to get their ideas on Maxwell Farnsworth's approach to fostering creativity. Howard Boyle, Vice President of Field Inspection had praise for Maxwell's unconventional approach to eliciting creativity from his subordinates.

"It would be fair to say that Maxwell is on to something important. Without his extra special emphasis on using your creativity, you could easily get trapped into solving every business problem in a mechanical way. When you're rushing from meeting to meeting, it's hard to be creative. Before Farnsworth came up with the Think Tank idea, I used to do all my thinking at home. I figured you didn't have time to think on the job. But thinking at home wasn't all that easy either. There are all kinds of distractions at home also. If you aren't shuffling papers other people in the family think you aren't working. People somehow don't equate thinking with working.

"Now, thinking is a formalized activity at the office. You are given a separate place to think in an atmosphere that helps you become creative. I wouldn't be surprised if Maxwell Farnsworth goes down in history as the man who brought creativity to the fast food business."

An executive who asked Honey Levine for anonymity had another view of the creativity inducing programs at Maxwell's Mini-Subs: "Face it, this is a modern day reenactment of the fairy tale, 'The Emperor's New Clothes.' In that story everybody knew that the Emperor was mistaken, that he was really naked and not dressed in fancy clothing, but nobody would face up to the fact. Maxwell Farnsworth is a great guy, but his ideas on making executives creative are far-fetched. People go along with his ideas ot make him happy. I would venture to say that nobody would enter the Think Tank or the No Distraction Room if nobody was around to observe them enter. They would simply take their little problem back to their office and work out a solution.

"What really happens with Maxwell's gimmicks is that people go through the motion of entering the Think Tank or receiving the head massage just to humor Farnsworth. If they do come up with a workable idea in one of those creativity sessions, it has to be refined further anyway. The person coming up with the idea usually then takes it to a few others to refine it in group discussions.

"It might even be that going off to a formal creativity exercise is counterproductive. Although I certainly do enjoy having an attractive woman stroke my head, I could think of a better way to finance the expansion of Mini-Sub shops without having her fingers run through my hair."

Questions

1. Should the dissenting executive confront Maxwell Farnsworth with his perception of the effectiveness of the company creativity training program? Why or why not?

2. What factors (related to the Maxwell Mini-Sub Company) other than the creativity inducing techniques may be eliciting creative behavior from company executives?
3. In what ways might these creativity training sessions be counter-productive?
4. One of Maxwell Farnsworth's former executives described him as "An old cornball who lucked out. His creativity bit is just hog-wash." Based on the limited information provided in this case, what is your opinion of the preceding statement?
5. What approach would you recommend that Mr. Farnsworth (or his subordinates) use to determine if the creativity inducing techniques are functional to the organization?

Case 6
Baton Rouge is a
Long Way From Home*

As an electrical design engineer with Surety Electronics, I'm faced with making at least one important decision every day at work. Each decision is unique, but all follow the same format. I do what I can to clearly identify the problem in my mind, search for innovative ways to solve the problem, mull over each one of these alternatives carefully, and make a choice. Within three months I'm able to discover if I made a good or bad decision from a technical and/or business standpoint. Recently, I faced a decision relating to my work that at the time appeared much more complex than an engineering design problem. My family and my future would be touched by the outcome of this decision.

One Monday night a few months ago, I was sitting at home relaxing and watching television. The children had been tucked into bed, the bills had been paid, and no emergency repairs were necessary around the house. In fact, things seemed unusually tranquil. Suddenly, the phone rang. Terry, an old college and fraternity friend I hadn't seen or heard from in about four years, was calling from Baton Rouge, Louisiana. For the first five minutes we exchanged the usual social amenities; he asked how I was doing and I asked how he was doing. Finally, Terry got to the point of why he had phoned. He

*Ronald A. Luchetti researched and wrote this case, with the exception of a few editorial changes.

wanted to know if I might be interested in a job with his employer, Baton Rouge Enterprises, Inc.

My first reaction was that he was joking. As the conversation continued, I began to take him seriously. Terry's company needed an electrical engineer to design and develop some automated machinery to manufacture the line of home power tools they wanted to sell. The type of work was identical in many ways to the work I was presently doing and which I found satisfying. Baton Rouge Enterprises was a small company, but their line of home power tools was selling well beyond expectations. According to their analysis, the only way they could keep pace with customer demand was to install automated, faster machinery to produce the product line. Up to this point, they had no electrical engineers on the staff; they were looking for one, and I was their first candidate. For many years, I had wondered what it would be like to be the "resident electrical engineer" in a small, promising company. From what I had heard, that kind of situation often leads the way to a vice presidency.

Despite the appeal of the position, I told Terry I couldn't take the job because I liked my present one so well. Also, it would affect my family if we just picked up and moved to Louisiana. We would be farther from our families than we were in our present location of Indianapolis. Terry insisted that I at least consider the job. Partly out of curiosity and partly out of courtesy, I said I would give the proposition some thought and would get back to him with my requirements for salary, vacation, relocation expenses, and job security. There I was, faced with a more complex problem than almost any problem I faced at work.

My wife, Loretta, and I discussed the offer that seemed like a golden opportunity. She told me to do what I wanted, but I knew that deep down inside she was reluctant to move farther away from her parents. She finally admitted this feeling, but still insisted that I should do what I felt was best in the long run for my career and for the family. I thought about my present position with Surety Electronics and how happy I was. Here I was an electrical design engineer, doing exactly what I wanted to do.

Out of college for only four years, I had almost doubled my starting salary. I was now eligible for three weeks annual vacation. Overtime pay was becoming quite regular. From what I could determine, the benefits package at Surety was unsurpassed in the industry. Aside from the standard benefits, I received a substantial yearly bonus. Adding up all these items amounted to almost $25,000 per year, $17,500 of which was salary.

To add to the dilemma of making the right decision, I made a good initial effort in my pursuit of an MBA at a satellite location of Purdue University. The company footed the bill for this program. My work assignments were very challenging; I loved my job and the people I worked with. My job assignments gave me ample opportunity for travel, a rarity for an engineer.

My future with my present company looked very promising. Despite all these pluses there wasn't much chance of promotion to a managerial position, though the pay was substantial and my job security was solid. The logical next step was to see what Baton Rouge Enterprises had to offer. In the back of my mind, I felt that they would reject what I would require to leave my present job. I asked for a starting salary of $22,000, three weeks vacation, benefits commensurate with my present benefit package, relocation expenses, and a promise of a managerial position as soon as I automated their systems. I figured it would take two years to complete the automation project.

To top off my list of demands, I asked the company to take care of selling my home and finding my family a comparable one in Louisiana. It might have looked as though I were making unreasonable demands, but I was confident that my talents and experience were deserving of an unusual opportunity. I felt that a person could ask for much more in the way of a compensation package if he is asked to relocate. If Baton Rouge Enterprises wanted me badly enough to grant all my demands, I would accept the job offer.

After reaching this tentative decision, I began to ruminate over what would happen if I left my present job, accepted the new position with Baton Rouge, and it fell through shortly after my family and I had relocated to Louisiana. My guess was that I had about a 95 percent chance of being rehired by Surety Electronics without losing anything if I came back within a year. After a year back on the job, I would regain all my seniority, vacation, bonus, and retirement benefits. Should I return *after* one year, it would be tantamount to starting as a new employee with them.

Aside from what the company policy states about rehiring people, I had to consider what the management attitude would be toward me. It would probably affect my chances for promotion adversely. Very probably, I would be considered disloyal or ungrateful.

While I waited for a reply from Baton Rouge Enterprises, I had some research conducted into the past performance of the company and its future prospects. A lawyer friend of mine with a good background in analyzing the financial situation of companies did the investigation for me. His conclusion was that the future of the company appeared uncertain. He reasoned that the company would be successful or fold within two years because it only had one product line. I assume that every fledgling company gets a similar rating from lawyers or accountants, but I had faith in this man's judgment.

To my surprise, I received an enthusiastic reply from Baton Rouge Enterprises. They were willing to guarantee me everything I requested and urged me to visit them at their expense. My wife and I took a long weekend vacation to visit the company and the city. We both liked what we saw. To make my decision even tougher, they told me they thought I could complete the automated system within two years and after that I would become an executive in the company.

The topic of relocation dominated our thoughts for an entire week. It did seem like a unique opportunity, even better than that described in the initial phone conversation with Terry. When it looked as if I was turning in the direction of accepting the position, my wife again told me she felt uneasy about relocating to Louisiana because it would substantially increase the geographic distance between us and her parents. Living in Indianapolis, we could reach her parents in three hours by automobile.

Another letter and another phone call were forthcoming from Baton Rouge Enterprises. Although they told me to take all the time I needed to make my decision, they were pressing me. Financially, the situation looked incredibly good, provided that it all worked out well once I arrived down there. If within a year I decided to return to my old job — and it was available — nothing would be lost (to the best of my knowledge). But the anguish of moving twice within a one year period might be more than my family and I could bear.

Should I accept the position, stay more than a year, and then find that the position wasn't going to work out for the long range, I would have ruined my future with Surety. Assuming the new company fell through after two years, I would be out of a job, my children would be of school age, and the job market for engineers could conceivably be quite limited. A move at that point in life would be much more difficult than at present. Should the new job fall through a few years from now, my wife would probably want to relocate to the area where her parents live. Job opportunities for electrical engineers have never been good in Loretta's hometown.

After two more weeks of tossing the subject around with my

wife and two trusted friends, I made my decision. I turned down the offer at Baton Rouge Enterprises. As I look back upon it, I guess I turned down the decision because of the risk involved and for family reasons. My wife would probably be unhappy about living so far from her parents, but then maybe she would grow more as a person if she were less dependent upon her parents. My future with Surety still looks promising, but I still cannot help wondering if I made the right decision.

Questions

1. Based upon the information presented in this case, should the engineer in question have accepted the job offer? Explain your reasoning.
2. What would you regard as unusual about the job offer extended by Baton Rouge Enterprises?
3. How much concern do you think the engineer should have given to his wife's reluctance to move too far from her parents?
4. Are there any other sources of information the engineer seemed to overlook in making a decision about relocation?
5. What position should Surety have taken if the engineer wanted his old job guaranteed? In other words, if he wanted to know what his chances of getting his old job back should his new job fail, what should the company have said?

Case 7
Every Author Deserves a Publisher

Bart Belladonna, age 42, successful sales manager and man about town, sat looking out the den window of his San Francisco townhouse. It was Sunday afternoon and Bart was sorting through the correspondence about a three-year personal project he had undertaken — the preparation and writing of a manuscript called, "The Management Mystique." Bart mused to himself:

"I just can't figure this one out. My business sense is penetrating in the women's fashion field. I know my product line, I know my customers, and I know my sales staff. My income has skyrocketed since I took over this territory. Things have gone so well that I'll be Regional Manager next year. Yet I'll never rest until I put this project to bed. It's hard to believe that no publisher wants 'The Management Mystique.'

"What astounds me is that 'The Management Mystique' is life itself in the business world. Maybe nobody wants to publish a book that confronts reality square in the eye. Here it is in black and white, the true story of how so many people want to get into management. They think it's the big dream fulfiller. Almost any young man or woman I have met in a sales job claims he or she wants to become a manager. Even some doctors I've met tell me they want to run a hospital or become a business executive. Yet when you get there, when you find a management job, it usually turns out to be a can of worms.

"For most people, management is one headache after another.

Somebody is shortchanged 57¢ in a paycheck issued from the Home Office and they want the manager to spend an hour figuring out what went wrong. I know a vice president who was making phone calls trying to find a moving company to take care of an office relocation at a reasonable price. The manager's title may sound glamorous, but you can spend many a night shuffling around forms invented by people with nothing to do but invent forms. Maybe my book hits too close to home. Maybe it's a threat. Or maybe it's too obvious. Or maybe they figure a sales manager isn't an important enough person to write a book."

Bart now had a difficult decision to face. His hopes of finding a publisher were rapidly dwindling. Two alternatives seemed apparent. One was to publish the book himself — pay to have it edited, typeset, and printed. He would then be left with the task of personally marketing a room full of books. Bart dismissed that idea as too crass and unprofessional. Printing a book yourself, he reasoned, is about as prestigious as having name cards printed. It may look good, but anybody who puts up the money can own a set of elegant name cards. Another possibility was to contact one of the subsidy publishers who advertised from time to time in newspapers and national magazines.

Bart carefully reread an advertisement he had clipped from a newspaper: "New York City publisher coming to this area. Looking for worthwhile manuscripts of all varieties, fiction, nonfiction, biographies. Publish your book in four months. Join our growing number of successful authors."

A telephone call to the designated number resulted in Bart's communicating with a recorded message. Dutifully, he left his name and address after the correct signal. Five days later an elaborate package arrived in the mails. Mercury Press sent Bart a complete file of information on the operation of a subsidy publisher. Success stories were given of authors who were rejected by innumerable publishers and who finally invested some money in *themselves* by subsidizing the publication of their manuscript.

Bart decided to at least give Mercury Press a try. If they rejected his manuscript, Bart reasoned, then his manuscript did not deserve to become a published book. Off to the publisher went "The Management Mystique" in the postage pre-paid mailer provided by Mercury Press. Bart Belladonna eagerly awaited their response.

Ten days later a letter from the publisher arrived. An editor from Mercury wrote: ". . . Rarely have we seen such a refreshing and candid analysis of an important contemporary problem. The editorial board at Mercury is unanimous in its decision to offer you a contract to publish your book. Your manuscript requires almost no editing. A publication agreement is enclosed. Please sign it and return it with your first payment to help defray publication costs. . . . We welcome you to our list of authors and anticipate a large sale of your book."

Among the agreements stated in the book contract were the following: (1) Mercury Press would print a first run of 2000 copies of the book, (2) the publisher would assist in the promotion and marketing of the book, including the mailing of copies to book reviewers, (3) the author would receive 40 percent of the retail price on sales of the book (4) the author would receive 50 percent on subsidiary rights such as paperback editions or sales to movies or television, (5) the author would contribute $6000 in three equal installments to help defray the production and marketing costs of the book, (6) the estimated retail price of the book would be about $7.95.

Belladonna made some rapid calculations. If slightly less than 2000 copies of his book were sold, he would recoup his $6000. All royalties paid him beyond that point would represent profit. Should the book sell 100,000 copies (Bart had read about popular management books that had sold over 300,000 copies) he would earn as much from book royalties as he was earning as a sales manager.

Contract in hand, Bart was enthusiastic about the prospects of the world finally having an opportunity to sample his thinking. Through his merchandising contacts in Alfie's, a downtown department store, Bart arranged an appointment with the hardcover book buyer at the store. After listening to Bart's brief description of up-coming book and publisher, Loretta Antos, had some upsetting words to say:

"Mr. Belladonna, I hope you didn't give those people any money yet. We look upon Mercury Press as strictly another 'Vanity Press' operation. Your book may be an exception, but outfits like Mercury generally publish books of no commercial value. If an older woman with a few dollars to invest wants to write a history of her village or a biography of her pastor, a subsidy publisher will gladly take on her project. Men, too, are just as desperate. A man who had inherited substantial sums of money came in here one day asking me if I would like to purchase any of the four books he had published, each one from a different publisher. Each so-called book was a collection of poems — one book dedicated to each of his four children. He had been offered contracts by each of four different subsidy publishers.

"Nevertheless, if a local author thinks that he or she has enough friends to buy a good supply of books we will order a few just to try it out. But the author cannot expect us to put his or her books on the rack with books from regular publishers."

Dejected, but realizing that he had only heard one point of view so far, Belladonna waited for the promised galley proofs. Included in the galleys was a letter firmly indicating that further production on the book was contingent upon Mercury Press receiving the second $2000 payment. The printing of the book was intermediate in quality between the crudest form of offset printing and good book process. Nevertheless, it was a *book*, bearing the beautiful name Bart M. Belladonna!

Two months later (after Bart made the final $2000 payment) 25 copies of the first printing of *The Management Mystique* arrived at Bart's house. He could now either simply wait for the royalty checks to begin arriving, or take an active role in the marketing of his book. Bart chose the latter course of action. He felt that his basic knowledge of marketing and sales could readily be applied to his own book.

Strategy 1 was to have a flyer printed describing the book and including an order form to be mailed directly to the publisher. Bart had 6000 of these printed. He purchased several management lists from a mailing list company in New York. Bart also developed a personal mailing list which included the names of friends, relatives, and business acquaintances. The names of former girlfriends and bosses also found their way on to his list.

Strategy 2 was to directly telephone every person Bart knew might possibly be interested in purchasing a copy of his book. The reaction Bart received from friends was so neutral or negative that he discontinued this strategy after about 25 calls. One friend commented, "Bart, I thought you were peddling women's clothing, not your autobiography."

Strategy 3 was to give away copies of the book to a number of people Bart thought might possibly purchase copies for other people. His own company president and a district librarian were included on this list. This strategy cost Bart about $225 since he was able to purchase books from the publisher at a 40 percent discount.

Strategy 4 was to make calls on store owners and book buyers in larger stores. After 10 rebuffs, Bart concluded that Loretta Antos, his first contact at Alfie's, was correct in her assessment. Booksellers take a dim view of subsidy publishers. Two of the people he called upon were willing to try a few books on consignment. They would pay the publisher or Bart after they *sold* the books.

Two years later, Bart reflects upon his decision to publish his book with Mercury Press: "We have to consider first the financial side. After 24 months, my royalty statement shows a total of 700 books sold, not including the 75 or so I bought as gifts for friends and even a few enemies. I collected about $2226 in royalties. Figuring roughly, my total expenses were around $9000 including payments to the publisher, mailings, flyers, typing, gas mileage for trips to the bookstores, and travel in conjunction with research for the book. That has given me close to $7000 in tax deductions. Figuring that I'm roughly in the 35 percent tax bracket, my real out of pocket loss on this project has been about $4500. Who knows what I would have done with that $4500 if I hadn't published my book with Mercury Press. If I bought leisure with the $4500 I could have had a few grand vacations, but I went on vacations anyway.

"Was I fleeced? I don't know. Am I hurt? I'm not so sure. One day, in a fit of anger, I demanded to speak to the president of Mercury Press. He isn't a bad chap. When I asked him what justification he could offer for the type of business he was in, he told me simply, 'Every author deserves a publisher.' Maybe he has a point."

Questions

1. In retrospect, should Bart Belladonna have published his manuscript with Mercury Press?
2. What service do subsidy publishers really offer the public ("What business are they really in?")
3. To what extent do you think Belladonna was using sound business judgment in the marketing strategies he used to assist the publisher to sell *The Management Mystique*?
4. What statements made by Bart would you consider to be irrational? Why?
5. What tools of management science might Belladonna have used to assist him in making a sound decision about accepting the contract offered by Mercury Press?

looking at wrong factor in decision making real reason was personal gratification not monetary.

REFERENCES

Bouchard, Jr., Thomas J. "A Comparison of Two Brainstorming Procedures," *Journal of Applied Psychology*, Vol. 56, October 1972, 418-421.

Burack, Elmer H. *Organization Analysis: Theory and Applications.* Hinsdale, Illinois: The Dryden Press, 1975. See Chapter 11.

Carter, E. Eugene. "The Behavioral Theory of the Firm and Top-Level Corporate Decisions," *Administrative Science Quarterly*, Vol. 17, September 1972, 413-428.

Frew, David R. "Transcendental Meditation and Productivity," *Academy of Management Journal*, Vol. 17, June 1974, 362-368.

Glueck, William F. "Decision Making: Organization Choice," *Personnel Psychology*, Vol. 27, Spring 1974, 77-93.

Heller, Frank A. *Managerial Decision Making: A Study of Leadership Styles and Power Sharing Among Senior Managers.* New York: Harper & Row (A Tavistock Title), 1972.

Hornaday, John A. and Aboud, John. "Characteristics of Successful Entrepreneurs," *Personnel Psychology*, Vol. 24, Summer 1971, 141-153.

Maier, Norman R.F. *Problem Solving and Creativity in Individuals and Groups.* Belmont California: Brooks/Cole, 1970.

Maier, Norman R.F. and Sashkin, Marshall. "Specific Leadership Behaviors That Promote Problem-Solving," *Personnel Psychology*, Vol. 24, Spring 1971, 35-44.

Shull, Jr., Fremont A., Delbecq, Andrew L. and Cummings, L.L. *Organizational Decision Making.* New York: McGraw Hill, 1970.

4
Stresses in
Managerial and Professional Life

Case 8
The Price of Success

"Kevin, what has happened to that unswerving drive of yours toward working your way to the top of our company?" asked his boss. "You are almost there. We have offered you a division presidency. Three years of success in that job and we might be able to bring you back to the corporate office as a Senior Vice President of Marketing. You are big league timber, Kevin. You are destined for greatness in our company.

"Ten years ago you came to us as an eager young business administration major just out of college. What an impression you created! Eager, intelligent, and, even at age 21, with an executive aplomb about you. We grabbed you right away for our executive training program. After two years in the field as a territory salesman, you moved effortlessly into a marketing research assignment. Within one year you became a Senior Market Analyst. After two years of brilliance in that position, we made you a Branch Manager. Again, after several years of sterling performance you then became the youngest Regional Manager in the history of our company. We figure you are now ready for the big jump — a general management assignment where you will be operating a profit center of your own. What more can a young executive want?

"We are sticking our necks out for you. Should you fail as a 31-year-old division president, the company could look foolish. Our offer is real. You can become President of the Cosmetics Division if you will just accept the position. I hear the excuses you are making about not being experienced enough for the job, and that other people in the company are more deserving of the position, but I don't buy them. Something else is holding you back, Kevin. What is it?"

"Fred, you're pushing for a rapid answer to a major life decision. Becoming a company president isn't like buying a cabin cruiser or going on a two-week vacation to Bermuda. It's more like getting married or having triplets. It's one helluva change in your life style. An impulsive person shouldn't even be in such an assignment."

"Am I really talking to ambitious Kevin Brady, that hard charging, good-looking Irishman who hates to lose at anything? Two years ago, if I asked you to tackle a special assignment in Venezuela, you would have been on your way to the airport before we went over all the details of the job. I always had the impression that if you weren't in business you would be an automobile racing driver.

"Could it be that you are acting coy because you want us to up the ante a little. As I said, the job should pay about $42,000 a year in salary plus a healthy executive bonus, depending upon the profitability of your division. In a boom year you could increase your salary by one third with your bonus. Besides that, being a division president would give you a fast track to perhaps a bigger division presidency or the Senior Vice President of Marketing slot. It is conceivable that you could be set for life financially if you accept this assignment now."

"Fred, believe me. I'm not being an ingrate. I haven't turned down this magnificient offer. Yes, the challenge of a division presidency excites me. I believe in the product line of that division. For instance, my 14-year-old niece used that facial blemish cream and it really works. The improvement in her appearance actually raised her level of self-confidence. We are marketing something solid. Our cosmetic line does contribute something esthetic to society in its own way. I think our company performs a lot of social good, considering its record on environmental safety and equal employment opportunity.

"Yet a man contemplating becoming a president has to carefully evaluate what becoming a president will do to his life style. In other words, what am I really letting myself in for?"

"Kevin, you're speaking in generalities. Let's get down to the specifics of what's really holding you back from jumping at this once-in-a-lifetime opportunity. Be candid with me. I'm both your boss and your friend."

"A good way to begin, Fred, is to tell you about a recent experience my wife and I had at the Sales Executive Club. An industrial psychologist was giving a talk about the problems created by success-ful husbands. He wasn't putting down success, and he wasn't really putting down husbands. What he seemed to be saying was that being a successful career person can create a lot of problems in your per-sonal life, particularly with your wife and children. When he finished his talk there was tension in the air. Husbands were grinning sheep-ishly at their wives. Most of the wives had a surprised expression as if this man was revealing their personal case history. One skeptic said this psychologist was way off base, that he was dramatizing a few isolated case histories of obsessed executives and their neurotic wives. That was hardly the reaction my wife or I had to the theme of the talk.

"As an aftermath to the talk, my wife and I began some serious dialogue about our relationship. She has some real concerns that if I become any more successful as an executive I might become a flop as a husband. A woman quoted at the talk said something that really hit home with my wife. Something to the effect, 'I think the husbands with the least success in their careers make the best husbands, because their wives and families are all they have.'

"Noreen thinks that I have paid progressively less attention to her as I have advanced in my career. She told me that I'm so pre-occupied with business problems that I only pay surface attention to her problems. One night she told me that her gynecologist said she would need a hysterectomy. I expressed my sympathy. She retorted that this was the second time she told me about the pending hyster-ectomy.

"That conversation served as a springboard for an examination of many other things about our family life. Out of nowhere, she asked me to name the teachers of our three children. I struck a blank on all three. She then asked me what grade our daughter Tricia was en-rolled in. I told her I thought the third grade. I was off by one grade, which she used as evidence that I'm not really participating in our children's worlds.

"Worse than that, Noreen then pointed out that I have been out of town on her last three birthdays. I feebly pointed out to her that her birthday just happens to take place during the time of our annual sales convention. My opinion is that a good many husbands who are going nowhere in their careers — even a few unemployed husbands — forget their wives' birthdays. We can't attribute all my shortcomings to my business success. But it did make me wonder if a company president can ever remember his wife's birthday, or maybe even his own."

"Okay, Kevin, you have the standard problems at home that an executive can anticipate. Just pay a little more attention to your wife and things will straighten out on that front."

"Fred, the problem of success interfering with my personal life goes beyond my relationship with my wife. I'm also worried about my physical health. I'm not a candidate for an ulcer or a heart attack, but the attention I have been paying to my career lately has taken its toll on my physical condition. I notice that I've gained a lot of weight owing to the amount of time I spend in bars and restaurants with customers and colleagues. Those hefty business lunches add more calories than most people realize. Not only am I gaining weight, but I don't look as sharp as I did when I devoted less time to the job.

"Part of the problem, of course, is that you have less time to exercise when you're immersing yourself in your job. When I am home on weekends, I have so much catching up to do on household tasks that I get less physical exercise. I wouldn't worry so much about having gained a few pounds and looking a little pale, if I didn't see a steady deterioration of my golf game. A few years ago, I heard a statement about golf and business that passed by me at the time, but now it makes a good deal of sense. According to the fellow making this statement, if your golf score gets over 85 you have no business playing golf. But if your golf score gets under 75, you have no business.

"Now I know what that character was talking about. As my income and level of responsibility has increased, so has my golf score. When I do play, I'm more erratic. My putting is ragged, I slice more than ever, and I've added about 10 points to my average score. I used to pride myself on my golf. Now I'm just a duffer who plays recreational golf. To get my game back in shape, I'll either have to sacrifice my job or my family. I know that the stereotype of a golfer is an affluent executive. More accurately, the affluent executive fits the stereotype of a duffer. My career is very important to me, but so is my golf game. It would seem unfeeling on my part to chip away at my time with the family in order to bring my game back to snuff."

"Of course, Kevin, if you don't keep raising your income you soon will not be able to afford golf. A person needs a lot of money to keep a golf game going, perhaps a few thousand a year, depending upon the particular club. If we give you a job as a clerk your game might return to its former level, but you would have to play in public parks. You'd spend so much time waiting to tee off, golf would then interfere with your personal life."

"Fred, I'm glad you brought up the topic of money. So far, the ever increasing amount of money I've earned hasn't had an overwhelming impact on my standard of living. In the 10 years I've been working for the company my income has more than tripled, but my standard of living has hardly tripled. My cost of living creeps up every year, and I need that big 10 to 15 percent salary increase just to stay even. Taxes go up at a much steeper rate than does your income.

"At times I find it both disturbing and embarrassing when I realize how little real financial security my ever increasing income has brought me. People think that as a Regional Manager for a large corporation, I have no financial worries. My in-laws think I'm stashing away about $1000 per month for the kids' college and our retirement. The truth is that except for programmed savings like the company retirement system and a mutual fund plan I'm enrolled in, many months go by without my saving any cash.

"What eats away at my insides the most is that some people grossing half as much money as I do seem to live about the same. Maybe they drive a Plymouth Duster instead of a Chrysler Cordova, but their car still performs the same function. Noreen, the children and I took a week's vacation to the Poconos last fall. We met loads of people there, such as foremen and school teachers, who make less than half my income and they had more dough to spend at the nightclub than I do. I'm beginning to wonder if the financial rewards associated with moving up in the executive ranks are real or illusory. Most of the bankruptcies I read about involve executives. Maybe there is something wrong with our system that subtly pushes up your expenses to meet your income."

"Kevin, maybe you're just having a bad day. Most of the problems you allude to are not as serious as you make them out to be. Perhaps you're over-reacting."

"I don't entirely discount that possibility, Fred, but before I take the big plunge to a presidency there are certain things that would have to be ironed out in advance. Most important of all, what would be expected of a division president in this company? How many hours per week do I devote to the company? Who takes priority in my life, my company or my family? Do I get paid the same if I work 70 or 40 hours per week? What certainty do I have of that executive bonus? And how much of it will you guarantee?"

"Kevin, get hold of yourself. To succeed at the top you have to love every minute of the job. Digging in to the corporate problems should be your biggest source of kicks in life. All the concerns about the job and the little inconveniences at home are not the central issue. They are simply part of the price of success."

Questions

attitude, kept shooting him down no empathy

1. How should Fred handle Kevin's ambivalence about assuming a division presidency?
2. What should Kevin do about his own ambivalence?
3. What stresses does Kevin seem to be facing?
4. What errors does Fred seem to be making in handling his interview with Kevin?
5. What guarantees about the remuneration and working conditions do you think the comapny is obliged to give Kevin Brady as a precondition for his accepting the division presidency?

*# 3 career vs family
health
change in life style
luck of confidence*

Case 9
Is There No Justice
in the Retailing Business? *

Fred Hansen sat in his lawn chair one Saturday afternoon pondering over his career at L.M. Cartwright, one of the world's largest chains of retail stores. Joanne, his wife, spoke: "Tell me what all this grim-faced, heavy, heavy, stuff is all about. What's been weighing you down all weekend?"

"So long as you asked," Fred replied, "I'll lay it all out for you right now. I'm going to be 41 next week; I've been with Cartwright for over 10 years, and I don't think I'm moving fast enough in the company. Just to kind of feel things out, I've asked to be considered for a transfer. Right now, I'm a district merchandising manager for women's apparel and that's not a big enough job at this point in my career. I think I would benefit from becoming a merchandising manager in one of the retail outlets.

"According to my analysis, the opportunity for promotion at the store level is greater than the opportunity for a promotion on a district level. Besides that, money means a lot when you're in a low paying field like the retailing business. Depending on the size of the store, salaries are usually higher for a store than district job. But beyond the consideration of money, I want to get to a store because that's where the action is in the retailing business."

Two months after his conversation with Joanne, Fred learned

---

*John Day conducted the research for and wrote portions of this case.

that his request had been granted. His immediate superior, Larry, explained to Fred that he was being offered a position as Assistant Store Manager and General Merchandise Manager in a limited line store in Hartford, Connecticut. Although he had heard a few unfavorable stories about the Hartford Store Manager, Fred elected to make the move to Hartford.

Fred explains the next episode in his career with L.M. Cartwright: "I jumped into the Hartford assignment with terrific enthusiasm and a very positive attitude. My impression was that I would be in the Assistant Store and General Merchandise Manager position for only two years before moving up to a full line store doing twice the volume of the one in Hartford.

"After just a few months on the job, I began to notice that my new position was beginning to affect my behavior. Joanne accused me of not being able to relax, even on my day off. Quite often I spent part of my day off working on store problems because of the complaints I received from my Store Manager. He claimed that when I was away from the store a whole batch of minor problems cropped up. He held me responsible for everything. To my knowledge, no other assistant managers carry so much responsibility. To give you an example, I'll explain my new added assignment.

"We've stepped up our company advertising in Hartford, yet we don't have a professional advertising manager for the five Hartford stores, so it fell into my lap to coordinate newspaper, radio, and television advertising for our entire Hartford effort. This task alone could easily be considered a full-time position. At the same time the company was instituting new merchandise control procedures. As merchandise manager, I was responsible for seeing that these procedures were instituted and understood by the sales staff and the office record keeping staff.

"My Store Manager was, of course, interested in maximizing profits. To cut fixed expenses such as salary costs, he hired young inexperienced people as department managers. Aside from paying these people low wages, his policy was to keep the store understaffed on purpose. These young college graduate trainees became fed up with the tremendous work load, the low pay, the verbal harassment, and they quit. As you might guess, the work load was left behind and divided up among the other department managers and myself.

"The result of this ever increasing work load is that I put in five 10 to 11 hour days, and one 14 hour day each week to complete my job responsibilities. Many a Sunday I had to devote most of the afternoon to routine paper work instead of spending time with the family like a normal husband and father. Or should I say a man who works for a normal company?

"Yet as I describe some of these problems, I'm only scratching the surface of what was really wrong. As you can deduce from what I've been describing so far, I had a tremendous amount of responsibility. Yet my power was quite limited with respect to making decisions. My boss was an authoritarian personality who relished countermanding my decisions and undermining my authority right in front of subordinates.

"For instance, one day he told me right out on the floor in front of other employees that he thought my window display for garden furniture was hideous and that I should rip it out right away before anybody from the Home Office saw it.

"It was the same thing with in-store promotions, which were my direct responsibility. I would tell my subordinates that I was given approval by my boss and that they could go ahead with a certain plan of mine. Then, three days later, my boss would reprimand me and reverse my decision. He made me look like a low paid messenger in the eyes of my subordinates.

"Nothing seemed to work smoothly in this job. I usually led the Monday morning management meeting. The purpose of the meeting was to introduce major promotions for the week, announce any new regulations, discuss mutual problems, and build team loyalty and spirit. We hoped to accomplish the loyalty bit by having each team member make a short presentation on item exploitation in his or her area of responsibility. What really happened was that the meeting usually ended up as a put-down by the store manager of me or one of the team members. Whoever was put down, it still reflected on my ability as a manager."

After several years in this job, Fred lost most of his initial enthusiasm for his work. In place of the formerly spirited manager, there was a bitter, disappointed, disgruntled individual who treated his subordinates in a perfunctory manner. His loss of enthusiasm slowly began to permeate the whole management team. A mild-mannered individual, Fred almost never expressed anger on the job. He rarely stood up to the Store Manager in defense of himself or his subordinates. Fred's boss looked upon such passive behavior as a sign of weakness. Fred's yearly reviews reflected his opinion. In his confusion and disappointment, Fred decided to stay with L.M. Cartwright until a transfer to another store came through.

The transfer Fred patiently waited for finally was offered to him four years after he began at Hartford. Fred thought that his career had received an infusion of new hope. But things haven't worked out in exactly that way. Fred reflects upon his new assignment as Manager of the Jamestown, New York store.

"The Jamestown store has a yearly sales volume of one tenth the Hartford store, and a staff of only 18 persons. Although these stores have traditionally represented the backbone of the Cartwright organization, they are being phased out in favor of larger suburban units. My next move with the organization will only come about when they close down this pathetic little store.

"My first reaction was to flatly reject the transfer. Joanne and my children were against the move, and it would seem to others that I've been farmed out to pasture. After a few talks with my boss and a few people from the regional staff, it was apparent to me that I would have to accept the transfer. My family and I will drag ourselves to Jamestown, but only with a sense of disillusionment and failure."

Questions

1. Do you think Fred Hansen might be well-suited to running the Jamestown store? Explain your reasoning.
2. How should Hansen have handled his relationship with his boss in Hartford?
3. What should Joanne's position have been about the transfer to Jamestown, (assuming she had misgivings about making the transfer)?
4. What might the Home Office do to prevent reoccurrences of situations like that of Fred Hansen?
5. What should Hansen have done when he realized that he didn't have sufficient authority to carry out his responsibilities?

Case 10
Making Eight is a Hassle *

"My case is hardly unique," commented Jack Whitney. "But perhaps in telling it other people like myself will avoid the same trap. We've all heard this story many times, but it bears repeating. Engineers and the companies that employ them just don't seem to need constant reminders about this problem.

"When I was released from the service, I was looking forward to finally getting a chance to be a real engineer. I guess you could have said I was gung-ho. You see, I had spent a total of six years in college earning a masters degree in electrical engineering. Starting my engineering career had to be postponed for almost five years after graduation while I repaid Uncle Sam for financing my education, but now I was ready to go.

"I took a job with a large shipyard in Virginia that had several contracts to build Navy warships. I had almost four years of sea duty as a missile fire control and systems officer and felt I could apply my education and experience to building those ships and their missile systems. It was a rude shock to me when I was assigned to antisubmarine systems about which I knew very little. It was worse to realize a few weeks later that I wasn't expected to know or, for that matter, to do very much. I read more than one novel and many magazines just to have something to fill the hours. I was not alone in

*This case was prepared and written by Gerald J. Soltas.

68

my frustration either. Numerous other engineers referred to their time-filling activities as 'making eight.' To compound the aggravation, we were occasionally required to put in overtime because 'the project is behind.' Talk about waste, a masters degree in automatic control systems engineering, four years of experience on the Navy's newest missile systems, and I was reduced to checking plans from some jerk in Washington who probably had never seen the inside of a college or a ship.

"It really got to me. I was coming home from work frustrated and discouraged. I've never been particularly easy to get along with, but my wife said I was becoming even more of a grouch. I had to do something!

"More education wasn't the answer. An engineer friend in the same company took a year's leave of absence without pay, went back to the University of Virginia, and earned a masters in electronics. When he came back to work, he got his old desk, his old job, and his old salary. We held another going-away party for him two months later.

"About the time I had been with the yard a year, I started sending out my resume and talking to employment agencies. In 1970-71, however, things were not exactly rosy for engineers. Once, out of 75 resumes I mailed, I received not one reply. Not so much as a 'thanks, but no thanks' letter. Just nothing. I even tried to get back into the Navy. You can imagine how desperate I was becoming. Then, to make matters worse, I was pulled from my projects on anti-submarine warfare and placed in a submarine development group. Just so you won't get the wrong idea, I was doing excellent work according to my supervisors and had already been promoted, at very little increase in salary, incidentally, to Senior Design Engineer, a move which usually took six to eight years for an engineer just out of college.

"In the submarine development group, I was further from my missile background and was only pretending to be an engineer. I was assigned to write various chapters in a training and maintenance manual dealing with systems which had already been designed and constructed. I specifically remember the first chapter I wrote was on the ship's entertainment system. Talk about useless!

"That was the last straw! I doubled and redoubled my job hunting efforts. Finally, one of the companies I had interviewed in college eight years before responded with what seemed to be a perfect opportunity at a decent increase in pay, at least enough to cover the cost of living difference between here and Virginia. At this point, however, pay was secondary in my mind. I was going to seed in that job and would have taken almost anything that offered the chance of a challenge.

"I have been at my new job almost two years now and it is everything I had hoped for. I have more projects now than I have time for. The challenge is stimulating; I have to dig and push, but I get more done, enjoy it more, and come home refreshed instead of depressed. Don't get me wrong, I still have problems and there are days when almost nothing goes right, but I have never once wished I had my old job back."

Questions

1. Why does a problem like that of Jack Whitney's so often go unrecognized in work organizations?
2. How much blame should Jack Whitney accept for this situation? What is his responsibility for taking the initiative to work out a solution to the problem of his underutilization?
3. What practical, business considerations of Jack Whitney's company might have led to his underutilization?
4. What does this case illustrate about the relationship between job satisfaction and motivation?
5. What should management do if they find underutilized people in their organization, but have no other jobs to offer?

REFERENCES

DuBrin, Andrew J. *Fundamentals of Organizational Behavior: An Applied Perspective.* Elmsford, N.Y.: Pergamon Press, 1974. See Chapter 4.

DuBrin, Andrew J. *Managerial Deviance: How to Deal With Problem People in Key Jobs.* New York: Mason/Charter, 1976.

Herzberg, Frederick. "Motivation-Hygiene Profiles: Pinpointing What Ails the Organization," *Organizational Dynamics,* Vol. 3, Autumn 1974, 18-29.

Ivancevich, John M. and Donnelly, Jr., James H. "Relation of Organizational Structure to Job Satisfaction, Anxiety-Stress, and Performance," *Administrative Science Quarterly,* Vol. 20, June 1975, 272-280.

Kay, Emanuel. *The Crisis in Middle Management.* New York: Amacom, a division of the American Management Associations, 1974.

Keller, Robert T. "Role Conflict and Ambiguity: Correlates With Job Satisfaction and Values," *Personnel Psychology,* Vol. 28, Spring 1975, 57-64.

Levinson, Harry. "On Executive Suicide," *Harvard Business Review,* Vol. 53, July-August 1975, 118-122.

McLean, Alan (Ed.). *Occupational Stress.* Springfield, Ill.: Charles C Thomas, 1974.

Sorensen, James E. and Sorensen, Thomas L. "The Conflict of Professionals in Bureaucratic Organizations," *Administrative Science Quarterly,* Vol. 19, March 1974, 98-106.

Walton, Richard E. "Quality of Working Life: What Is It?" *Sloan Management Review,* Vol. 15, Fall 1973, 11-21.

5
Political Maneuvering in Organizations

Case 11
Give Me Equality, Not Favoritism

Although I have an important message to tell the world, I'm not making a complaint or trying to express dissatisfaction with the system. It's just that we need to continuously reevaluate how we treat certain groups of people. What I have to tell is not always complimentary, but it is the truth. It may seem at times that I'm trying to get back at my Black brethren who have done so much to help me. I would not want to communicate that perspective, but both Black and white do-gooders need to get feedback on how their efforts are coming across to the people they are trying to help.

A logical place to begin is Frederick Douglass High School in downtown Detroit. If you prefer, I'll use the term "inner city" or "ghetto area," but to me it was downtown Detroit. Our high school was wedged in between some broken-down or vacated factory buildings, but it wasn't the type of place that an "inner city" or "ghetto school" is supposed to be. Sure, we had a reasonable number of irresponsible citizens such as junkies, brawlers, thieves, and plain no-goodniks, but I was never rolled at Douglass, not once. The biggest crime most of our students were ever involved in was breaking a window in the process of playing stickball. Fellows and girls in my crowd both pitied and laughed at the small but vicious criminal element in our school.

Blacks were in the overwhelming majority at our school, so we were kind of in charge of things like getting the best seats in the cafeteria or holding student offices. Our school was big on athletics, and

74

Blacks dominated the teams. Only one white boy was on the basketball team. We nicknamed him "Harry the Honkey," but out of affection, not hatred. He and I both played forward on the team the year we got to the Class A Sectional finals.

I was a first-rate city basketball player in addition to playing halfback on the football team. My good grades and my athletic accomplishments gave me a "big man" rating with my fellow students. I was voted most likely to succeed in my graduating class — an event in my life that spurred me on to bigger accomplishments. By graduation I had 10 different scholarship offers to sort out. All were based upon financial need, but they also included the provision that I would play basketball and/or football.

I decided on Regional State University because they guaranteed me a good paying job during the times I was not playing ball. In addition to the job, I was informed that I would be able to rent a car for $1 per day due to a generous grant from an anonymous local new car dealer. R.S.U. was a good choice for me, too, because it meant I wouldn't be too far from my mother, father, and sister who were eking out a penurious existence back in Detroit.

At State I majored in chemistry as a follow-up to my high school interests in physical science. I fantasied myself as a research chemist for a pharmaceutical company, making the big discovery that would eradicate some dread disease. My high school chemistry teacher said that a person like myself, who was both a leader and a good student, had a mission to do some good for the world.

My first three years at State were wonderful times. I played third and fourth string on the football team, and I only started in one or two basketball games, but I was still a hero to my friends. At State we had a few high school All-Americans who were cut from the squad. It was a wonderful accomplishment just to be able to make the team, avoid being injured, and maintain decent grades. By my fourth year, things were still going well, but I had a shift in my thinking about what I wanted to do with my life.

At about that time a couple of friends of mine began talking to me about how well Black college graduates were doing in managerial jobs in large corporations. They told me stories of how Black college grads at these companies were out meeting people and dining on expense accounts. They told me about how much a good-looking dude like myself was in demand as a salesman. My roommate told me a story about a former football player who was making $30,000 selling beer to restaurants. He explained that that particular beer company was way behind its quota on Black people in good jobs. To top that off, the restaurant owners relished doing business with an athlete. According to my friend, the combination was unbeatable.

At the same time as my curiosity about office work was being aroused, I was becoming disenchanted with chemistry. Gradually, I was even developing an aversion to the smell of a chemistry lab. Chemistry began to seem like such an obscure discipline in the total scheme of corporate life. I also learned from some of the professors that without a Ph.D. it was unlikely that a chemist would obtain a high paying or responsible job in industry. My getting a Ph.D. in chemistry just made no sense to me. The thought of it seemed to me to be pointing my life in the wrong direction. My girlfriend at the time said I would be happier as a Good Humor man than a bench chemist for the rest of my life.

After conferring with people at the counseling center, a few friends, and a few professors, I made a career decision. I would finish my college days with my chemistry major. My cumulative grade point average was still good — just short of a B. Upon graduation, I would enter an MBA program. By this arrangement, I would have wasted no time, or money. My physical science background would always be useful, helping me to think logically. Besides, I was led to believe that some companies actually preferred an MBA with an undergraduate degree in physical science or engineering.

Once I declared my intent to apply for admission to graduate school in business, things began to happen for me. It was apparent that my name was being circulated on some sort of a list. Representatives from two companies wrote me that they wished to see me on one of their regularly scheduled visits to the university. It seemed flattering to me that General Copper Company and National Urban Bank wanted to talk to me about a management training position before I had even been accepted to a college of business.

My meeting with the recruiter from General Copper Company gave me a strange feeling, somewhat because the recruiter seemed ill at ease. He kept talking about the company actively looking for a person of my background for its management training program. He made some reference to the fact that a chemistry major would have an edge in a copper company. That was definitely "jive talk." I confronted the representative and asked him if he had any interviews lined up with white chemistry majors. He hedged again and alluded to the fact that people of my "background" were in demand at the company. I wanted him to admit that my Blackness was of interest to him. I wouldn't have been offended at a white interviewer referring to the fact that I'm Black.

The woman from National Urban Bank had more class. After about 15 minutes of chatting about my future plans and how banks had become much more exciting places to work, she looked me straight in the eye and said that her bank much needed a 4-B applicant. I bit, and asked her what a 4-B candidate was. She told me, "We're looking for people who are Black, Beautiful, and Business Bound." After a good laugh, I told her that I would be pleased to write her when I was close to getting my MBA. I recognized that our interview was exploratory, and that the bank was not making a commitment to me. But it still struck me as unusual that banks were so intensely interested in cultivating Black people for their management training programs.

Shortly after those exploratory interviews, I settled down to the serious business of finding the right MBA program for myself. It did not seem necessary to send out a flood of applications, so I proceeded to apply only to a couple of schools of particular interest to me. After gathering the appropriate information, mailing out my applications, and arranging to take the admissions test for graduate school, I encountered another big surprise.

One night I received a phone call from a man who said he represented an association of graduate schools, and that he wanted to talk to me in person — something about financial aid. Mr. Algonquin and I met five days later. He informed me that my record was so outstanding that the Association was willing to give me substantial financial aid (about two-thirds of my tuition) if I would attend one of the member schools. Algonquin did point out that I would have to go through the normal channels for admittance to whatever school in the Association I attended. The financial aid was only for qualified students.

In response to my questioning, Algonquin explained that the Association program was designed to give minority students an expanded opportunity to attend graduate school in business. I asked him if this program of encouraging minorities was open to Egyptians, Portuguese, Swiss, and Eskimos, or just to Blacks. Maybe I shouldn't have come on so strong, but I was beginning to tire of people using the euphemism, "minority," when they really meant poor Blacks and Puerto Ricans.

Things went quite well at the B-school I chose to enter. My courses opened up new vistas to me. I picked up information about topics that I had no idea were part of a future manager's repertoire. My former vantage point as a chemistry major gave me very little insight about the workings of big business. People at the B-school were terrific, both classmates and faculty members. What particularly impressed me was how enthusiastic these professors were about their particular disciplines. The only time my Blackness came up during my course work was in an organization development exercise conducted by my behavioral science professor. A white gal in the class confronted me with the fact that she admired the way I could be Black without being self-conscious or militant about it. I explained to her and the rest of the group that I had nothing to be self-conscious or militant about. I was trying to make a go of it in the world as a person, more than as a Black person.

My only unusual incident in B-school about being a Black man came about during registration week. I was contacted by two different groups who offered me their help. A specialist from the reading and study clinic was assigned my "case." He told me that entering graduate students who attended inner city high schools were being offered an intensive reading improvement program. At first I didn't know if I was being patronized because I was raised in the city or because I was Black. I explained to that cat to check out my verbal score on the graduate school admissions test. He then explained that the service was strictly voluntary.

Two weeks after classes started I heard from a representative of the Association. He inquired how I was getting along in my program of studies. I told him that my course in quantitative decision analysis seemed hairy, but other than that things were going well. He then informed me about a tutoring program offered by the Association at no cost to the student. It was obvious that this special program was for Black people only. I informed my friend that I would ask a classmate or the instructor for help if I couldn't resolve things myself. In slight irritation, I told the man to go find a more worthy cause.

After graduation, I did make connections with the National Urban Bank. A management training position was open at one of their major suburban branches. One week before my scheduled interview, another member from the Association telephoned me to ask me how my job search was going. I informed him that before looking further I would first see what transpired at National Urban. He explained that the purpose of his call was not to help me line up interviews, but to see if I needed some money for a suit. "Appearances are very important," he explained. Sarcastically, I told him that the Baptist Church back home had already taken up a collection to buy me a suit.

My first inkling of preferential treatment because I was Black took place about four months after I joined National Urban. A white friend in the management training program and I were chatting about the impact of inflation and high taxes upon a young person's earnings. He made some comment about how well he thought he could do on $16,000 a year, but that after four months at the bank he was disappointed. He and I were the same age and both began the training program on the same day, yet I was being paid $17,100. Unbelievably, the bank seemed to be paying me an $1100 premium for being Black. In a way I was grateful, because it could have been my athletic accomplishments or my B.S. in Chemistry that prompted the bank to give me a higher starting salary than my colleague. Rather than cause my friend any embarrassment or appear ungrateful, I dropped the topic.

At the end of the one-year management program, I saw some long range possibilities for myself at National Urban. You might even describe the environment as dynamic, particularly in some of the departments. I had my short range goals set on getting assigned to the marketing department. I could see a real need for finding new groups of people and new types of enterprises eligible for borrowing bank money.

My level of enthusiasm was somewhat dampened by the next incident, which I thought brought special attention to my Blackness. I was the first person in the training program to be given the formal title "Manager," although I would not be managing anybody, at least for a while. Accompanying the promotion, a photographer from the communications department called to tell me he was assigned to shoot a picture of me as one of the youngest managers in the bank's history. After thinking for a moment about what he was saying, I told him to call me later in the week.

I enjoyed the special treatment I was getting at the bank, but somehow I wish the treatment had more to do with my accomplishments than my Blackness. I realize I was being singled out for being a successful young Black person. Despite all these good things that were happening to me, I couldn't help telling my boss one day to give me equality, not favoritism.

Questions

1. How might a company implement a policy of "equality but not favoritism" with respect to Black people?
2. If you were Jesse Harris (the individual narrating this case),

would you remain with National Urban Bank? Why or why not?
3. Is Jesse Harris being politically naive in his demands to be treated with equality but not favoritism?
4. What would be a tactful and effective way of offering a Black B-school student specialized tutoring?
5. Was the bank justified in giving Jesse Harris a higher starting salary than his white counterpart? Explain.

Case 12
The Maladroit Firing

It will be difficult for me ever to forget that Monday morning in late November. As usual, I took my brisk walk across town from our east-side apartment to my office on the 35th floor of company headquarters in Rockefeller Center. Hurriedly, I sorted through the morning mail. Among the predictable items was a bevy of mail from civic groups and charities asking for funds from our company. As Vice President of Public Relations at Blasdell Corporation, I receive about 50 of these requests weekly. As I was focusing my attention on the proposed revised format for our annual report sent to me by the Manager of Financial Relations, I was interrupted by a signal on the intercom. Betty Hughes, my secretary, relayed the message to me that my boss, President Coleman Anderson, wanted to see me at 11 a.m. in his office.

Coleman's pattern is to speak to me directly when he wants to confer on a non-emergency situation. When something really big is up, he tends to set up an appointment with me through my secretary. Enjoying the challenge of trying to predict what Coleman has on his mind, I made my best prediction. I assumed he wanted to talk to me about the rumors circulating that he would be thinning out our management ranks to help adjust for a disappointing earnings picture. It's always been a strong contention of mine that any news about a reduction in force, at whatever job level, should be coordinated through the public relations function. Without a carefully worded press release and a consistent statement from company officials, the organization can look pretty bad to the public.

As I entered the waiting room outside the President's office, his secretary picked up the intercom and announced in her officious voice: "Greg Sampson is here to see you now."

Coleman Anderson, looking somewhat perturbed, immediately launched into the topic of the conference: "Greg, business conditions are not good at Blasdell Corporation these days. Our earnings per share is getting low enough whereby the financial community is becoming disenchanted with our stock. Our stock has dropped from $81 to $47 in six months. Our earnings have declined 27 percent from the same period last year. It all spells trouble. There is going to be a lot of management shuffling taking place around here."

Recognizing the gravity of the situation Coleman was describing, I asked how I fit in the picture; how my staff and I could make a contribution to improving this difficult situation. Anderson became almost ashen, then commented:

"Greg, we're going to have to sacrifice a lot of people to improve our profit position. We are going to thin down and realign in order to cope with our changing business circumstances. Immediately, we are going to trim about 75 salaried employees from our corporate staff. Plus, we are going to have to sacrifice about four or five vice presidents. It's not a rosy picture; it's not something I enjoy doing, but it's for the good of the corporation.

"Your services are terminated as of the end of the year, but we are giving you three months severance pay. You've made a fine contribution to Blasdell in the 10 years that you've been here and your leaving will be a big loss. Do keep in touch with us in case our business situation changes. Please try not to take this development personally."

Stunned, I felt a wretching sensation in my stomach. Perspiration instantly oozed out all over my body. I felt as if I had just finished an hour of squash. All I could retort was, "I'm happy that you think I've made a contribution around here. So do I."

The rest of the day was a combination of anguish and tension. I felt silly taking care of my job responsibilities since it was apparent the Corporation felt they could get along well without me. Yet, I was being paid and I couldn't just sit in my office staring out the window. It took me two hours to write a simple memo that I would send to each member of my staff after I had discussed my situation with my family. It read:

"With considerable regret, I wish to announce that I will be leaving Blasdell Corporation effective December 31 in order to pursue my personal interests. Thank you for the splendid cooperation I have received from everyone of you during my years with the company."

What a paradox! Here I was falling on my own bureaucratic sword. This kind of deceptive, euphemistic statement is the kind of pap we often release to the press when we fire somebody. Here I was pulling the same transparent sham tactic on my own staff.

It took me two martinis at "The Bull and the Bear" to brace myself for that evening's announcement to Donna and our two children, Garth and Shana. All three were home — a rarity for a given Monday night. After a brief ceremonial "Hello," I made my grand announcement:

"I've got a bomb to drop. I've been let go from Blasdell. That's right, I'll be out on the street right after the Holidays. I'm sorry. I feel I've failed you, but I'll begin my job search tomorrow. Don't anybody worry about anything."

"Why, those bastards," blurted out Donna, "who needs them anyway? I've often said you were too good for the Corporation."

Garth and Shana conferred together briefly, and then presented a unified front with Garth as the spokesperson:

"Dad don't worry about anything. We love you very much. Both of us will enroll in public school starting in January. Who needs these stuffy private schools anyway? It will be a good education for us to attend a city high school." Although intended to help, that comment made me feel that sending your children to a public school in New York was tantamount to voluntarily placing them in a reformatory for juvenile delinquents.

By the next morning, my self-confidence was creeping back up to its normal level, and I was ready to tackle the biggest assignment of my career — finding a suitable job before my resources were depleted. Provided I found a new situation by April 1, I would not have lost even one paycheck in the process. My first step was to telephone colleagues of mine in other companies to see if any opportunities for a person of my background were available.

It became apparent after the third phone call that I was speaking to the wrong people. How could a public relations head with a smaller job than mine tell me about a job opportunity for myself? If they knew of one, they would apply for it. As one friend of mine working for a petroleum company put it, "Greg, if you were making $16,000 a year as a public relations specialist we might be able to help you. But a VP like yourself is looking for a compensation package of $50,000. Even if I knew where to slot you into a smaller job, I couldn't sell it to my company. Rightfully, their reaction would be that you would probably up and leave when you land the right situation for yourself."

As a sounder strategy, I made contact with all the corporate officers I knew of who were not in the public relations field. I figured they would be less threatened that I was really after their job. Larry Hastings, president of a chemical company, gave me a message I was soon to hear in 10 different versions: "Greg, I'm sorry to hear about the retrenchment at Blasdell. But it's almost just as grim around here. Everybody I know of is counting pennies and tightening belts. However important public relations is, it's not something that we're looking for to beef up in uncertain times."

My next standard approach to finding a job was to scan the classified advertisements in trade journals, the big city newspapers, and the *Wall Street Journal.* No job near my level could be found listed in any of these places. The few lesser jobs I responded to with a resume and cover letter produced only a few polite "Thank you for your interest; we are currently reviewing a number of people for this position," type of reply.

Two weeks after I began my job search, I tried a bolder approach — placing a "position wanted" ad in about 10 different newspapers and trade magazines. It read:

> 47-year-old Public Relations Vice President for 2 billion dollar conglomerate seeks new position. Heavy record of accomplishment in all phases of corporate p.r. Available immediately, compensation negotiable.

Responses were large in number but from the wrong people. Instead of a flood of inquiries from potential employers, I received a number of responses from employment agencies and career counseling firms. For a fee, a large number of people were willing to help me find a job. By now a month had passed, and I felt that almost any fee that would secure me a job would be a bargain.

I decided to register with the employment agencies, several of whom were executive agencies where the hiring company pays the fee. I was even willing to gamble on the few agencies where the job seeker pays the fee. It appeared doubtful to me that an employment agency of the ordinary variety could come up with a Public Relations Director job for me at anywhere near my salary requirements.

Perhaps I made a mistake, but I finally decided not to become involved with a career counseling firm at that stage of my job search.

My case would cost about $2300 considering my job level. For this fee they would help me conduct my job campaign and counsel me about making the right kind of career decision. They were quite honest in not guaranteeing that I would be placed as a result of my sessions with them. Although it may have been myopia on my part, it appeared to me that a person in a specialized field such as public relations would need less help in sorting out his job potential than would a generalist type of executive.

In the first 40 days of my job campaign, I had turned up only one warm lead — a Director of Community Relations position at a company that was polluting the environment and wanted to get the government off their backs. The job paid $25,000, was located in a factory town, and the three previous incumbents resigned or were fired in the last two years. It was difficult for me to even fake enthusiasm for that job. Not unlikely, once the incumbent helped them out of the bind with the government the position would be terminated. My lack of enthusiasm must have shown through. I never heard from them again.

By the end of two months, I took a step I would never have believed possible for myself — even in my most bizarre nightmares. I registered at the unemployment insurance bureau and was soon receiving weekly checks for $95, the maximum allowable at the time. My first reactions were that I was hitting rock bottom, that I was dropping out of society. However, I was far from the only person with an executive appearance at the State Unemployment Bureau. Armed with their attache cases, most of the management personnel tried to look like state officials rather than unemployment insurance claimants.

One morning my wife entered my den at home, which I was now using as my base of operations for finding a job. Angrily, I shouted, "Don't bother me at the office." Suddenly I realized that I really was not at the office and that I really wasn't making much progress at finding a new position. My tensest moment during the day occurred when I sorted through the mail, hoping that an encouraging letter, even a job offer would be found among the bills and polite negative responses to my letters of inquiry.

As my fourth month of unemployment ended, I began what I now consider a truly desperate tactic. Daily, I picked names of corporations and their presidents out of the Dun & Bradstreet Directories. This served as the basis for a mailing list of about 1000 companies. Each was sent a copy of my resume, a general purpose cover letter (typed with an automatic typewriter), and a stamped self-addressed envelope. At least this gave me a steady trickle of mail to riffle through and a few remote leads. A few letters were returned with the statement that the addressee was deceased.

Finding a job became a preoccupation. It became hard to face friends or converse with my wife or children about any other serious topic. I sold my car, which saved me $100 per month in garage bills alone plus the cost of maintenance and payments. My wife took to making enormous stews that we ate for several days in lieu of the usual steaks and chops. We eliminated meals at restaurants, drinks in bars, cancelled all planned vacations. I did not renew my subscription to five magazines as they came due. Donna sold off half her wardrobe to a "Next to New" shop. To give us some working capital, I sold my $5000 in municipal bonds. We refused all payments to charities. Donna gave up smoking. Garth and Shana found jobs in McDonald's to provide themselves money for school expenses.

People have told me, and I have read, that adversity brings a family closer together. I found the opposite to be true. The simple query from Donna, "What's new?" aroused me to anger and despair. Shana's inquiry about what she could do about applying for college sent me into a tirade about her lack of awareness of how desperate our situation had become. My interest in sex, sports, current events, and even the stock market dwindled. I would ruminate for hours over my growing pile of letters of rejection. I would conduct a telephone follow-up campaign every day between the hours of 10 and 12 a.m. and 2 and 4 p.m. My executive experience had told me that these are the times executives are the most receptive to unanticipated phone calls.

As my job hunt entered its sixth month, my self-confidence sank to its lowest level. It became increasingly difficult for me to even look like a person who ever expected to work in an executive capacity again. Gradually, I realized that I was doing something wrong in my approach to finding new employment, but my mind was so fogged I couldn't figure out what it was. Could it be that it's not my fault? Perhaps our system of utilizing executive talent, of matching up jobs that need doing with people that can do them, is too helter skelter.

Questions

1. Assuming Blasdell Corporation found it necessary to release Greg Sampson, what approach should they have taken? Why?

2. What criticism can you offer of Greg Sampson's job hunting campaign?
3. What contingency planning might Greg Sampson have engaged in to have better prepared himself to cope with the possibility of someday losing his executive position?
4. What criticism would you offer the President's concern that unless they take drastic action, Blasdell Corporation will become a less attractive investment?
5. In your opinion, should Greg Sampson receive unemployment compensation? Why or why not?

Case 13
The Compulsive Career Planner

Mickey Cain looked forward to his scheduled visit with Dr. Allen Raymond, an industrial psychologist specializing in career planning. As Mickey explained to his wife, "I'm not particularly convinced that anybody can tell you how to manage your career, but I would like an outside professional to take a peek at what I'm doing, to see if my plans and dreams are realistic or unrealistic. I'm flexible. I listen to good advice."

By way of preparation for his meeting, Mickey pulled together a career dossier including a resume and a collection of notes to himself about his career progress. His intention was to make the best possible use of his career counseling session. Mickey felt more comfortable in the interview than he would have predicted, due partially to Raymond's reassuring manner.

"I'm Allen Raymond. What type of help are you seeking?"

"I want to know if I'm planning my career correctly. I want to know if there is something I should be doing that I'm not doing. I also want to know if I'm doing something that I should not be doing. I guess I'm looking for an outsider's view of how well Mickey Cain is doing in his master plan to become a corporate biggie."

"I take it you want to become a high ranking corporate officer?" replied Raymond.

"Sure do, that's why I'm here. I want to run a company by the time I'm 48 or 49 at the latest. I've read that if you don't make it by then, you can forget your chances of greatness."

"Of course, that depends upon how you define greatness. Why don't we begin by your giving me a running history of your career so far, including your education and job experiences. I'll take a few notes. Later on I may ask you for more details about some of the things you mention."

"Wow, a chance to talk about myself," said Mickey. "If I'm boring you at any point, let me know. My feelings don't hurt very easily. Where should I start?"

"Begin at the beginning. Start with your early childhood."

"I was raised in Seattle, the second child of five children. My father was a supermarket store manager. He worked long hours to eke out a modest living for the family. It seemed we were all happy. I don't recall having any big hangups as a kid. I enjoyed my early days at school, and I was a reasonably good student. I don't recall spending any time in the Principal's office, nor did the school request that my parents come in for a visit."

"At that period in your life did you have any idea of what kind of work you wanted do as an adult?" asked Dr. Raymond.

"My earliest notion about what I wanted to do seemed to originate in high school," answered Mickey. "As soon as I was old enough to get working papers, I started bagging groceries in my father's market. On occasion, an executive from the Home Office would come by to visit the store. Kind of like a General Manager of the Cincinnati Reds making a yearly inspection of the lowest ranking farm team out in the boondocks. I noticed that these executives seemed so cool, so unharassed, so in charge. And you could tell people looked up to these execs. If they stood in line, some poor working man-type would beckon to the executive to get ahead of him just because the executive looked so important. I decided then that I wanted to be an executive in a big company."

"Tell me about your high school days."

"By the time I reached my senior year in high school, it was apparent that I was just not the ordinary Joe. I played baseball; I wrote for the school newspaper; I got good grades; I was president of the G.O. (student government). In fact, I was voted the most likely to succeed.

"I entered the University of Washington in Seattle in the Fall of 1958, majoring in industrial engineering. My purpose in majoring in industrial engineering was to give myself a solid background that would help prepare myself for bigger jobs.

"My grades at college were pretty terrific considering I was majoring in engineering. I think my final grade point average was something like 3.45. I studied hard because I found the course work fascinating. My extracurricular activities kind of tapered off at college. For the first two years I worked 10 hours per week at the supermarket. Then I obtained a job in a machine shop as kind of an industrial engineering aide, for about 12 hours per week.

"While at the machine shop, I could clearly see that you have to play some kind of success chess to get ahead in corporate life. There were some very bright people, nice guys, sitting in dirty offices grinding out solutions to engineering problems all day long. After 10 years on the job they were still brown bagging it. A few of the people I met in the front office didn't seem any brighter. Perhaps they just had a better understanding of what it takes to get ahead.

"I graduated from the University of Washington in 1962 — not a bad year for finding a job. A subcontractor to Boeing offered me an industrial engineering position. After one year as an industrial engineer, I caught on to the idea of using my engineering background as an entree to sales. I recall reading an article that the best route to the executive suite was through sales rather than engineering. Six months later, I landed a job as a sales engineer for a company selling automatic car wash systems. The company was called Robot Systems. These robot-like mechanisms needed an engineering-minded person to help explain their technical features to prospective customers. Most of the people willing to lay down about $18,000 of their own capital had a good working knowledge of mechanics, having been in some phase of mechanical work themselves."

"How did you do as a salesman? How well did you perform?" asked Raymond.

"My track record as a salesman was something to be proud of. I was second in total sales out of 20 salesmen one year. The other two years, I was somewhere in the top five. The travel was a little heavy, but I really enjoyed the excitement of tying down franchises. Our units were mechanically sound, so I didn't have to feel any guilt about putting something over on people. The franchisees who followed the guidelines we gave them in our management training program could make a good living from their automatic car washes.

"By 1966, I was itching to get into management. As they say, by the time you're 26 years old you have to make your move into management if you're going to get anywhere. I spoke to the management at Robot Systems about my ambitions and, to my surprise, they were very obliging. They told me that a person of my vitality should be managing other people. Besides, business was going so well that they were thinking of expanding. I was appointed Western

Regional Manager with five sales representatives reporting to me. We decided that San Francisco would be a suitable place for the office.

"After about three years in the job, things started to go a little stale. I was becoming tired of training people to sell car wash franchises and negotiating some of the bigger deals myself. My income was moving along. But I could see my head hitting the ceiling pretty soon. My Regional Manager title sounded very impressive, but don't forget we did not have branches or districts at Robot Systems. The only logical upward progression was a Home Office executive job, and they were in short supply.

"Another serious concern I had about the company is that they were rapidly approaching market saturation. A few franchises went under in towns where we allowed one or two franchises too many. Our corporate group was ethical. They did not want people to suffer because of miscalculations on our part, so a minor retrenchment was forthcoming. Putting all the facts together, it appeared time for me to make my next move. I knew this would be a big one because I was approaching age 30.

"One criticism I could make of my career at that point was that I had neglected to play 'ping pong.' According to the ping pong theory of career mobility, an executive should go back and forth between line and staff jobs, even though emphasizing line assignments. All my experience had been in direct line jobs. I registered with an executive placement agency, and they came through like a tiger.

"After rather rapid negotiations, I was offered a job as Assistant to the President of Sterling Automotive Replacement Corporation. They are the third biggest muffler, shocks, and brakes replacement chain in the country. Particularly attractive was the fact that they were on a growth curve when I was offered the job. Before taking the job, I hit the President head on with my interest in becoming a high ranking corporate executive. He assured me that I would not have been hired if Sterling did not think I was executive timber. My starting salary was $27,500 plus a modest bonus based upon the profits of the firm."

"How did that job go for you, Mickey?"

"Sensational. It was just what I needed at that point in my career. I had an inside peek at the problems that plague a company president of a $90 million business. As he became more confident of my capabilities, he let me handle more of his work. I was dealing with environmentalists, lawyers, major suppliers, and even helping to formulate policy on brake system warranties. I would go to the office in the morning feeling like I was a company president, and that was a great feeling.

"But you can't go on being an 'assistant to' for very long. It could put you into a dependency mode that would be hard to shake when the time came to handle an independent job. So I asked my boss for a line assignment when it met their schedule. Within four months I was made Eastern Regional Manager. That's my present job, and I've held it for close to three years. It seems though that the amount of new learning on the job is beginning to flatten out."

After a short pause in the flow of conversation, Dr. Raymond asked Mickey Cain what standards he used to judge his progress. "For instance, how do you know if you are a success or a failure? To whom do you compare youself? How high up the corporate ladder is good? What are your thoughts here, Mickey?"

"I guess you could say I'm kind of a fanatic about measuring my career progress. In some ways I think I'm doing very well, and in some other ways I'm not quite as convinced. In general, I think I'm doing well, but I often hear about somebody younger than myself who has a bigger job or who is making more money.

"I'm right on target with respect to making my age in thousand dollar units. A successful person — one who is going to make it big in corporate life — is supposed to be making $35,000 per year at age 35, and that's precisely where I am. Maybe that figure should be adjusted up for inflation, but as a rough guide it does show I'm earning the income of a successful person."

"What about non-monetary measures of success?" Allen Raymond asked.

"Following the thinking of one management expert named Gleason, I think I should be managing a broad corporate function by the time I'm age 40. I've already passed the milestone of having been through with the first level of management by age 30. Wait, let me get my career graph from my attache case. I plot income, level of responsibility and age on my graph, all in different colors. According to Gleason's analysis, I should be through with the second level of management by age 35. It looks like I'm slipping behind here, being Eastern Regional Manager at age 35.

"Whether or not I can consider myself a big success depends at this point upon how sure I am that I'll be managing a major corporate function by 40."

"What are you doing to improve your chance of reaching that goal?"

"First of all, I'm keeping my eyes open for opportunities outside Sterling. There doesn't seem to be an apparent slot beyond the Regional Manager level. We don't have a large corporate set-up with separate marketing and manufacturing functions. All the action seems to be out in the field.

"Second, I'm making myself known to executives in related industries, such as our suppliers. I make it to the trade shows, even taking my turn at managing our booth. I try to have lunch with a big executive in the automotive supply field at least once a month. As they say in the trade, I'm staying visible.

"But I'm doing all the talking, Dr. Raymond. I've paid money to get your critique of my career planning. What do you think of my approach to managing my career?"

Questions

1. What recommendations would you offer Mickey Cain about managing his career?
2. What is your opinion of the validity of the measures of success used by Cain?
3. What errors (if any) do you think Cain is making in managing his career?
4. Should Allen Raymond give Cain an outsider's opinion of his career progress? Why or why not?
5. To what extent do you think Cain is over-emphasizing income in measuring his progress?

will mickey ever reach a point where he is satisfied. Internal pleasure.
If he doesn't make it to top "mid career crisis"
what happens when he retires.
good to have goals, but enjoy trip also.

Case 14
You Need Connections to be Obnoxious

Falcon Aircraft of Memphis, Tennessee, has shown a record of steady growth since the sale of its first private airplane to a business corporation in 1962. Falcon manufactures and sells a line of small aircraft to businesses who (a) believe that ownership of private planes is economical when all costs (including cost of executive time) are analyzed, and/or (b) value the status associated with the ownership of aircraft. In recent years, five different sports and entertainment figures have purchased personal jets, suggesting an expansion area for Falcon.

Steve Christie, President, and Allan Garfinkel, Vice President of Marketing, look forward with optimism to the future of the executive aircraft business. Among the reasons they cite as harbingers of good times is the trend toward larger and larger commercial aircraft. Although the larger airplanes have more luxury appointments, many executives resent being packed in with 200 or 300 other passengers. Steve Christie calls these new oversize commercial transporters, "subways in the skies." Another factor underlying the anticipated expansion of sales is the cost factor of not using private aircraft. An innovative cost analysis prepared by the Falcon financial analyst has demonstrated that the true cost of purchasing a Falcon Jet is quite often much less than that incurred by using commercial airlines. The analyst's figures include such costs as depreciation and the fact that one key sales person can cover much more territory in less time using personal air transportation. A national advertising campaign of this nature produced better than expected results in terms of inquiries and actual sales.

An international sales meeting (eight United States and two European sales representatives) was called in the context of prosperous business conditions. A feeling of camaraderie pervaded the group as the executive team and the sales reps met in a posh Pocono Mountain resort. Steve Christie keynoted the meeting with an after-dinner talk titled "Good Times Ahead for Falcon." Ten o'clock the next morning the non-inspirational or business side of the international meeting was underway. Allan Garfinkel conducted this meeting, accompanied by his administrative assistant, Ginger Baston. Dressed in casual attire, and equipped with red vinyl loose-leaf binders embossed in gold with "Falcon," the sales force listened with anticipation to Allan Garfinkel's presentation, "A New Marketing Outlook for Falcon." Smiling, he began:

"Gentlemen, gentlemen, and my trusted aide Ginger, thanks so much for all flying here to the beautiful Poconos. I see that a couple of you have bloodshot eyes. Perhaps, against company advice, you arrived here by commercial airlines or the Greyhound bus. That only proves that even a Falcon representative can at times be a slow learner." (After a mixture of laughs and boos had subsided, Allan continued.)

"My marketing knowledge tells me the best time to make changes, to strengthen something that already works is when times are good. And friends, times are good right now. But if we don't make a few modifications in our business approach right now, maybe times won't always be so good. I'm here to talk about positive, constructive changes which can keep Falcon in orbit. Nothing would be more discouraging to me than to see Falcon go into a tailspin after the enviable record we have established so far. I see three areas in which we need either to make some changes in our way of doing business, or to be mindful of some strategic mistakes we might be making.

"I note with some concern that we have been falling behind schedule in getting our sales-by-objectives program off the ground. As we explained in our last meeting, from now on we would sell by objectives. Everything we do must fit into some overall company objective. We are a modern organization that must utilize modern management techniques. I see a hesitancy on some of your parts to suggest some objectives that we can use as a starting point. I detect an almost superficial amount of attention being paid to this program. Yet a sales force without specific objectives could become a ship without a rudder."

Pete Zigafoo, the Western Regional Manager (all sales representatives at Falcon are called Regional Managers), raised his hand
and began to speak without an acknowledgment from Garfinkel:
"Allan Baby, who are you kidding? Objectives are for neophyte
salesmen. We know why we are all here. My job is to peddle
airplanes. Does a surgeon need objectives to tell him to remove a
hurting appendix? Does a big-league baseball player need an objective
to tell him to raise his batting average? We have enough paper work
around here already without the addition of a sales-by-objectives
packet. Are we here to sell airplanes or to fill out forms?"

Allan replied weakly, "I didn't solicit your opinion, but thanks
for your candor. However, please, let us not dismiss the value of an
important new management system because one seasoned cam-
paigner has been achieving decent results by an intuitive approach. I
know Ziggy quite well. He sells by objectives, but he writes his
objectives down on the back of an envelope or sometimes on his
cuffs. His wife wrote me a nasty letter complaining that objectives
written in ball point pen don't come off white-on-white cuffs!

"My second concern is that some of us — and I'm not naming
names — are forgetting that the role of a sales representative is
undergoing a transition — even in the executive aircraft business. The
sales representative of today is a true business or technical consultant
to his or her customers. When you are talking to a prospective
purchaser of an executive jet, you are often talking to a person with
sophisticated knowledge of aircraft. You have to have some updated
answers. You have to be able to converse intelligently with an
engineer the customer might bring in as a consultant on the purchase
of the airplane.

"And not only do you have to speak intelligently about the
technical properties of the aircraft, you have to do head-on battle
with the cost accountants. You have to be able to rigorously defend
the position taken by our financial people about the cost effectiveness of our product.

"I know you have all done a good job in the past. Yet there is a
need for continuous updating of your knowledge in both aircraft
technology and financial analysis. Self-improvement of this nature
can be incorporated into your sales-by-objectives program. I am not
here to point a finger at anybody, but I have a record of an instance
where we lost out on a sale because the Regional Manager did not
have the right information at his fingertips. He could not talk the
language of the aeronautical engineer who consulted on the purchase
of that piece of equipment. We lost that sale to a competitor.

"In another instance the customer decided to continue using commercial scheduled flights because one of our Regional Managers could not handle the pointed questions asked by one of the prospect's accountants. In both instances an updating of knowledge most likely would have resulted in consummation of the sale by the Regional Manager. I recognize that everybody who sells for Falcon is a licensed pilot. However, being a pilot is not enough. Your base of knowledge about aircraft and financial analysis must continue to expand."

"Hold on, Allan," interrupted Pete Zigafoo, "you're hitting at one of my pet peeves. A lot of salesmanship is going down the drain these days because the salesman forgets his true function. A good salesman exercises personal influence. People still buy airplanes from you because they like you. If you can't make that company president a fan of yours, he'll take our ideas and buy from a competitor. If you try to dazzle the customer with technical information, he may get suspicious. If a customer needs some more technical information, I have the guy speak to somebody in Memphis.

"But, Allan, don't feel alone in your mistakes. A lot of marketing managers these days have forgotten what good old-fashioned selling is all about. Whether it's vacuum cleaners or $250,000 jets, you have to be a likeable peddler."

"Ziggy, you might be talking about a style that is comfortable for you, but the idea of a technical consultant replacing personal salesmanship will work for most people in today's business. I'm not denying that you are successful, yet, we must adopt a sales strategy that will work best for most people in the long range. I hope that the rest of you in this room can see my point of view.

"A third topic I want to talk about for now deals with a rather indelicate issue. We all want to increase sales, and we all recognize that lavish entertaining is part of this business. Prospective customers expect to be whisked around the country for a demonstration ride, and perhaps have a fine meal at an exotic restaurant. Nevertheless, we have to be careful about what kind of token of appreciation we give them. Certainly, sending someone a gift pen set with the inscription 'Falcon Jet' is not out of line. Nor is flying someone to the World Series and giving him box seats at our expense. Recently, information came back to me that one of us seated in this room — and he shall be nameless — was attempting to influence sales by furnishing a prospective customer with call girl privileges at our expense."

"Hold on, Mr. Garfinkel," said Pete Zigafoo in a strident tone. "You wouldn't want to take some of the fun out of buying a $250,000 piece of equipment, would you? One customer I'm familiar with is a very lonely man with a very unfriendly wife. When he makes a big purchase he expects a little entertainment on the side. If you enforce a policy of not charging call girls to entertainment expense, some Regional Managers will simply have to charge that kind of entertainment to our miscellaneous category. Allan, I think you should learn to overlook a few things. Get my point?"

"Pete, I get your point, but it will not influence my judgment about what is sound business practice versus what is a low-level way of making a sale. I want everybody in this room to be proud of the methods he used to obtain a contract for Falcon Aircraft."

Two months after the national meeting, Dick Clapham, Eastern Regional Manager and youngest member of the sales team, was paid a visit by Allan Garfinkel. The purpose of Garfinkel's trip was to critically review Clapham's performance. Among Garfinkel's points of contention was that Clapham had made almost no progress in implementing his sales-by-objectives program. Neither had he taken steps to upgrade his knowledge of aircraft technology or financial analysis. Garfinkel addressed him sternly, "Dick, didn't you get the point of our national meeting? It's been several months since the meeting and you have done nothing along the lines that I recommend about upgrading yourself. I would even say you are ignoring the objectives program."

Dick Clapham replied, "Come off it, Allan. I got the impression that you don't take this program seriously. You're probably doing it just to look good in the eyes of Steve Christie."

"You're absolutely wrong," countered Garfinkel. "I'm dead serious about every thing I said at that meeting. That's why I'm here visiting with you to get things straightened around. Right now you are on a collision course with failure. Even some of your entertaining expenses are getting out of line in relation to your sales volume."

"Come off it, Allan. Look at the way Ziggy toyed with your plans at the national meeting. It looked to all of us as though he wasn't taking you very seriously."

"Dick, what I'm going to tell you next is just between you and me. If you repeat this conversation, I will deny that I ever said it. Old Pete Zigafoo has much more power in this company than you would realize. His situation and yours are not comparable. We can bend the rules a little bit for him for a couple of reasons. One, he has a tremendous hold over a number of major customers who update their equipment every couple of years. He sells more Falcon Aircraft than any other three Regional Managers combined. Two, he has a very close tie-in with the President. The story I have heard is that Ziggy lent Steve Christie $35,000 in cash to help him get into this business.

"What I'm telling you, Dick, is that you don't have the connections of a Pete Zigafoo. And only people with connections can afford to be obnoxious."

Questions

1. What should Allan Garfinkel do about Pete Zigafoo's disregard for organizational policies?
2. What should Dick Clapham do about his confrontation with Allan Garfinkel?
3. What should Steve Christie, the President, do about his indebtedness to Pete Zigafoo?
4. How should Garfinkel have handled Zigafoo in the national sales meeting?
5. Evaluate the probable effectiveness of Garfinkel's "confession" to Clapham.

REFERENCES

DuBrin, Andrew J. *Survival in the Sexist Jungle.* Chatsworth, Calif.: Books For Better Living, 1974.

DuBrin, Andrew J. *Fundamentals of Organizational Behavior: An Applied Perspective.* Elmsford, N.Y., Pergamon Press, 1974. See Chapter 5.

Eden, Dov. "Organizational Membership vs. Self-Employment: Another Blow to the American Dream," *Organizational Behavior and Human Performance*, Vol. 13, February 1975, 79-94.

Jennings, Eugene E. *Routes to the Executive Suite.* New York: McGraw-Hill, 1971.

Kaufman, H.G. *Obsolescence and Professional Career Development.* New York: Amacom, a division of American Management Associations, 1974.

Marcus, Philip M. and House, James S. "Exchange Between Superiors and Subordinates in Large Organizations," *Administrative Science Quarterly*, Vol. 18, June 1973, 209-222.

Pfeffer, Jeffrey and Salancik, Gerald R. "Organizational Decision Making as a Political Process: The Case of a University Budget, *Administrative Science Quarterly*, Vol. 19, June 1974, 135-151.

Robbins, Stephen P. *The Administrative Process: Integrating Theory and Practice.* Englewood Cliffs, N.J.: Prentice-Hall, 1976. See Chapter 5.

Rosen, Benson and Jerdee, Thomas J. "Sex Stereotyping in the Executive Suite," *Harvard Business Review*, Vol. 52, March-April 1974, 45-58.

Stolzenberg, Ross M. "Education, Occupation, and Wage Differences Between White and Black Men," *American Journal of Sociology*, Vol. 81, September 1975, 299-323.

PART III
SMALL GROUPS

A substantial share of organizational behavior takes place within the context of small groups. This section of the casebook concentrates on those aspects of small-group behavior that the author feels are crucial for understanding and predicting the behavior of people at work. Emphasis is again placed upon cases that have the most relevance for knowledge workers—managers, professionals, technical and sales personnel.

A degree of arbitrariness is necessary to place a given case in one particular chapter or even in one particular part of this casebook. "The Group Decides in Brazil," for example, is placed in the chapter about small-group behavior because the emphasis is upon a type of participative management that accomplishes organizational objectives via small work groups. It could be argued reasonably that this case belongs in the leadership chapter or in the chapter about organizational change (or climate).

6
Small Group Behavior

Case 15
The Puzzle
Block Work Teams *

The Atco Company is a large producer of children's plastic toys. Annual sales exceed $100,000,000, and they are growing at a yearly rate of 10 percent. One of their best selling products is a small plastic puzzle block. The Puzzle Block Department employs approximately 130 people. Organizationally, there is a department head, assistant department head, a general staff person, and three foremen—one per shift. Hourly employees work in teams which are headed up by a team leader. The main function of the department is to assemble the puzzle blocks, which have been one of Atco's most stable products over the last 10 years. Sales forecasts show that the puzzle block is expected to continue selling well and that sales volume should keep growing at a six to seven percent rate yearly for the next five years. Long range forecasts show a modest but continued growth of this product over the next 15-year period.

In the early stages of department growth, the puzzle blocks were assembled manually. Color coded plastic parts were fed into a small workplace and an operator would assemble the pieces in order to form the block. Indirect labor people were used to transport the plastic parts to the workplaces. They also transported the finished blocks into storage before they went on to the packaging department.

*I. R. Trojan researched and wrote this case.

Within three years, as sales grew, the Atco Company could see that the product had to be produced by a more automatic process if sales forecasts were to be met. An automatic assembler was designed, built, and debugged by the company's Engineering Division. As the assembler was installed, maintenance personnel from the Solid Plastics Division (the Puzzle Block Department is part of this division) were trained to properly maintain it. These mechanics would do preventive maintenance and repair any breakdowns which might occur. At first, only one mechanic per shift was assigned to the department and he was on call for any breakdowns that might occur, as well as for performing routine maintenance work.

Within five years the department had grown from the initial three machines to a total of 20 machines. These were staffed with one operator per machine and one support person per four machines. Each mechanic assigned to the department was responsible for the maintenance of four machines. This included trouble calls and routine maintenance functions required to keep the machines operating as efficiently as possible.

The support person was responsible for a variety of functions. He or she performed all the handling functions associated with the product, such as supplying parts and moving and storing the finished product. The inspection operation for four machines were also done by the support person, and he or she was responsible for the final quality of the product. If any of the machines was not producing a quality product the support person would shut down the machine and have a mechanic check out the situation and make any necessary repairs.

At this time in the department's history, a new department head was appointed. Glen Aldridge, age 30 and with past experience as an industrial engineer, was appointed to the position of Head of the Puzzle Block Department. Having been the department's industrial enginer for the last five years, he was intimately familiar with its operation, equipment, and personnel.

During his years of work as an industrial engineer, Glen had developed a good working relationship with many of the operators in the department. Though production continued to improve at the rate of one to two percent annually, he thought this level could be improved. He also sensed that the operators were not overly satisfied with the type of work they were doing. As he saw the picture, Glen was faced with two problems which had to be solved in order to improve department efficiency and morale.

During his years in school, Glen had been exposed to behavioral science approaches to understanding management. As an industrial engineer he gained more knowledge of work groups or teams. He often felt that the team approach to the Puzzle Block Department's organization might help to improve efficiency and morale. After careful consideration he decided to try this approach to management.

Interviews held with the operators upheld Glen's hunches. The operators felt that they had no control over what they were producing due to the power held by the support person. They didn't know what level of quality they were producing because they didn't get to examine their final product. The support person also had control over their machine, and this gave the operators an uneasy feeling. Operators also alluded to feelings of boredom. Once the parts were loaded into the assembler, the machine cycle gave them approximately 10 to 12 minutes before it had to be tended to again. They felt they could be given more responsibility than they presently held.

After the interviews, Glen and the rest of his department supervisors discussed how teams should be organized and what other types of responsibilities might be given to the operators. They decided to organize around a six-person team. According to their analysis, six people would be capable of operating five machines, performing all quality testing, handling all supplies, and following production schedules. It was reasoned that a team leader should be chosen for each group to organize the team and assist department supervision in evaluating departmental personnel.

Before the change was made, Industrial Engineering was asked to evaluate the plan's feasibility. A careful study of the operators and equipment was made. During this study the service provided by maintenance was also examined. The industrial engineers discovered that the mechanics, also, were not fully utilized. When the study was completed, the following recommendations were made:

1. The department should establish the work teams on an experimental basis.
2. The mechanics assigned to the department should be reassigned and given responsibility for five machines instead of four. It was also suggested that the given machines alotted to the mechanic would be those of a single work team.

These recommendations, along with Glen's, were taken to division supervision and approved. Shortly after division approval, work began to select an initial experimental team. Participants were carefully chosen to maximize the probability of success. The team was organized and prepared to operate three months after the initial idea.

The first month of operation showed little or no difference between the team operation and the normal operations. As time passed and the team became more of a unit, production began to show increases. The quality level also showed a modest increase. Within a five-month period, the work team was producing at a 10 percent increase over the rest of the department and the number of blocks rejected had dropped by 20 percent.

The next step was to establish two more teams, one per each of the other two shifts, and chart their results. The same pattern showed itself with the two new teams. It was at this point that supervision felt the change to work teams should take place in the entire department. In order to form the new work teams, one individual from each of the original teams was appointed team leader. He or she helped to organize the group and to start it into production. Within a two-year period, the entire departmental organization had been changed to a work team format. Production as well as the quality level of the product increased over the next two-year period. Employee satisfaction (measured through question-naires administered after introduction of the work teams) was at a higher level than it had been previously.

In the later part of the second year and in the early part of the third year, two of the groups showed a productivity somewhat higher than the other groups. Performance was reviewed at mid-year, following the customary policy of the Atco Company. Shortly after this performance review, department supervision began to notice feelings of dissatisfaction coming from the two superior groups in the department. In the following two months, open dissatisfaction was visible in these two groups and productivity began to decline. Department supervision began to investigate the cause of this performance turnaround.

In the course of the investigation department supervision dis-covered that the main reason for the dissatisfaction was the perfor-mance evaluation system used and the way the department applied it to the teams and their members. When evaulating personnel, a 1-10 rating system was used, 1 being the highest rating and 10 being the lowest rating. Increases were based directly on the numerical value an individual received, with some discretion (1-2%) allowed the depart-ment head. Industrial Relations studied the work done by the operators and classified the job performed into a wage bracket, the only exception being team leaders, who were classified at a higher bracket. As one experienced worker explained her objections to the system:

"If we are all in the same wage bracket, we all get the same amount of money no matter how hard we work. It's fun to outperform other teams, but if putting out more puzzle blocks doesn't lead to more money, working hard gets old pretty fast."

As the work teams were started, Glen Aldridge and his assistants had to decide upon how the teams would be evaluated. Consensus was reached on the following plan:

1. Teams would be rated as a team in comparison to each other. The discretionary part of the pay increase would be determined by this method.
2. Individuals would be evaluated on their effectiveness within the team rather than in the entire department.

When this plan was reviewed with the existing team members they had no objections and felt it was an equitable way to evaluate department personnel. However, the members of the two clearly superior teams felt that this program of evaluation did not treat them in an equitable manner. As a team individual in a superior team, the "poorest performer" might be rated a 3. As a member of one of the other teams, one of the employees may also be rated as a 3 in comparison to the other members of the group. Yet, when these individuals would be compared, not actually done by the department, the 3-rated individual in the superior team would be a higher caliber employee than the 3-rated individual in one of the other groups; but both of the employees would receive equal increases and their records would show equal capabilities.

Glen realized that in order to eliminate the dissatisfaction in his two top teams he would have to solve this problem. He was deeply committed to the team organization in the department and felt that evaluation had to continue in its present manner in order for teams to function as teams. He felt that if he began to rate each employee as an individual again rather than as part of a team, the organization which had been instituted would no longer function in the team manner.

Questions

1. What should Glen Aldrich do to enable the superior teams to regain their former levels of job satisfaction?
2. Would you recommend that Atco organize other toy departments into team operations? Why or why not?
3. In what specific ways does it appear that the puzzle block assembler jobs at Atco were "enriched"?
4. What possible structural or technological factors might be mediating the high performance of the two superior work groups?
5. What is a plausible underlying reason(s) that the team arrangement actually raised job performance?

Case 16
The Group Decides in Brazil

Miguel Sanchez, Executive Vice President of Services Electricos del Brazil, reports with pride how his company — the largest electrical supply company in the country — has introduced a unique form of employee participation in decision making. His analysis of his company's experience with self-management was presented at an international conference on innovative management. A management researcher was able to tape record the presentation made by Sanchez. With some editing and deletions, Sanchez's presentation was as follows:

"My company is owned by the state and supplies nearly 33 percent of all the electrical energy produced in Brazil. We have had worker directors on the board since 1969. Our latest innovation in management, in operation for about one and one-half years, hopes to involve worker representatives in the decision making process at all levels of management in the company from first-line supervisor to top executive. We call the system self-management or participative management.

"Our system calls for the heads of departments and sections to work with management committees, the committees to serve as guides and auditors. Their role is to insure that decisions made by management integrate the point of view of the 30,000 member work force. Each self-management committee includes representatives of the light and power union to which over 80 percent of the workers belong. S.E.B.'s 2000 supervisors also appoint their own representatives to the committees. Top management sends representatives and so does the medical department. Thus, a full cross section of all points of view is represented in our self-management committes.

"We (other members of top management and myself) are beginning to notice some improvements in the efficiency of S.E.B. It appears that our customers, who number close to 3,000,000, are getting better service and things are running more smoothly in our offices and power plants. We seem to have fewer equipment breakdowns, less absenteeism, and fewer communication snarls — a big problem in our industry.

"One of my vice presidents reported to me last week that he thinks all the employees in our firm now work with one major purpose in mind. They are aware of our goals, thus, they know what we want to achieve. They feel that they are participating in our growth and they realize that, as we grow, so will their opportunities.

"Please do not think that everything is perfect in our company. We have considerable progress to make and we still have people who doubt that what we are doing will work in the long range. One Board member told me that she doesn't believe we have our feet on the ground. She told me she has respect for what we are doing, but she is concerned that the consumer is footing the bill for our brave experiment in management. In her evaluation, electricity costs more per kilowatt hour in Brazil than in any other South American country.

"There are definite signs that the greater sense of involvement among workers is bringing benefits to S.E.B. Several months ago, two of our key generators broke down under the strain of unanticipated electrical demands. A breakdown of this nature can even precipitate a health crisis, and we were close to that point. Repairs to the two broken generators were conducted in record time even though the generators were in sorry shape. Our service engineers dug into the problems with a fervor that I had never seen before. They looked upon the company's problems as their problems. It was self-management at its best.

"Another big change I noticed since we introduced the self-management committees is a reduction in overtime. Employees now seem to be making better use of time during normal working hours. Because of this increased efficiency, there is less need for overtime work.

"The question will inevitably come up, so I will address it myself. People often ask me to explain how a union leader can function as the President of a public utility. Our President, Juan Garcia, was appointed to his job by the Brazilian Government. Garcia was a respected union leader and a respected person. I think the respect people have for him would not change if he were strictly a company man and had never been part of the union. He is a big help in getting our self-management program to work, but I think it would work even if he were not present. People basically believe in self-management.

"Our self-management committees meet regularly twice a week with the manager or section head concerned. Should agreement not be reached on an issue, it is referred to a higher management level. With my committee, unresolved issues are referred to the Board. After one year's experience we have not had to refer an issue to the Board.

"What we are trying to do is to improve the efficiency of the company, not purely through the directives of management, but with the cooperation of everybody, regarding them as a community of workers. We think we have the right system, but as a rational person, I must express some doubts."

At this point in Sanchez's presentation, there was an unusual silence in the room. People moved to the edge of their seats as if to ask Mr. Sanchez, "What kind of doubts?" He obliged by putting down his prepared talk and making a few extemporaneous comments:

"Please don't misinterpret my concerns. The general picture is a very positive one. Our experience so far already indicates that workers are responsible and capable enough to have a say in important decisions. They are not going to make coffee bean plantations out of our power plants. Every decision made in our utility is related to the operational running of the company. It is our employees who know the daily operations of the company best. They should, therefore, be making decisions about running the company.

"What does concern me is whether or not we are creating a procedure that could become cumbersome and time-consuming as time goes on. Right now everybody on the self-management committees is still enthusiastic about the idea. But what's going to happen in a few years when the process becomes old-hat? Will people begin to say 'How unfortunate, it's my turn to serve on the self-management committee. I wish they would leave us alone and put the company back in the hands of the people who are paid to make these big decisions. Who wants to sit in on a committee meeting on a warm, beautiful afternoon and second-guess management's decisions?'

"As I ponder over the future of Services Electricos del Brazil, are we really just creating a monster type of bureaucracy where we have subcommittees checking the work of committees?

"Whenever I have these doubts, I take comfort in the analysis of our capable vice president, Mr. Garcia. He does not worry about self-management committees becoming too cumbersome and slowing down our decision-making procedures. His point of view is similar to that of Japanese executives. Mr. Garcia contends that it may take more time to reach decisions with self-management, but, once you have a consensus, nobody argues about the implementation from that point forward. Before we shifted to self-management it was very difficult to get some decisions implemented because of resistance to change at lower levels in the firm.

"Ladies and gentlemen, before I answer any questions from the floor, I want to state that I share Juan Garcia's viewpoint, but I must admit that self-management sometimes sounds too good to be true."

Questions

1. Would you recommend continuing the wide-scale program of self-management at S.E.B.? Why or why not?
2. Would you recommend a similar program of self-management for the electrical company serving your geographic area? Why or why not?
3. How did appointing a union leader as president of the utility influence the results obtained with self-management?
4. What should management do about the problem of the high cost per kilowatt hour charged by S.E.B.?
5. What is your position on the statement, ". . . are we really just creating a monster type of bureaucracy where we have sub-committees check the work of committees?"

Case 17
The Corporate Office

Olympia Insurance Company is the third largest stockholder-owned insurance company in the United States with total assets of close to $10 billion. In addition to providing a comprehensive program of casualty and life insurance coverages, Olympia also offers the public a diversified package of financial services, including consumer and commercial financing. The company has experienced a long and distinguished history and is an acknowledged leader in the insurance field. During upturns in the economic cycle, Olympia has acquired its equitable share of increased revenues and increased profits. During downturns in the economic cycle, Olympia has experienced substantial increases in life insurance sales and demands for consumer and commercial loans. Over the last several years, the company has both increased sales and trimmed costs. One stock analyst publicly stated that "Olympia is truly an insurance behemoth without a significant problem."

Despite its healthy status, Olympia Insurance Company underwent a minor change in its top corporate structure one year ago. All major executives of the company were retained, but, in place of the traditional division of responsibilities among top executives, a corporate office was formed, staffed by four key executives. By name they are: Bertram L. Logan, Chairman and Chief Executive; Stanley V. Edelstein, President and Chief Operating Officer; Alexander L. Cupolo, Executive Vice President, Insurance and Mutual Fund Operations; Simon M. Clarence, Executive Vice President, Financial Services.

Bert Logan was pleased with the improved operating results he was achieving with the team approach to top management; nevertheless, he had some gnawing concerns that this was less than a perfect system of management. His concerns prompted him to confer with Dr. Allan Glass, a psychological consultant to management.

LOGAN: "The reason that I've invited you here to discuss some concerns I have is not that Olympia is in any kind of trouble. And we don't have any misfits on the staff that I want you to help me rehabilitate or reassign. We have been experimenting with a new way of running a major financial institution and I'm trying to decide if we are moving in the right direction. My personnel vice president told me you have published some very sound work about organization design."

GLASS: "I'll accept that as a compliment, Mr. Logan. After you called my office to arrange for a conference, it came to mind that I read something about your new top management structure in the *Wall Street Journal.* I was able to retrieve the article and I read it again this morning. But perhaps you could give me an inside picture of what prompted you to form a corporate office."

LOGAN: "Like many well-known companies, we sometimes appear more dynamic to outsiders than we do to ourselves or some of the very sophisticated financial analysts. I think that enthusiastic stock analysts painted too glowing a picture of our company. True, we don't have any major problem, but there was a valid reason that we changed from the standard top management arrangement to the corporate office.

"Our now retired chairman, and my predecessor, felt that Olympia was becoming a little sluggish. Perhaps even slow on our feet and unimaginative. A few smaller stock companies, and a handful of mutual insurance companies were making more creative decisions about what to do with assets. I would never tell the public these words directly, but one of the biggest problems an insurance company of our size faces is what to do with all our assets. We could buy out the stock of a major company all at once if we wished. We could erect an Astrodome that would make the ones in Houston and New Orleans look small in comparison, if we decided to go into the sports arena business.

"Our retired chairman and I both agreed that maybe what we needed to achieve a more creative flair to our financial decision making was to get more input into the decisions. In the past, Jonathan Anderson (the former chairman) made too many of the big decisions himself. Anderson and I talked to a few other large business corporations that had gone the corporate office route. We also talked to two management consulting firms that are well-known for their organization planning studies. It seemed that such a top management arrangement would make sense for Olympia. Equally important, it seemed to be the type of management suited for my individual preferences. I'm not an arbitrary person nor a unilateral decision maker.

"Just because I have the most exalted job title around here doesn't mean that I should make all the top decisions. Any decision we make about what to do with a major portion of our assets can have reverberations across the country."

GLASS: "What kind of decisions do you and your three colleagues make as a team?"

LOGAN: "We attempt to use the corporate office in its finest tradition. We try to avoid dealing with normal operating decisions. Our purpose is to focus upon major problems and opportunities. It's almost as if we are the corporate long range planning group, yet some of our planning concerns itself with the short range. Typically, we are concerned with things like acquisitions and investment strategies. We work over the topic to everybody's satisfaction, then the person whose major responsibility that area is makes the final decision.

"A recent example was a possible acquisition of Environmental Funds. They are a mutual fund company that caught onto the tail of the ecology movement. All their money is invested in companies that have a substantial stake in the ecology field. We agonized over this decision because an insurance company investing in the environment would indicate deep social concern on its part. Alexander Cupolo was very enthusiastic about the prospect, but Stanley Edelstein pointed out to Cupolo that he wasn't being rational and objective. His concern for the social good was clouding his judgment. Environmental Fund had been investing in a good many marginal outfits that would most likely never turn a profit. They needed us more than we needed them. In that situation, we used the team approach to step back from a proposed opportunity.

"At other times we have argued ourselves into doing something or going ahead in a particular direction that one person making the decision might have avoided. About one and one-half years ago, Simon Clarence talked to us about the possibility of starting up an executive and professional loan company. He reported to us that this was a promising new form of consumer financing that was potentially quite profitable. A company of this nature does all its business by mail. You get your customers through selected media advertising in such as *Business Week*. Money is lent in amounts up to $25,000, at an interest rate of close to 18 percent. You only lend money to people making over $28,000 per year. The default rate on these loans is less than two percent.

"We gave Clarence a good deal of encouragement on his idea. We went ahead and formed Executive Loan Service. It appears to be one of our healthiest new business ventures. Without the team approach, I think Clarence would have passed this idea by. He considered it a little on the risky side for a staid institution like ours."

GLASS: "So far, you have painted a positive picture of the corporate office concept at Olympia. From the information you have presented, I would say things are working. How about some of the problems?"

LOGAN: "I was coming to them. One concern I have relates to the problem of equal contribution to the corporate office. I often get the impression that Al Cupolo is not making a full contribution to the group. If something lies outside of his natural area of decision making, he tends to rubber stamp the opinion of the person whose area of responsibility it is. For instance, Edelstein, our president, came up through the life insurance end of the business. Cupolo seems to go along with any opinion Edelstein expresses about future ventures in life insurance.

"Edelstein is a terrific president. I'm just wondering if he is truly functioning as a member of the corporate office. I wonder if he is really adding creative input to our ideas outside of his own areas of responsibility.

"I'm also concerned that the rest of our management task force will get the idea that this is a company run by a committee. It really isn't. A person who is not serving as part of the corporate office would have a difficult time appreciating what is happening up here. But it is not management by committee."

GLASS: "What makes you so sure?"

LOGAN: "The difference between a committee and our version of the corporate office is a real one. Each member of the four-man team makes a contribution to the decision making process, but we all have our own areas of responsibility. For instance, we may all kick around the idea of merging with a big industrial company, but that decision would have to be mine. I am still the chief executive. I don't want our lower ranking managers to think that the corporate office means we are avoiding decisions at Olympia. We want sharper decisions all the way down the line, not the kind of compromise decisions you often get with a committee approach."

GLASS: "Any other concerns?"

LOGAN: "A final one is almost unanswerable. Our corporate office has one meeting scheduled for each week. At almost every one of those meetings I ask myself silently, 'Are four people a large enough group to act as representatives of $10 billion in assets? Or are they too many? At $185,000 per year, should I be making these decisions?"

GLASS: "I agree, your other problems might be more answerable."

Questions

1. How might Bertram Logan evaluate the effectiveness of Olympia's corporate office?
2. How could Logan go about determining the optimum size for a corporate office?
3. What should Logan do about his concern that Cupolo is not carrying his weight?
4. How might Logan guard against the possibility that his management force will use the corporate office as a model to "manage by committee"?
5. What should Logan do if the consultant advises him to abandon the corporate office because, in his opinion, it is an inefficient way to run a business?

Case 18
The Petty Group *

Camille Widmer vividly recalls how enthusiastic she was about her new position as a medical transcriber in the Medical Records Department of a 625-bed hospital. Age 27 at the time, she had earned a two-year degree from a business school. Coupled with her academic training was seven years of job experience in the medical field in such diverse locations as New York, Florida, and Alaska. Camille reports:

"Medical transcribing is a lot of fun and it has plenty of built-in challenges. The job basically consists of typing patient histories (and some of these are lulus), physicals, discharge summaries, and routine and emergency procedures and operations. A transcriber has to take this information from belts or tapes and transfer it directly onto patient records. Your job is made more difficult because many doctors speak in a garbled, hurried manner.

"The work of a transcriber demands a high degree of typing skill, a complete knowledge of medical terminology, and a strong command of general English. I take a lot of pride in all the skills and abilities I have developed during my years of work. I've been told that my work is outstanding, and that certainly gives me a good sense of achievement.

"Over the years I've developed my own set of values about what

*Stephen F. Taylor researched this case and is responsible for most of its writing.

is good or bad, or right or wrong, or terrible or wonderful. A good share of my values comes from working with a wide range of people. I can accept the fact that different people have different values. But watch out when somebody does something that rubs my value system the wrong way. I'll speak right up to such a person and tell him or her where to get off.

"I consider myself to be at least a moderate feminist, so I can make some objective criticisms about women at work, particularly women involved in clerical or secretarial work. Whenever you put a group of women together in a work situation you're going to get some clashes of interests. This is evident by the jealousies and malicious gossip that take place in an office. I was determined to circumvent these problems when I took my new position at the hospital.

"There were five other transcribers in the Medical Records Department. All were younger than I, generally by about six years, but all of them had at least three years of experience at the hospital. On my first day at work I was warned by Alice, my assistant supervisor, to be wary of certain people with whom I would be working. I thanked Alice, but I thought to myself, 'My God, I've only been here two hours and already the segregation has begun.' I resolved to keep an open mind and to stay free of any partisan activity.

"The women Alice had in mind were Bonnie, Norine, and Judy. These three transcribers were the youngest in the office, but all had worked there three or more years. They had formed their own clique, united by the fact that they worked at MRD strictly for the money and had very little interest in or concern for their work. Bonnie, Norine, and Judy were concerned primarily with stretching their coffee and rest breaks as long as possible, and to do the minimum amount of work necessary to survive in the job. No doubt, these women had worked out a comfortable daily routine for themselves.

"According to Alice — and my own observations later bore this out — their daily work output ranged from 20 to 40 tape-minutes of dictation transcribed to manuscript. They rationalized that this low output was justified because of the importance of quality transcribing in a medical department. According to their analysis, an increase in quantity would be accomplished by a decrease in quality.

"Alice and Diane, the other transcribers, were serious workers who took considerable pride in doing an excellent job. They enjoyed being productive for its own sake. On a good day, these two women can put out 100 tape minutes of dictation transposed to manuscript. They scored high on both quality and quantity at the same time. Alice and Diane were older and had more experience at the hospital than did Bonnie, Norine, or Judy. The older women were not respected and perhaps even despised by the three younger women. I suspect Alice and Diane were kind of threats to the younger women.

"The two small groups of women almost never got together on anything. Diane, however, had no hesitation in speaking her mind to Bonnie, Norine, or Judy. Quite often, she would make some blunt statement like 'You girls represent a roadblock to progress in this department,' or 'Why don't you three try and sandwich in a work break tomorrow? Your rest breaks must get monotonous.' Alice, in her minor supervisory capacity, attempted to be polite and pleasant in her dealings with them, but she was unable to achieve their trust or respect because she was an outsider to the group. Anyway, Alice really preferred to associate with Diane.

"I plunged into that office situation with the vow that I would be friendly with everyone, yet remain uninvolved with and impartial to the two small camps in the office. I, therefore, kept my nose to the grindstone, my ears to the transcribing belts, and my fingers to the keyboard. Within a few days, I was familiar with the new equipment. I was so involved in my work that I frequently worked right through my break periods. I had little occasion to speak with the others except to collaborate with them in their work. When I did take a break or go to lunch, I alternated between the two groups. My sincere purpose was to avoid showing partiality and to be friendly to all.

"When I went to lunch with Bonnie, Norine, and Judy, the talk centered on Diane and Alice. I quickly learned that Diane, or Alice, or anyone who cared about her work and expended a great deal of concern and effort was considered devious, 'square,' and unworthy of respect. These women told me their honest conviction that no one seriously believed in the so-called work ethic today, and that anyone who overtly demonstrated such a belief could not be trusted.

"Bonnie, Norine, and Judy believed that people who worked hard didn't really care for their work. What was really on their minds was an ulterior motive for working hard, such as trying to put other people down, trying to get promoted, or trying to get a raise in pay. Nobody really got a kick out of work, according to these occupational misfits.

"The result of these differences in attitudes between the two groups was malicious and suspicious speculation about Diane's and Alice's motives, actions, personalities, and even private lives. I got the distinct impression of being 'left out' for my personal attitudes and values. I think they were testing me to see if I would come over to their mode of thought and join their perverse little group. Although I could hardly stomach what they were doing, I remained determined to be tactful and impartial. I listened to all that was said, but I was noncommittal in my actions and words.

"When I went to lunch with Diane and Alice, I found that they were not the miscreants the other women in the office had made them out to be. Neither of the two women engaged in malicious or even petty gossip. They preferred to talk about their work, homes, hobbies, private lives, as well as politics, economics, and other current affairs.

"Although they were aware of the attitudes and actions of the other three transcribers, they preferred to ignore the matter and talked about the problem only if something unusual occurred.

"I found myself identifying more strongly each day with Diane and Alice. All three of us had similar attitudes about work and what it meant to us. Our avocational interests were reasonably similar, as were our outlook on life. As my closeness with Diane and Alice grew, it became increasingly unpleasant to associate with Bonnie, Norine, or Judy. After a short while, I only had contact with them on a formal basis, in the office, when the work so required.

"As a result of all this, it became clear to the three-woman clique that I had chosen sides and did not like them, despite my friendly attitude and sincere attempts not to show partiality in the office.

"When the conflict between the two groups became more intense than I could tolerate, I complained to Marge Holcomb, the manager of the Medical Records Department. I told Mrs. Holcomb that not everyone was doing her fair share of the work load and also that 'some people' were overstating the amount of their output in the record book.

"I was hesitant to name names, but when it was apparent that Mrs. Holcomb was totally unaware of the situation, I knew I had to document my allegations. I gave the manager a diary-like analysis of what was going wrong in the department. I felt an obligation to attempt to rectify an unfair situation and achieve equitable treatment for everyone. Why should Bonnie, Judy, and Norine get credit for work they did not do? Why should they get paid for nine and ten-hour work days when they only did three or four hours of work?

Why should they take long breaks and lunches when others had to skip theirs to do work that should be done by everyone?

"Soon Bonnie, Norine, and Judy found that I was an interesting topic for speculative and malicious gossip, which made its way to other areas of the hospital. The way they saw things, I was a hypocrite — pleasant and sweet to everyone's face, but behind their backs I was doing everything I could to get them fired so I could get jobs at the hospital for my friends. To them it was obvious that the reason I worked so hard was to show everyone else to be inferior, and maybe get them fired. Perhaps, they figured, I was bucking for the position of assistant supervisor.

"Bonnie, Norine, and Judy knew in their minds that quality was the important factor in their work and they thought that anyone like me, Alice, or Diane who achieved such high levels of output could not possibly achieve the accuracy and perfection that can only come at slower typing speeds.

"Ten weeks after I began working in the department the sides were clearly drawn: Bonnie, Norine, and Judy versus Alice, Diane, and Camille. All we had in common was the fact that we were doing the same kind of work in the same department. The situation was a stalemate, and I think the hospital and ultimately the patients were the losers."

Questions

1. What should the department supervisor do about the differences in productivity between the two sub-groups within the Medical Records Department?
2. State at least three conclusions about small group behavior that can be reached from an analysis of this case.
3. Can you think of any other approach (to improving upon the problems within the department) that Camille might have taken besides going to her supervisor?
4. Critically evaluate Camille's strategy of trying to be friendly and pleasant but impartial.
5. Do you think Camille was justified in explaining to the department supervisor the problems that were taking place within the department? Why or why not?

REFERENCES

Fine B.D. (now Dov Eden) "Comparison of Work Groups with Stable and Unstable Membership," *Journal of Applied Psychology*, Vol 55, April 1971, 170-174.

Franklin, Jerome L. "Relations among Four Social-Psychological Aspects of Organizations," *Administrative Science Quarterly*, Vol. 20, September 1975, 422-433.

Friedlander Frank and Greenberg, Stuart. "Effect of Job Attitudes, Training, and Organization Climate on Performance of the Hard-Core Unemployed," *Journal of Applied Psychology*, Vol. 55, August 1971, 287-295.

Gibson, James L., Ivancevich, John M. and Donnelly, Jr., James H. *Organizations: Structure, Processes, Behavior*. Dallas, Texas: Business Publications, 1973. See Chapter 9.

Hampton, David R., Summer, Charles E., and Webber, Ross. *Organizational Behavior and the Practice of Management*, revised edition. Glenview, Ill.: Scott Foresman, 1973. See Chapter 5.

Hrebiniak, Lawrence G. "Job Technology, Supervision, and Work-Group Structure," *Administrative Science Quarterly*, Vol. 19, September 1974, 395-410.

Johnson, Doyle P. "Social Organization of an Industrial Work Group: Emergence and Adaptation to Environmental Change," *The Sociological Quarterly*, Vol. 15, Winter 1974, 109-126.

Leavitt, Harold J. *Managerial Psychology*, third edition. Chicago: The University of Chicago Press, 1972. See Part Three.

Roe, Betty Boyd and Wood, James R. "Adaptive Innovation and Organizational Security," *Pacific Sociological Review*, Vol. 18, July 1975, 310-326.

Rosenberg, M. "Which Significant Others?" *American Behavioral Scientist*, Vol. 16, December 1973, 829-860.

7
Leadership Styles

Case 19
The Peripatetic C. E. O.

Granger B. Allport sits at the head of a freshly oiled fruitwood conference table surrounded by water colors and oil paintings of boating scenes. His office window in downtown Chicago peers out over Lake Michigan. From this restful, comfortable setting, Allport directs the activities of United Products, Inc. Despite his gracious office, Granger Allport is a restless, energetic leader who spends a minimum of time there. He is on the move and so is his empire. After seven years as chairman and chief executive officer of this organization behemoth, he is in the middle of the second stage of the sweeping changes he has brought to one of the largest food company empires in the world. Phase I involved masterminding an elaborate network of affiliated companies that doubled sales from $450 million when he took charge to close to $1.1 billion in the last fiscal year. Phase II involves the delicate task of meshing the old operations with the new, building an integrated, mutually supportive, synergistic combination of food and non-food companies.

To help achieve this integration, Allport explored many different types of organizational structures for the top of the organization. Upon the advice of a leading management consulting firm, and a group of inside organization development specialists, Allport established an Office of the Chief Executive. In essence, he split up his responsibilities with Vice Chairman John Luchetti and President Earl Coolidge. The new organization arrangement allows Allport to pursue what he describes as a "humanized approach to running an operation" by divesting him of many day-by-day operating decisions. Despite his unloading of routine responsibilities, Granger Allport has little discretionary time. He is an involved, busy top executive, whose time behind the controls of his luxurious cabin cruiser has diminished steadily since he took over the C.E.O. position at United Products.

Among his colleagues, Allport is noted for long range thinking. In establishing the Office of the Chief Executive, he has given some forethought to his retirement. His new organizational arrangement allows him to scrutinize the performance of Luchetti and Coolidge, both of whom are in competition for Allport's job when he retires in about two years. Internal critics have mentioned that this arrangement essentially "pits two people against each other for a reward that only one can win." Allport disagrees:

"Competition is healthy at any level in an organization. Competition leads to harmful conflict only when the people in conflict are self-serving or immature. I wouldn't have those types of people at that level in my organization. The same principle works with some of our food products. In several instances we have two brands in head-on compeition for their share of the market. Grandma's Oven Baked Bread competes directly with Ranchero Bread; Marvelo Cereal is pitted against Super Hero Nuggets."

Under the forceful leadership of Allport, United Products has grown from primarily a baked goods manufacturer to a diversified, far flung corporation with divisions engaged in production and sale of fountain pens, toys, furniture, sporting goods, restaurants, and publishing children's books.

Recognizing that rampant diversification can lead to a confused, unmanageable empire, Granger Allport gradually began to apply the brakes to diversification two years ago. In his words, "It was time to slow down, to assimilate, to pontificate, and to see where we were. Several major conglomorates in recent years have developed a bad case of corporate indigestion because diversification became an end in itself. A few of these multidivision firms have sold off the same companies they paid through the nose to acquire just a few years ago. Unrestrained growth can be worse than stagnation. I'm willing to reverse a trend if it is for the good of the corporation.

"I received some flak from a few of our executives and some of our biggest stockholders when it was released in the news that United Products had applied the brakes to diversification. My opinion is that they were overreacting. Policy must be capable of reversal if it is to be viable policy. A strong tenet of mine is that all policy is subject to cancellation once it is apparent that it is no longer serving the good of the corporation."

Allport considers monitoring the performance of his division heads to be one of his major responsibilities — a belief that necessitates travel in excess of 150,000 miles per year. He has developed an elaborate system of measuring performance that is not dissimilar to a standard management-by-objectives approach used in many business and not-for-profit organizations. Division heads provide substantial input in establishing goals for themselves and the companies they manage. Allport then compares their performance against these goals. Results can be expressed in financial, sales, manufacturing, or sometimes in "human" terms. For instance, one division head established a goal of reducing labor-management conflict in his plant.

"Without some kind of harmony in his operation," said Allport, "the long range picture could only be disaster. In a one-year period the head of that division spent an incredible amount of time hammering out compromises and reaching new understandings between management and labor. His contribution was far in excess of what he could have achieved by increasing the number of cup cakes coming out of his plant."

Allport receives monthly analyses of divisional operations expressed in the language of modern business. He stuffs these reports into his brief case and carefully reviews them in transit between divisions, or in his motel room at night. Yet he contends that his most valuable input data stems from his personal contacts with divisional personnel. "I can tell more about the manufacturing capability of our toy division by chatting with their plant superintendent than I can by studying their fanciest computerized analysis. Face-to-face meetings are indispensable for understanding both the problems and the strengths of a company."

Allport visits every operating unit at least once a year, which keeps him on the road an average of 12 to 15 days per month. "A top officer of a conglomerate can only be effective if he spends a considerable portion of his time out in the field. If you want to stay behind your desk, stay out of the multicompany or multidivision business."

In addition to these in-person appearances, one member of the Office of the Chief Executive — quite often Allport himself — sits down every 13 days with 17 middle managers from field locations. Each representative of the top office makes a 10 minute presentation followed by a free flowing discussion. United Products has discovered that these meetings represent a vital communication medium for the organization. Middle management personnel are frank in their discussion of the problems facing them.

Among the topics discussed in recent meetings are problems in implementing equal employment opportunity programs, high employee turnover in one division, slim profit margins on a brand of cat food, corporate social responsibility in relation to food preservatives with unknown side effects, and the amount of division earnings absorbed by costs of centralized administration (world headquarters). When a problem discussed at the division level seems of unusual significance to a representative of the Office of the Chief Executive (including Allport) it may become a top management project.

One such project currently being pursued by President Earl Collidge is how to provide division of more of the benefits that are allegedly forthcoming from being a member of a multicompany corporation. For instance, most of the division heads are not fully aware of the kinds of problems for which the World Headquarters is prepared to provide help. As one division head expressed it, "What problems should I bring to your attention? If we think the plant needs complete modernization, do we ask you for the capital to finance such a venture? Or do we deal with local banks? If we need to recruit more women for supervisory and managerial positions, do we go to you for a packaged program, or for the names of a few likely candidates?"

A tentative solution to this problem has been the establishment of a Corporate Coordinator who regularly telephones (and sometimes visits) field installations to attempt to match up field problems with corporate resources to solve such problems. As Granger Allport describes this function, "If it works, we'll keep it. If it just adds overhead with no real purpose, the new position will be folded."

Allport's style of leadership, characterized by his face-to-face encounters with a wide range of divisional personnel, has received its share of praise and criticism. A manufacturing head in New Hampshire represents the positive point of view. He states:

"You can best appreciate the efforts of Mr. Allport by contrasting the present with the situation that existed before he was on the scene. He had limited, almost non-existent communication with Corporate. Somebody from Chicago would visit us only when we were in big trouble on something. Usually, it was their opinion that the situation represented big trouble. Now we have a top executive group who really cares about what's going on. Mr. Allport is a very busy man, perhaps one of the busiest executives in America, yet he knows me personally.

"You cannot help getting the impression that most big shot executives don't really care much about manufacturing. They figure it doesn't take much imagination to turn products out the door. But Mr. Allport is different. He appreciates our problems, and I can level with him about some of the gut issues that we face. He cares, and he gives us an ear.

"Another facet I appreciate is that the Office of the Chief Executive, and particularly Mr. Allport, makes us realize that we really are part of the bigger picture. If you don't even know who the Corporate people are, you hardly feel that it makes sense to belong to United Products."

A division head in another plant takes a less charitable view of Granger Allport's style of management. He says:

"What Allport is really doing is glorified snooping. He's not content with our written reports describing our operations. He wants to get a peek himself. He figures he has some kind of crystal ball that will give him an instant analysis of your problems just through a one-hour conversation. He smiles a lot, shakes hands with a lot of people, but he's really absorbing a lot more information than he's giving out. Worse than that, there is a distinct tendency among some of our field managers to hold back on making important decisions until they have direct contact with somebody from the Office of the Chief Executive. I know one Division Manager who phoned Allport's secretary inquiring when he would next visit their division. The strategy worked. Granger Allport paid a visit to their installation three weeks later and the Division Manager asked for concurrence on his plan to automate away about 20 production jobs.

"Granger Allport is a capable executive who has done a lot for United Products, but I fear he has become Big Daddy who won't give his little children the freedom they need to become mature adults."

Questions

1. Assume Granger Allport were aware of the criticisms about his field visitations, what should he do?
2. Do you believe that Granger Allport over-emphasizes the importance of face-to-face contact with field personnel? Explain.
3. How might members of the Office of the Chief Executive guard against division personnel looking to them for concurrence before making a major decision?

4. Comment upon the probable functions and dysfunctions of the "Corporate Coordinator" function.
5. Assuming that United Products continues to grow, should the once yearly field visitations be split equally among the three top executives? In other words, is it necessary for Allport to have personal contact with all the divisions of United Products? Explain your reasoning.

Case 20
A Different Style of Leadership*

In my new position as Systems Engineer with BBG Industries, my initial assignment was in the Glass Research and Development Automations Section. My immediate supervisor, Al Sirroco, was given the mission of providing computer services for laboratory personnel and production, thus bridging the gap between data processing and process control. With a background in chemical engineering and computer sciences, Al was instrumental in pioneering the powerful and beneficial use of the computer as an aid to scientists and engineers. Utilizing a rented time-shared terminal, results were obtained that maximized calculation thruput and accuracy, thus providing concise historical records so vital in the research environment. Upper management was very impressed by Al's initial success in the realm of automation. The formation of the automation section was concrete evidence that management encouraged further growth in this field for BBG Industries.

Al faced the basic problem of obtaining group cohesiveness and coordination in order to build it into an effective organization. People in our group had diverse backgrounds, including a Ph.D. in mathematics, computer operators with high school diplomas, electrical engineers, and operations research personnel.

To overcome possible communications barriers among members

*Robert E. Gmitter researched and wrote this case, with the exception of several editorial changes.

of such a diverse unit, informal group meetings were held once a month. During such meetings each member could openly expound upon any problems requiring clarification, without any fear of retaliation. These staff meetings created an air of openness and relaxation of the status differences caused by differences in rank in our group. Each member had ample opportunity to make an informal presentation of what he or she was contributing to the group effort. Talk about work often spilled over to talk about personal life; the net effect was to produce a feeling of togetherness. After awhile one got the impression that any group member would help any other member with any kind of problem. One weekend, five of us helped bail out Tim, a computer operator, whose basement flooded in a rainstorm.

Our group obtained its first real surprise about Al's approach to managing people following a once-in-a-lifetime incident. An unfortunate situation occurred at the computer center which required the immediate dismissal of a key senior analyst. Although quiet and seemingly introverted, the analyst was held in high esteem because of his diligence and his record of accomplishment. Everyone in the group wondered what violation necessitated such drastic action on Al's part.

Rumors spread that perhaps the systems analyst had been engaged in sabotage, physical attack upon a fellow worker, criminal activity, drug abuse, or maybe a combination of several of these. The day after the incident, Al summoned the group into his office for an important announcement. He informed us that the extreme dedication to job performance shown by this systems analyst had caused him to suffer a nervous breakdown. Al maintained that it was necessary for his safety and the safety of the group for this man to be immediately separated from the company.

Evidence to corroborate Al's explanation was discovered when the individual's desk was cleaned out. A note was found buried beneath some papers in one of the drawers. His writings reflected several approaches to suicide. Al instigated efforts, and received approval, for the analyst to undergo psychiatric help immediately at the company's expense. In addition, severance pay of six month's salary was granted to him, and the company agreed to help him find future employment once his condition improved.

Al's explanation and the suicide note seemed to satisfy everyone's curiosity. However, several weeks later the real cause for the dismissal of the systems analyst surfaced via the company grapevine. One night when the analyst was working late, the only other employee in the building was a female computer operator. While she was walking down the aisle between the office and the computer equipment, he unzipped his pants, exposing himself. Upset by the incident, the computer operator reported the analyst's exhibitionism to her father, a manager in the laboratory. The father demanded retaliation and subsequent criminal prosecution.

Al's handling of the situation was unique and the termination of the systems analyst placated the father. By firing the analyst, the operator was spared the embarrassment of confronting him again at work. Yet, a couple of people in the group felt that Al's handling of the situation was bizarre. Irv, a mathematician, expressed it this way:

"Al sure is cool under pressure, but he's also quite a moralist. Sure, the poor guy exposed himself once that we know of. We cannot estimate the probability that he would expose himself again given the same circumstances. Maybe the father who complained so bitterly was really just jealous of the systems analyst. Worst of all, I question the value of Al making up a phony story just to bury the incident. If we fired everybody in this company who displayed a little deviant behavior once in their lives, we would probably have a pretty thin work force."

Al's approach to leadership can also be understood in his handling of overtime work. Many times crucial projects required extended periods of late hours in order to meet critical deadlines. For exempt professionals, the lab rule stipulated that no compensation would be given, regardless of the time expended in discharging one's responsibilities.

Al informally modified the rule for his group. The term "E-Time," for earned time, could be accumulated by each member for extra hours worked. This was an honor system with responsibility left entirely to the individual. Earned time could be cashed in by trading it for time off with pay when the project load lessened. Al's policy minimized the long, arduous hours of extended toil and promoted excellent group morale.

Al strived constantly to support individual accomplishments and to foster creativity in the glass industry. The Director of Research required a monthly meeting to discuss his group's progress, concepts, improvements, and future goals. Although key projects were mandatory in the agenda, voluntary participation and the initiation of topics were allowed at these important meetings. Each member of the group was encouraged by Al to make his contribution.

Al's impact upon people can be illustrated in his dealings with Kiwabi, a senior mathematician in the group. Kiwabi was advised to present a radical technique for the regression analysis of process data which reduced the time and amount of data, yet maintained qualitative accuracy. His brief presentation in the limelight impressed upper management and paved the way toward Kiwabi obtaining a fully-paid leave of absence to obtain his Ph.D.

A study I had made of various computer systems for process control, as to their power and cost, was scheduled by Al for one of these meetings. My presentation led to future study of this same topic, which verified my findings. Not only was my career as a systems engineer brightened because of it, but the company benefited by obtaining more efficient computer systems with the latest technology at the maximum return upon investment. I honestly believe that without Al's prodding and guidance this study would not have come to fruition.

Supplementing our exposure at meetings, Al would circulate, via interlab memos, accomplishments and proposals of his personnel. By this mechanism, all pertinent managers and head scientists were made aware of the existence of group members. It also provided a first-rate opportunity for interface with groups requiring our supportive capabilities in the field of automation.

Al also scheduled trips to the plants to introduce us, explain our function, and relate our specialties. Plant associates could depend upon our expertise to assist them with problems. One such problem solved by our group was the correct depositing of raw materials, such as sand and dolomite, into holding bins. Predetermined amounts of raw material are required for each raw batch composition of glass before heating. The existing manual method had caused production upset due to the wrong ingredients in the bins. An automated, batch unloading protection system was designed, developed, and implemented by our group.

You can understand Al's comprehensive approach to managing people only by sampling the kind of things he did for people. Al would arrange trips for us to other companies, such as Mead Paper, to exchange technological applications and broaden our knowledge of automation. Al also encouraged a few of us to write articles for trade journals, and even provided help in this area. On the basis of these efforts a couple of us have achieved some national recognition.

Al had a keen sense of the ever persistent technological changes taking place in the world of automation. To maintain the group's expertise, Al would submit a list of appropriate courses relevant to each individual's background. Participation and attendance at symposia and conferences were integrated into the work schedule.

One of Al's pet projects was to get us involved in the Process Control Workshop at Purdue University. The Workshop consisted of international representation dedicated to standardization of the principles of process control automation.

For my money, Al is a top manager. But not everybody agrees with me. One of the skeptics in our groups said, "If Al walked into my office at 4:30 and reminded me to brush my teeth because it was good for me, I wouldn't be surprised. It would fit his leadership style."

Questions

1. How would you characterize Al Sirroco's leadership style? Use whatever framework for viewing leadership style you think is appropriate.
2. How should Al have handled the situation of the systems analyst involved in the incident of exhibitionism?
3. Do you agree with the case writer about the implied excellence of Al's leadership approach? Why or why not?
4. Even if you agree that Al is an effective leader, what criticism can you offer of his leadership style?
5. What is your evaluation of Al's technique of "advertising" the capabilities of his group to potential users throughout the organization?

Case 21
A Fund Drive Needs the Right Leader

For a number of years Paul Callahan worked as a Campaign Director at Russell & Blackwell, Inc., a nationwide fund raising firm. Headquartered in New York City, the firm had branch offices in key cities throughout the United States. The essential business of R&B was to supervise and direct for a flat monthly fee, and for a specified period of time, the fund raising efforts of its client organizations. R&B's clients were usually nonprofit organizations, such as churches or schools. When hired by an organization, R&B would assign a full time Campaign Director, an assistant, and a secretary (all salaried employees of R&B) to each campaign. This staff would organize and direct the raising of funds, with most of the actual soliciting being done by members of the client organization. R&B carefully evaluated the probability of success of each campaign undertaken by the firm before signing a contract for its execution.

Paul Callahan had successfully directed several campaigns for R&B. Eventually, he decided to start his own fund raising firm, Callahan's Campaign Direction. Happy Acres Retirement Home, his first client, wanted to raise $750,000 to build an extension to their existing physical facilities. This new building would provide improved recreational areas, a hobby room, a new chapel, and living areas for 20 new residents of the Home. Happy Acres had originally applied to R&B for assistance with their campaign. R&B had conducted their usual feasibility study and decided that the campaign had a very good chance of success. However, because of an overload of clients at the time, they were willing to assign the campaign to Paul Callahan's new firm.

A six-month campaign was planned. Callahan hired an assistant and secretary, and established on-site headquarters at Happy Acres. The standard procedures in an R&B fund raising campaign (and now practiced by Paul Callahan's campaign) were as follows:

1. Obtain a list from the client of potential donors. Segment this list into categories according to presumed amount of donation (for instance, $5000 or greater, $1000 to $5000, down to the $10 or less category).

2. Make up a list of foundations likely to contribute to this type of campaign. Visit the director of each foundation personally and make a formal request for funds.

3. Design and print a brochure about the campaign. Take photographs and write a script for a slide show; or make a film about the campaign explaining its goals and describing what the campaign would accomplish.

4. Present a series of lectures to volunteers from the client organization, explaining the most effective techniques of getting people to contribute.

5. Write personal letters and make visits to all the potential substantial donors. Present the slide show, read them the brochure, dine them, and above all don't take "no" for an answer. A specific illustrative procedure for raising donations would be, "If they are considering giving $500, tell them that if they will allow you to put them down for $5000 instead, you will set up a handsome plaque with their name on it in the new building."

The Happy Acres campaign was well-suited to this type of approach. Happy Acres is a private institution and is affiliated with one of the largest Protestant sects in the area. Each member church was assigned a dollar goal to reach in its own parish. Paul Callahan was able to make his pitch to the whole congregation at once during Sunday Services. He appeared in each church on successive Sundays.

Callahan's campaign had a definite goal ($750,000) and a definite reason for raising the money (a new building). Foundations were highly receptive to helping this fund drive — improving the lives of elderly people was becoming a popular cause. Wealthy members of Happy Acres residents and wealthy members of the community contributed heavily. The slide presentation showed architectural renditions of the new building and included photographs of elderly people strolling about the spacious grounds, attending a Christmas party, happily weaving baskets, and engaging in other pleasant activities associated with senior citizens.

Paul Callahan so impressed the Ladies' Auxiliary with his slide show and eloquence that they pledged $50,000 to the campaign. Prior to the meeting, the Auxiliary stated that the largest amount of money they could raise would be $5000.

The campaign proceeded according to schedule. By the end of six months $750,000 had been raised for the new building. Happy Acre's management was pleased and attributed much of the success of the campaign to Paul Callahan's fund raising expertise and personal leadership abilities. Callahan's newly formed firm met with success on its first venture.

Callahan's Campaign Direction was next hired by a university located in the same city. Originally a private institution, Elmwood University had become state supported about 10 years ago. Declining enrollments and increasing costs put Elmwood in dire need of unrestricted, privately raised funds. Among the uses of these antici-pated funds were scholarships, special campus events, and financial inducements to well-known professors to bring them to the Uni-versity. Private funds were necessary because the state would not support this type of expenditure.

Paul Callahan was given a six-month contract to improve the fund raising results at Elmwood. Following the procedures he had learned with his previous firm (and that had worked for the Happy Acres Retirement Home), Callahan hired an assistant and a secretary and set up office on campus. From that point on things did not proceed as smoothly as they did at Happy Acres. At least six things seemed to go wrong.

First of all, there was no manageable list of potential contribu-tors. An enormous computerized list of alumni was available but only one quarter of one percent of these people had ever made a donation to Elmwood University. Second, directors of foundations informed Callahan that making donations to state-supported institu-tions was against their policy. Third, there was no stated fund raising goal in mind with respect to purpose or amount. As Callahan's assistant commented, "It's difficult to put together an effective slide presentation when the funds to be raised will be used for many small undefined purposes — especially when none of the purposes tug at a person's heart strings."

Fourth, there were no volunteers particularly interested in helping with the solicitations. Callahan was hired by a Board of Advisors who felt they had made their contribution by hiring him. He was expected to perform all the other tasks required in a fund raising drive. Fifth, the climate for donating to colleges was bad.

Student riots of about 10 years ago and the unemployability of some recent college graduates had decreased public sentiment for students. Furthermore, alumni felt that their state taxes represented sufficient support for a state university. Sixth, (and perhaps most important of all) considerable infighting existed about the expenditure of funds that already existed. For example, the Medical School and the Law School each insisted that contributions from their alumni belonged to them and not to the university as a whole.

Paul Callahan doggedly kept trying to apply the same formula that had been used at Happy Acres and all his other successful fund raising campaigns. Nothing seemed to work well — even a favorite trick of fund raisers. Callahan ordered $1000 worth of beautiful walnut plaques to be engraved in gold with the names of large donors. The plaques sat in the storeroom unused. Callahan put together a slide presentation which showed picturesque views of the campus. No potential contributors made themselves available to see the showing. He spent weeks designing a brochure to be sent out to alumni during the annual Loyalty Fund Drive. Results were disappointing — the amount of money collected by the Drive was approximately the same as the year before. In addition, costs were much higher than the year before. A full-color brochure printed on high quality paper was used this year in contrast to a mimeographed flyer the previous year.

An observer commented, "Paul Callahan could not understand what was going wrong. University people tried to point out to him that the problems of Elmwood were complex and required a deep analysis and a fresh approach to fund raising. Walnut plaques and expensive brochures simply weren't enough to turn people's attitudes around.

"Paul responded to the criticism by saying that he was the fund raising professional. He knew his methods worked and that people were being unfair. He began to blame everyone else for his problems. Eventually, he began absenting himself from his office for days at a time. His assistant and secretary were left in the office to field complaints. Embarrassingly, they were left with no good excuses to tell people about Paul's whereabouts."

When the contract expired, Callahan requested a six-month extension. He reasoned, "People have not given my methods a fair chance. All I ask for is a fair chance to get this campaign off the ground." The Board of Advisors issued a formal statement in response to his request:

"In our considered opinion, Mr. Paul Callahan's knowledge and understanding of Elmwood University's fund raising needs is minimal. Furthermore, he has demonstrated no leadership qualities during his period of employment by the University. His contract is therefore not to be renewed."

Questions

1. What would you regard as Paul Callahan's biggest mistake in managing the Elmwood University campaign?
2. What style leader would be best suited to handling the Elmwood University Campaign?
3. To what extent were some of Callahan's problems at Elmwood University caused by his lack of sufficient formal authority to attain his objectives? Explain.
4. What factors were responsible for Paul Callahan's great success at Happy Acres and lack of success at Elmwood University?
5. Was the Board of Advisors justified in refusing to renew the contract of Paul Callahan? Explain your reasoning.

Case 22
Our Leader is too Charismatic

CASE WRITER: "Joe, please give me a brief description of your company president."

JOE: "Before I give you my description, it's important to recognize that my vantage point is that of a middle manager in the Home Office. I'm manager of financial planning, which boils down to my reviewing operating results for each of our 25 different supermarkets. It's a demanding job that keeps me so busy that I may miss out on some important observations about our president."

CASE WRITER: "Don't worry about accuracy at this point. I want your perceptions. I will have a chance to talk to different people and cross-check observations."

JOE: "Barry L. Linder, our Chairman of the Board, is the chief executive around here. He very much is the person in charge of Linder Food Markets, Inc. Mr. Linder is a tall, handsome, athletically built man, in superb physical condition for his age. You get the impression from his appearance that he is in his late 30s.

"Under Barry's direction, Linder's has grown from a corner grocery store operation into a multimillion dollar business. We plan to open three stores in this region this year. At one time we were strictly in the grocery business. The stores have expanded to the point where they contain small department stores within the supermarkets. We have also moved into the garden and home building supply business. We sell gas and oil outside of a few of our biggest stores. Through Barry's forward thinking, we have set deals with a large bank for them to have branch offices right in a couple of our stores.

"Barry's business sense and financial resourcefulness are unquestionable. Coupled with that elusive mystique that you might call charisma, he is a powerful leader. He operates as a leader not only on the local level, but nationally as well. He has been president of various national food market associations. He has even gone to Washington, D.C. to serve on some governmental commissions.

"Barry Linder has a combination of personal charm, mannerisms, and physical presence that elicits 100 percent effort from most of his employees. He never seems to have to use coercion. He wins the respect of his peers because he projects himself to be a cut above them. He is clearly accepted as a leader."

CASE WRITER: "Are you describing the ideal leader?"

JOE: "Not really, now that you put it that way. Barry does have some tendencies towards the authoritarian type of leadership. His tendencies toward authoritarianism are more likely to be evident at the upper levels of the corporate structure. I hear he is not authoritarian when he is dealing with the store managers. He takes periodic field trips to visit his installations first-hand.

"Although I describe him as somewhat authoritarian at the corporate level, even there he comes across as someone quite out of the ordinary. He is considered by other members of the executive team to be a firm, forceful, and effective businessman, not an authoritarian. He simply overwhelms people with his very presence. He is the type who is immediately in control of any situation in which he finds himself."

CASE WRITER: "You are certainly describing an influential and successful leader. It sounds as if the company is doing miraculously well and Mr. Linder is well-liked. But no leadership style is without its adverse consequences. Let's get on to some of the problems associated with Barry Linder's charismatic leadership."

JOE: "You make a good point. Linder is a highly effective leader, but I think we do have problems with him. My evaluation of Barry Linder cannot overlook the fact that his charisma and dynamism have led to some major problems in the corporation. His projection and image have led people to believe that he alone is capable of making the critical decisions affecting the corporation."

CASE WRITER: "How does that problem present itself on a day-to-day basis"?

JOE: "The standard statement in the corporate office when a big decision has to be made is "Let's wait until Barry comes back, so we can get his opinion. Unfortunately, it is not just the opinion of Mr. Linder that people are seeking, whether they realize it or not. What they really want is a decision from "the man." When Barry Linder makes a decision, the corporate people regard it as a decision incapable of being in error."

CASE WRITER: "Do you have a specific incident in mind"?

JOE: "A local brewery was going out of business. They called us to give us first shot at buying off virtually their whole stock of beer already canned or bottled. Since we were close by and had the biggest number of outlets, it would have been a quick clean deal for them. Their president wanted action and he was willing to take a very low price for his merchandise.

"Our head buyer thought this was too big a deal to make without Barry's consent. Barry was out of town for a few days, and their Marketing Manager wanted action. We lost the deal due to the time delay. It was no corporate crisis, but things like this can weaken a company. How many good opportunities can you pass by without it having some negative side effect"?

CASE WRITER: "One thing about your organization that confuses me is the fact that you have a president, yet the chairman is making day-by-day operating decisions."

JOE: "How right you are. Brian Linder is Barry's younger brother, and president. Yet, he defers to Barry on many critical decisions. Brian is in his late 40s, the president of a $120 million corporation, but he is fearful of making those big decisions that a president must make. My analysis is that Brian fears two things. First of all, he worries about making the wrong decisions. Second, he is actually concerned that his big brother will be angry with him if he does make the wrong decision. It's like an old-world European family, where little brother is under the control of big brother so long as big brother is alive."

CASE WRITER: "It's not unusual in a corporation the size of Linder Food Markets, Inc. for the management team to check with the chief executive on all big decisions. That brewery selloff might even be considered a big decision since it departed so radically from normal policy. You would have been pushing so much Buckeye beer at reduced prices that the major breweries might have been aggravated. You might have had problems in even storing all that inventory."

JOE: "I take it you want a few examples of little decisions that the management team asks Barry to make. Ah, don't laugh, these are all true.

"Our Consumer Affairs Manager, Janet Billings, suggested that we hang some plexiglass over the produce to act as a filter between the customer and the merchandise. The idea here is that people wouldn't be buying produce that other customers had breathed or coughed upon. Maybe it wouldn't work 100 percent but it would have some excellent public relations value. It would look as if we really cared about the health of the consumer.

"The manager in charge of facilities improvement wouldn't even seriously consider getting bids on the plexiglass covers until Janet had checked out the idea with Barry Linder. To him, any idea is far-fetched until Mr. Linder has given it his divine approval."

CASE WRITER: "I don't see that as such a trivial decision. No supermarket I have visited used plexiglass germ barricades."

JOE: "Well, here's a decision a Chairman of the Board shouldn't have been making. Last September, a saleswoman, Mildred Stein, came to the corporate office. Her pitch was that the Linder's sell all kinds of Christmas merchandise, from Christmas trees to little plaster-of-paris figurines of baby Jesus. Yet, at least 20 percent of our customers are Jewish. She had developed an attractive "Chanukah Wagon" that she wanted us to allow into each of our stores just for the holiday season. It contained Chanukah bushes, candle holders, Chanukah cards, and a few other things, all done in good taste. We would get the standard markup. We wouldn't be tying up too much floor space. Most of all, we would be progressive in our thinking.

"You would think poor Ms. Stein was asking us to merge with a manufacturer of rat poison. After a brief consultation between our head buyer and the president, they both agreed that the woman should come back when the Chairman returned. He finally approved the idea, but our company received the merchandise later than other area stores. We also ordered later than other stores."

CASE WRITER: "Can you give me another example of a small decision that rightfully should have been made without clearance from Barry Linder?"

JOE: "Two years ago there was a horrendous flood in our area. Many lower and middle-income people were left temporarily homeless. Food supplies were also ruined by the flooding. Somebody came up with the humanitarian and sensible idea of having the large supermarkets in the area donate food to the flood victims. They supplied the trucks and the people to dispense the food. All that was required of the store owners or managers was to donate some food.

"It seemed that all the stores cooperated. When we were

approached, Barry Linder was out of town. His brother told the relief volunteers that a decision like that couldn't be made until the Chairman returned from a business trip. This bit of indecisiveness resulted in a rumor circulating that Linder's didn't want to help the flood victims.

"Ours is a great supermarket chain, a model for others to follow. I guess our major problem is that our leader is too charismatic."

Questions

1. What should be done about Barry Linder's leadership approach and who should do it?
2. What are some of the dysfunctions of Linder's leadership style not mentioned by Joe in the case?
3. If Joe is correct in his assessment of Brian, what should be done about Brian and who should do it?
4. Assuming that Linder's continues to grow in size, how well is Barry Linder's leadership style suited to the future of the organization? Explain your reasoning.
5. In your opinion, what types of decisions should require approval from Barry Linder, Chairman of theBoard of a supermarket chain with over a $100 million sales volume?

Case 23
The Disorganized Practitioner *

Naomi Miller, a friend of mine, is now happily ensconced in a large company as the manager in charge of word processing. She has the reputation of being a model of personal efficiency, and some of these attitudes and behavior rub off on her subordinates. Naomi learned some useful information about management from her college courses, and she has the right natural characteristics to run things. But Naomi thinks she learned the most about what mistakes to avoid as a manager from her summer and part-time work experiences while attending college. Naomi can describe her experiences better than I can. Please recognize that she is not a hostile person, just a careful observer of management practices. Fortunately, Naomi was willing to provide me with a written report of her experiences. With some editing, the report follows:

"If the person who reads this report is to fully understand my experiences in working for Dr. Wilbur Emmet, he or she will first need some insight into the personalities involved and how the office was organized.

"Our main character, Dr. Emmet is a small-town, highly dedicated practitioner of internal medicine. Due to the shortage of doctors in his area, he generally functions as a specialist in family medicine (or "family doctor" as these same people used to be

---

*Dede Argenteri conducted the research for this case.

called). Many people identify his medical acumen and behavior as better than that of Marcus Welby. Unfortunately, unlike the good Dr. Welby, he is prone to erratic emotional behavior in his handling of subordinates.

"Dr. Emmet is also a terribly disorganized, undisciplined, and unscheduled person. For example, one day he called me into his office to ask me where the prescription pads were to be found. I told him they were in the in-basket directly in front of him. He then requested that the prescription pads be placed on the side of the desk. I complied. I found out the next day that he had placed them back in front of the desk, deciding that this would be to his advantage.

"Wilbur Emmet's medical ability is of the highest caliber. He spends virtually all of his working hours either at the office, at the hospital, or driving between them. I can cite occasions when he would not go out of town because one of his patients was in critical or serious condition. My hunch is that if Dr. Emmet treated patients the way he treats subordinates, he would find himself either without many patients or with a large number of malpractice suits.

"Gloria Emmet, the business manager, unlike her husband is extremely competent and efficient in business matters. Her business-like manner does not prevent her from conveying an attitude of concern for the patient. Mrs. Emmet works in the office during the morning hours. Aside from taking care of many business matters, she relieves Francine Wilmot on the incessantly ringing office telephone.

"Mrs. Wilmot, the head secretary, has worked for Wilbur Emmet for the past 11 years. She is a kind, consoling, emotionally warm individual. Friends of hers converse with her for hours about their personal problems. Her personality exudes trust and confidence. Because almost all of the patients request to speak to Francine, her main responsibility is answering the telephone and functioning as the receptionist. Although she could efficiently handle other work in the office, such as assisting the nurse, she is kept too busy performing her regular activities to get involved in anything additional.

"Mrs. Maria DeJong, another full-time secretary, has worked in the office for a year and one-half. Maria handles insurance forms, dictation, and billing. An efficient and competent secretary, she is usually current on all of her work assignments. She also fills in any position that is backlogged. Her concern for promptness means that she begins work and leaves the office at exactly the same times every day. This practice is an irritation to other members of the office — particularly when the office is experiencing a peak patient load.

"Our last two nurses were Dorothy Bellina and Joan Melesko. It seems as if there is a quarterly turnover of nurses. Very few nurses who consider themselves to be professional will tolerate working for Dr. Emmet for long. He is a firm believer in absolute supremacy for the male doctor. His nurses are given no decision making authority on anything related to patient care. I remember one day his saying to Mrs. Bellina, right in front of a few patients, 'Here, Nurse, please fill my fountain pen.'

"My duties consist of filling in where I am needed. I have worked in the office for the past five years, generally during the summers or on Saturdays. Thus, I have developed an accurate understanding of the requirements for different positions in the office. I balance the books and prepare patients for their office visits. My main job, as I see it, is to insure that the office runs smoothly. A high school student does the filing on a part-time basis.

"A major problem we have around the office is that none of us get the backing from management we really need to carry out our jobs. Here is a good (or should I say, bad!) example of what I am talking about. On many occasions when we speak to a patient over the phone about his or her bill or appointment, the patient becomes angry. The anger is triggered by the fact that we cannot work the patient in for that particular day, or he or she thinks that the bill is too high.

"Dr. Emmet has given us instructions to hang up the phone on anyone who is hostile and uses abusive language. We ask the patient to call us back when he or she is prepared to speak in a civil manner. After such an incident, the doctor is informed of the patient who had this outburst. Wilbur Emmet would then reassure the office member involved that she did the right thing and not to worry about the situation.

"Frequently, the patient involved in such an incident would go down to the hospital to see Dr. Emmet or would wait for his next office visit to discuss the situation with him. At this time the doctor would almost inevitably support the patient, and imply that one of us was in the wrong for being so impetuous. All of this places a lot of pressure on the secretary. She is caught in the middle because the patient takes great delight in telling her that the doctor took the patient's side.

"I'll give you another example of how we need more authority to do our jobs. We have a rule in our office that if a person is a consistently delinquent billpayer, he or she is not to be given an appointment for an office visit. When a patient with a record of delinquent payments calls for an appointment, we refer the call to Dr. Emmet. He frequently makes an exception to his own rule and agrees to see the patient.

"When the doctor does follow his rule about delinquent payers, the matter is still not always settled. Cases have arisen where the patient will go to the Emergency Room and request to see Dr. Emmet, instead of the doctor on service. Rather than tell the patient he or she will have to pay his bills, Dr. Emmet will examine the patient. He then reminds one of us to make sure to inform the person again about bill payments. But if a confrontation between the patient and one of us occurs, there is no assurance that he will support us. When Gloria Emmet hears of the incident, she will call the patient herself and back our judgment. Temporarily, at least, faith in our judgment is reinstated.

"One develops the distinct impression that Wilbur Emmet does not know how to lead a medical office. The consequences of this misdirected leadership approach can be disastrous. Our office is organized so that if one person is lagging behind in her work, another will pitch in. Generally, this keeps the office running smoothly. When the doctor is in one of his volatile moods, he may decide to reassign our job responsibilities.

"Chaos is created by such a decision, particularly so because two people may be assigned the same job. It makes us feel as if the doctor has very little confidence in our ability to carry out the job we were hired to do. Two people don't need to perform the same task in such a small office. Besides, we are hardly being used to our full capacity when we are sharing the same job.

"Much of our work is dependent upon the doctor to complete some form, or to read and analyze reports. When Dr. Emmet is lax in finishing his paper work (many things in a medical office require a physician's signature) it holds us up. "Erratic" is the word that best describes his approach to his paper work. One week he will keep all his dictation and records up to date; the next week he might not finish any of it. Thus, when the doctor schedules his time properly we work to capacity. Since this is not usually the case, we waste a lot of time during normal working hours.

"Were it not for the big demand for medical services in his town, I think Dr. Emmet would go out of business. Either that, or let somebody who knows something about management run the office."

Questions

1. What should Naomi (and, or her coworkers) have done about Dr. Emmet's erratic leadership behavior?
2. What do you think are the reasons that Dr. Emmet is more considerate of his patients than of his office workers?
3. How would you characterize Wilbur Emmet's leadership style according to any theory of leadership you choose as a framework?
4. What administrative changes (things relating to structure, not changes in people's attitudes or behavior) can you suggest that might ameliorate some of the problems described in this case?
5. How might the concept of shared leadership (divorcing technical from administrative leadership functions) help resolve some of the problems described in this case?

REFERENCES

Berlew, David E. "Leadership and Organizational Excitement," *California Management Review*, Vol. 27, Winter 1974, 21-30.

Day, David R. and Stogdill, Ralph M. "Leader Behavior of Male and Female Supervisors: A Comparative Study," *Personnel Psychology*, Vol. 25, Summer 1972, 353-360.

Fiedler, Fred E. "Validation and Extension of the Contingency Model of Leadership Effectiveness," *Psychological Bulletin*, Vol. 73, March 1971, 128-148.

Greene, Charles N. "The Reciprocal Nature of Influence Between Leader and Subordinate," *Journal of Applied Psychology*, Vol. 60, April 1976, 187-193.

Gruenfeld, Leopold and Kassum, Saleen. "Supervisory Style and Organizational Effectiveness in a Pediatric Hospital," *Personnel Psychology*, Vol. 26, Winter 1973, 531-544.

Hunt, James G. and Larson, Lars L. (Eds.). *Contingency Approaches to Leadership.* Carbondale, Illinois: Southern Illinois Press, 1974.

Lawler, D.J. *Effective Management: A Social Psychological Approach.* Englewood Cliffs, N.J.: Prentice-Hall, 1972.

Sims, Jr., Henry P. and Szilagyi, Andrew D. "Leader Structure and Subordinate Satisfaction for Two Hospital Administrative Levels: A Path Analysis Approach," *Journal of Applied Psychology*, Vol. 60, April 1976, 194-197.

Stogdill, Ralph M. *Handbook of Leadership: A Survey of Theory and Research.* New York: The Free Press, a division of Macmillan Publishing Company, 1974.

Vroom, Victor H. and Yetton, Phillip W. *Leadership and Decision Making.* Pittsburgh, Pa.: University of Pittsburgh Press, 1973.

8
Improving Subordinate Performance

Case 24
Why Do I Need Objectives?

"Mona, there is something I want to review with you," said Sam Williams, President of Biotronics, to his private secretary. "I want to make sure that the management-by-objectives system is moving on schedule. Also I'm very interested in learning how the program is being received throughout the company."

"You told me to set up a special file for the program. I have, and it seems to be up to date. Almost everybody has submitted his forms on time. People seem to be filling out the forms, so I assume that the program is at least in operation."

"So far, so good, Mona. But still we don't know if the program is working. Just because people are filling out the forms doesn't mean that we yet have an effective mbo system."

"I recognize that, Sam, but the feedback I'm getting is that people are accepting the program as a sensible way of doing business. To my knowledge, people are not grumbling about participating in the program."

"Maybe we need some more direct feedback on how the program is operating. Mona, could you set up meetings for me with any three managers you choose? My only restriction is that you select one manager from marketing, one from engineering, and one from manufacturing."

Sam met first with Lloyd, the Western Regional Sales Manager. Asked about his experiences with the newly created mbo program, Lloyd replied: "Sam, it's too early to tell how well the program is being received, but so far the reaction is positive. You know sales people, they tend to be good sports. They can roll with the punches. Field people want business for the company and they are willing to go along with almost anything the Home Office thinks can help them."

"That's certainly an unusual interpretation of an mbo program — something the Home Office thinks can help improve performance in the field. It is intended to be helpful, but the developers of mbo look upon it as a system of management."

"Sam, if the mbo program is supposed to be a system of management, it could lead to some very rigid management practices. We have found that in the field you have to be more flexible than the mbo program seems to allow. We plan our objectives the best we can, but we don't take them too seriously."

"What do you mean, you don't take them too seriously?"

"Don't misinterpret what I have to say, Sam. I'm glad mbo has replaced subjectivity, but a field person can't predict his life as neatly as a staff person. We chase after things that seem important at the moment. Our customers' needs change so fast that our objectives become obsolete pretty quickly."

Sam met next with Oscar, the Factory Superintendent. In his usual deadpan manner, Oscar described his experiences with the mbo program: "No sweat, Sam. We in manufacturing are used to working under quotas. It's the same ball game with a different name. One of my general formen called the mbo program old wine in new bottles. I have to go along with him. I do like the forms better than the ones we used with the old appraisal system, though. It prevents us from playing favorites. It's hard for my men to rate somebody very high just because of a friendship. My managers now have to look at a man's results."

"Oscar, it looks like you're using the program just as it was intended. Keep up the good work."

Sam then met with Elmer, the Manager of Development Engineering. At first evasive about his department's use of the program, Elmer then commented: "As far as I and my three project engineers are concerned, this program is a waste of time. You're the boss, so we'll go along with it. But I still think we could be putting our time to better use."

"What do you mean by that, Elmer"?

"It may be hard for you to understand our position, Sam, but an mbo system was not meant for creative people. You can't set up objectives for creative work. We are all professionals who know why we are being paid. It makes no sense to straight-jacket us with a complicated set of forms. It seems to me that mbo is better suited for people performing routine chores."

"You're entitled to your opinion, Elmer, but I think you have a lot to learn about mbo. Perhaps we should call back the consultant who help set up the program to do some reeducating."

The following morning Sam discussed the results of his survey with Mona: "It looks like our program is meeting with mixed results. I see some people taking it seriously and benefitting from it, but I also detect some resistance. In some ways, I'm encouraged and in some ways I'm discouraged. Still, I think we must move forward with the program on a company-wide basis. Can I see you this afternoon at three to get you further involved in the program?"

Arriving promptly at three, Mona asked Sam. "You mentioned something about my getting further involved in the program. Does that mean I'm going to take on more administrative responsibility for it? I'm all for that. I hope to have my job reclassified as an administrative assistant sometime in the near future."

"Maybe giving you more responsibility for the program would be a good idea. But that's not what I had in mind for today's conference, Mona. I think it's time you and I set up some objectives for you. I doubt the system will be fully effective until everybody in the company is involved."

"Sam, are you serious? Or is this a good-natured joke Mr. Williams has sprung on his private secretary?"

"Of course, I'm serious, I believe in mbo."

"Well, Sam, I believe in it too. If I didn't believe in it, I wouldn't be the company coordinator. But I cannot understand how you would use the program on me. Why do I need objectives? Haven't I been doing my job well?"

Questions

1. What factors account for the different perceptions of the value of the mbo program?
2. Should Mona be personally involved in the mbo program? Why or why not? Should Mona be the coordinator?
3. How should Sam handle Mona's resistance to the program?
4. What is your opinion about the applicability of mbo to creative work?
5. How should Sam handle Elmer's resistance to the program?

Case 25
The Age of Accountability

At 4:30 on a Friday afternoon, Brad Williams gestures to the bartender that he and Sam Levy, a Board member, would like another round of martinis. One year has passed since Brad arrived on the scene as the new Executive Director of Children's Assistance. "Brad, you look like you have a lot on your mind," said Sam. "Why don't you go over the highlights of what has happened in your shop since you took over the reins last Janury."

"Okay," said Brad, "but I'm not in the mood to be diplomatic. I'll give you a rundown of what has really happened, as I see the situation."

"Don't worry about my saying anything unfavorable to other Board members. I think you've done a fine job, Brad, considering what you've had to work with."

"We can't stay in this bar all night, so I'll just sketch over the highlights.

"To begin, you have to understand my management philosophy. People have called me a hardnosed, tough-minded executive. A few of my critics have even described me as being more abrasive than carborundum, but they could be missing the point. You might say my background is in the humanistic tradition, but that doesn't mean I don't care about results. I remember, when I was a minister running my own parish, I used to ask myself if I was really saving any souls or having some kind of an impact on the parishioners. My attitude was that I didn't belong as a minister if I wasn't achieving measurable results. Can you believe it? I fantasied installing a religion-by-results program in my parish. Thinking like that got me interested in agency work. As a department head, I was all enthused about management-by-results. Part of the reason I was selected for the position as Executive Director of Children's Assistance is because of my business-like approach to public service.

"Two weeks after I took over as Executive Director, I could see some very clear signs of organizational pathology. In other words, that organization was *sick, sick, sick!* Above all, the entire shop was run without any accountability. Nobody seemed to know how much direct or indirect time case workers were spending on children's problems. We didn't even have breakdowns of the average amounts of professional and non-professional time required for different kinds of services. Nobody dreamed of measuring whether or not a particular type of service was performing any good. One counselor demanded a salary increase because she saw 100 more children in one year than the year before. When the case was brought to my attention my response was, 'Did you produce better or worse results by seeing those 100 additional children'?

"A second major problem facing me was a sticky personnel situation. The man I replaced was a kind, non-management type agency head. He preferred a two-hour luncheon with Board members to grappling with internal problems. Because of his lack of interest in administrative work, he allowed his Assistant Director to function as the informal head of the agency. Al, the Assistant Director, was ineffective for different reasons. He tried to do everything himself, and because of it wound up accomplishing very little. He tried to keep abreast of all problems throughout the agency, but wasted much of his time on inconsequential things. I found an inch of correspondence in the file relating to the purchase of new waste-baskets for the agency, all with his signature. Because Al was so busy picking nits, he didn't spend much time with the department heads below him.

"The first big change I made in running Children's Assistance was to install a formal Management Information System. It included a daily reporting of hours allocated to different tasks, both professional and non-professional. I upgraded a secretary to the task of Management Information Coordinator. Al tried to block the system by demanding that Sheila (my MIS Coordinator) review all her input data with him before formally entering it into the system. In addition to my Information System, I launched a management-by-objectives system in which everybody in the shop above the clerical level would work toward some very specific targets. If they achieved these targets or goals, they could say they were doing a good job. If they missed, they goofed. It's that simple.

"Al represented a real problem of organization planning. I couldn't live with the situation of his being my direct assistant, so I placed him in charge of training and new projects. My hope was to put him where he could do the least damage, but I'm still not sure if I did the right thing. Al could do damage in any position. One of the training specialists complained that Al was telling him to switch the slide projector model he was using. Somehow, people listened to Al, maybe because he was really in charge for so many years.

"Reactions to my new programs and procedures varied all over the lot. On the positive side, one of the department heads said to me after I had been on the scene five months, 'Brad, when you arrived, we lost Santa Claus, but we gained a manager.' I considered that a profound compliment. On the negative side, I also received a lot of flak and sniping. One day a small package arrived on my desk. Inside was an inexpensive stop watch, probably bought at a pawn shop. A note was attached which stated, 'Dear Brad: Use this stop watch in good health. We all know that you could measure the output of social workers more precisely if you only had a more accurate measuring device. P.S. Watch out for Jane. Last seen, she was spending three more minutes than the national average social worker requires for driving back from a field visit.'

"In a staff meeting one day, the chief social worker said he finally figured out what was wrong with the United States. 'Factories have become more like social agencies, and social agencies have become more like factories.'

"Because of the constant undercurrent of flak, I formed a committee to help set objectives and implement the management information system. Members of the committee included representation from all levels. Professionals, paraprofessionals, clerical help, and even a Board member. I think the level of cooperation is improving, but things are not yet running smoothly. Al still carries a lot of weight in the agency. Many people still check with him to get approval on things."

"Brad, I agree with you," said Sam. "You've had an eventful year, and a hard year. But you're moving in the right direction. I guess we live in an age of accountability."

Questions

1. How might Brad have better managed the situation with Al, the former Assistant Director?
2. Might Brad have approached installing his Management Information System in a different manner? How?
3. How appropriate is Brad's leadership style for running a social agency?
4. What is your reaction to the comment that "Social agencies shouldn't be run like factories."?
5. What do you see as the key issue in this case? Why?

Case 26
The Full Court Press

Newport Mutual Insurance Company has a regular program of superior-subordinate counseling that has been in operation for close to five years. The core ingredient of the program entails a three-way meeting of the person being counseled about job improvement, his or her boss, and a human resource specialist on assignment from the home office. Prior to the meeting, according to the format of the program, the superior confers briefly with the human resource specialist to discuss the plan for the subordinate's development.

Bonnie Fraser, Branch Manager of the Richmond, Virginia Office and a 16-year veteran in the casualty insurance business, was scheduled to meet with Rudy Bonbright, the Human Resource Specialist from the Home Office. As Branch Manager for the last three years, Bonnie's performance was rated as satisfactory by her superiors. Any criticism about her performance seemed to center around her devoting an unusual amount of attention to the personal development of her subordinates, sometimes at the expense of performing some of the other functions required of her position.

With this criticism about her performance in the back of his mind, Rudy Bonbright began his discussion of the development of personnel at the Richmond Branch.

RUDY: "How are things going for you here, Bonnie? I mean how are your people coming along?"

BONNIE: "Quite satisfactorily, I would say. Our sales are up slightly and we are getting a better mix of business. We have added substantially to our commercial lines and are getting our share of the desirable lines of coverage. Nobody in the office is in danger of being dismissed for poor performance and most of the 20 people here are showing signs of making positive strides in their development. I am personally working with six of the people on their development. The other people are being helped along by their supervisor, but sometimes I'm concerned that part of their development gets lost in the press of everyday business matters. I do what I can to insure that such a situation does not happen with the people reporting directly to me."

RUDY: "Maybe we could begin by talking about a specific person among the six you are working with directly. With whom shall we begin?"

BONNIE: "A good starting point would be Russ Atkins, my Field Sales Manager. As you know, he is responsible for most of the recruitment, selection, and training of our new sales personnel. I assist him on many of the selection decisions, but maintaining a field force is mostly his job. He's a good man, with potential for advancement, provided that he overcomes a few developmental needs."

RUDY: "In your opinion, what are his developmental needs?"

BONNIE: "Number one, I don't think Russ is a very effective planner. There are times when he honestly comes into the office with no plan of attack for what he should be doing. He just waits for an assignment or for the phone to ring. One phone call can send him into a three-hour diversion. He also doesn't seem to have a master plan for recruiting a steady supply of new sales personnel. He figures enough people are eager to sell insurance to make it unnecessary for him to draw up elaborate schemes for recruiting new personnel.

"I'm developing a gnawing concern that part of Russ's problems — one thing that is holding him back — is that he is less self-confident than a Field Sales Manager should be. Maybe this could be the factor underlying his other developmental needs."

RUDY: "And what might that be?"

BONNIE: "I think that Russ lacks a killer instinct. He's not mean enough, and this rubs off on the sales people he is trying to develop. Of course, I don't believe in the old-fashioned stereotype of an insurance salesman who badgers prospects into buying more insurance than they need. In my branch, I try to disseminate the idea that a representative for Newport Mutual is a professional insurance consultant — somebody who has the good of the client in mind at all times. Yet, there are times when a prospect needs a little convincing.

"As part of our sales training program, the Field Sales Manager accompanies the inexperienced salesperson on as many sales calls as may be needed. It is crucial for the Field Sales Manager to demonstrate how important it is to close a sale. Not much skill is required in talking to insurance prospects about their insurance problems. A salesperson is paid to close a few big ones. And here is where a little bit of the killer instinct is required. After the prospect is in clear view, you have to get that harpoon in and wheel him on to your boat."

RUDY: "How does Russ Atkins feel about your diagnosis of his needs for development?"

BONNIE: "Russ has a mixed reaction to some of my observations. I think he partially agrees. He seems to be at least fairly responsive to some of our agreed upon action plans for overcoming his developmental needs."

RUDY: "What are these action plans that you have developed?"

BONNIE: "They involve some reading, some attendance at the right kind of training program. But rather than go into detail about them now, why don't we wait until our three-way conference. We can carefully review them in Russ's presence. Then we won't be going over the same ground twice."

RUDY: "Good idea. Why don't we meet with Russ now. Can we use the conference room? It's somewhat neutral territory. If we meet in your office, Russ may unconsciously interpret it as a use of double authority to exert force to get him to improve."

(Bonnie, Rudy, and Russ meet in the conference room.)

BONNIE: "Russ, you have met Rudy before. He's the human resource man from the Home Office who's here to help us with the superior-subordinate development program."

RUSS: "Oh, sure, I remember you came by about six months ago. I understand that today is my turn. I've been looking forward to this meeting. It's always good to get an objective third party's opinion about something as important as your career development."

RUDY: "To begin, Russ, could you review for me what your career goals are?"

RUSS: "Sure thing. I'm in field sales now and I see it as a logical stepping stone to reaching my ultimate goal of a top management position in the marketing wing of an insurance company. At age 28, a Field Sales Manager is a fine perch for further advancement. I would assume that if things go well, I will be eligible for a Branch Manager position in a couple of years or less."

RUDY: "I see. That sounds logical to me. Statistically speaking, a very small proportion of people ever get to be Vice Presidents of Marketing, but it's well worth aiming high."

BONNIE: "As things stand now, what will you need to do as an individual to reach those heights? In other words, is there anything that could be blocking you from reaching your goal?"

RUSS: "It's mostly a question of more of the same. More experience that will improve me across the board. We all need improvement. Just like anybody else in business, I could benefit from being more intelligent, creative, and luckier."

BONNIE: "But what about some of the specific needs for growth that apply to you, Russ Atkins, as an individual?"

RUSS: "Yes, I almost forgot about them, didn't I? Number one, you told me that I should plan my activities more effectively. That might be true to some extent, but my job as Field Sales Manager doesn't lend itself very well to careful planning. You never know which sales representative is going to ask for your help or which of the big customers might want to talk to you. Aside from the duties of a Field Sales Manager, I also handle my share of key accounts."

RUDY: "What action plan have you worked out to improve your skills as a planner?"

RUSS: "I believe that just by being aware of the importance of planning, you can improve your skills in that area. Also, at the request of Bonnie, I've been reading a couple of books that give a manager a lot of good tips on planning his work day. One I recall is an old book of Drucker's, *The Effective Executive* (1967). I've made some progress in reading it and it looks useful. Bonnie, of course, has her own sure-fire techniques of forcing me into becoming a better planner."

RUDY: "What are those?"

RUSS: "She bought me a huge Executive Daily Planner which requires that you keep a meticulous diary of what you do and everything you plan to do. One section of each month's diary asks you to list your plans for the week, month, year, and, finally, a three-year projection. The idea is sound and I make casual use of it. At least every other day, Bonnie asks me how my Executive Planner is going. She follows my diary very closely while I interpret it as a rough guide for action."

BONNIE: "Yes, I do think that such a desk planner is a useful step in improving your planning skills on a day-by-day basis. It requires careful follow-up, otherwise it is easily forgotten."

RUSS: "Okay, now let's talk about Bonnie's insistence that I need to be more aggressive, more of a killer. She also tells me that I should be more self-confident. I agree to some extent, but I don't want to overdo it. A fine line exists between assertiveness and being obnoxious — particularly here in Richmond. I think you can get away with more assertiveness in the New York area. It's a cultural expectation."

RUDY: "What improvement programs have you worked out to match these developmental needs?"

RUSS: "Bonnie has influenced me a lot here, too. First, let's take the self-confidence angle. I don't feel lacking in self-confidence, but I do agree that I, like anybody else, could benefit from acting more self-confident in more situations. Bonnie was helpful in arranging for the company to pay my tuition to the Dale Carnegie Sales Program. I found it effective, even though it is somewhat on the emotional, rah, rah side. Excuse the expression, but I don't want to come across to others like the stereotype of an insurance salesman.

"Bonnie's follow-up to my experiences at Dale Carnegie is worth talking about. She would ask me every week if I felt I was getting anything out of the program, if I were becoming more self-confident. That kind of follow-up can get annoying."

BONNIE: "I didn't mean to annoy you. It's just that any kind of developmental experience requires frequent attention. If you ask yourself periodically what you are getting out of a training program, you are more likely to derive some benefits from it. It's another way of reminding yourself to put into practice the principles that you learn during the training sessions."

RUDY: "Are there any other concerns you have about the way Bonnie monitors your developmental program?"

RUSS: "Yes, I think she plain puts too much effort and time into the development of her subordinates, particularly me. She can get a little cloying at times, despite her good intentions. Another thing she's been pushing is for me to attend assertiveness training. Her point is that perhaps this is just the kind of growth I need to become more self-confident and more of a 'killer.' I'm not so sure I'm that unassertive, but I was willing to give it a try. As things worked out, I did attend a few sessions and I found them intriguing. For one, I learned that I'm much less of a basket case than Bonnie thinks. Most of the other people in the group are far less assertive than I am."

BONNIE: "Then you did get something out of the program. It gave you more confidence in yourself. You realize some more of your strengths."

RUSS: "I guess I should be thankful for that. I'm not objecting to the fact that you pointed me toward an assertiveness training program. What does irritate me is the way you keep a weekly check on my progress. At least once a week you ask me, 'Do you feel yourself becoming more assertive?' "

RUDY: "Then you object to Bonnie's coaching techniques."

RUSS: "At least some aspects of her coaching. What I dislike most is her full court press."

RUDY (After the meeting): Bonnie, I think you are pressing too hard with Russ. He may be showing some resistance to being overdeveloped by the company. We want our managers to participate with enthusiasm in human resource development, but we also have to watch out for an overemphasis in this area. Remember that all development is really self-development.

Questions

1. What should Bonnie Fraser do about Russ Atkin's opinion that she is maintaining a "full court press?"
2. What recommendations might Rudy Bonbright, the Human Resource Specialist, make about the superior-subordinate relationship between Bonnie and Russ?
3. Do you think it is legitimate for Bonnie to expect Russ to become more self-confident and assertive?
4. To what extent do you think the presence of Rudy Bonbright in the superior-subordinate relationship represents an invasion of Russ Atkin's privacy?
5. How committed does Atkins seem to the developmental goals mentioned by Fraser in her meeting with Bonbright?

REFERENCES

Beatty, Richard W. and Schneirer, Craig Eric. "A Case for Positive Reinforcement," *Business Horizons*, Vol. 28, April 1975, 57-66.

DuBrin, Andrew J. *Fundamentals of Organizational Behavior: An Applied Perspective.* Elmsford, N.Y.: Pergamon Press, 1974. See Chapter 8.

DuBrin, Andrew J. *Managerial Deviance: How to Deal With Problem People in Key Jobs.* New York: Mason/Charter Publishers, 1976.

Fein, Mitchell. "Job Enrichment: A Reevaluation," *Sloan Management Review*, Vol. 15, Fall 1973, 69-88.

Hackman, J. Richard. "Is Job Enrichment Just a Fad?" *Harvard Business Review*, Vol. 53, September-October 1975, 129-138.

Ivancevich, John M. "Changes in Performance in a Management by Objectives Program," *Administrative Science Quarterly*, Vol. 19, December 1974, 563-574.

Jamieson, Bruce D. "Behavioral Problems with Management by Objectives," *Academy of Management Journal*, Vol. 16, September 1973, 496-505.

Kaufman, H.G. *Obsolescence and Professional Career Development.* New York: Amacom, a division of American Management Associations, 1974.

Reddin, William J. *Effective Management by Objectives: The 3-D Method of MBO.* New York: McGraw-Hill, 1971.

Slusher, E. Allen. "A Systems Look at Performance Appraisal," *Personnel Journal*, Vol. 54, February 1975, 114-117.

9
Interpersonal Communications

Case 27
The Unisex Job Title

A diagonal slice of the management of Comfortware Mills awaited with curiosity the report of Jean Hammond, Manager of Equal Employment Opportunity. As described in the management newsletter distributed two weeks earlier, Ms. Hammond had done an extensive study of job titles at Comfortware, and her report would be issued verbally in today's meeting. Attendance was mandatory. Jean Hammond spoke:

"Good morning, members of management. I am happy to notice what a large turnout we have for my presentation. My professional assistants, my word processing technician, and I have worked diligently to assemble my report in time for today's meeting. If this were not an important issue, one that could have consequences far beyond the confines of Comfortware Mills, we would not have asked for a personal audience. As a supplement to my oral report this morning, every member of management will receive a written summary of our findings.

"As the memo indicated, the nature of my study was to determine if Comfortware was engaging in sexist practices through the use of job titles. Many other organizations have been guilty of this subtle form of sex discrimination. I suspect that every person in this room can give an example of a company that uses the antiquated title 'salesman' to really mean 'salesperson' or, better yet, 'sales representative.' Here we are in the year of the Bicentennial and we still use anachronistic and discriminatory job titles in our company.

Comfortware has a favorable record in providing equal employment opportunity to males and females, a record that we can all be proud of. Yet, I fear that some widespread sexist practices still exist in the way we address people.

"Please hold your comments until the end of my formal report. My topic is so emotionally laden — though it shouldn't be — that I know you all have some worthwhile reactions to the points I raise.

"As my assistants and I scanned each and every job title in our policy manuals and personnel handbooks, I came up with a grand total of 27 different discriminatory labels. These, of course, do not represent the true extent of sexist labeling of people in our employ. A fair number of sexist *informal* labels was also revealed in our study. I will return to that topic later. To begin the core of my report, let me share with you some of my representative findings of discriminatory job titles. I will recommend an acceptable alternative in each case and give you a hint of my reasoning for suggesting the alternative.

"Unfortunately, Comfortware Mills is guilty of using the term 'salesman' when referring to both males and females. One monstrosity I encountered was 'woman salesman.' Let's modernize and use the term 'sales representative' at all times. I recognize that we use this term most of the time. An unfortunate connotation of the term 'salesperson' is that it refers to a retail sales clerk in the minds of many people.

"We found a job called 'yardman' used for an individual who tends to the lawn and related matters. Please, let us refer in the future to the one holding this job as 'yard person' or 'yard custodian.' There is no biological reason why a person who tends a yard must be male. Better yet, let's just use the term 'gardener' and let that serve as a model for seeking out neutral terms for every job or position at Comfortware.

A term widely used at our manufacturing sites is 'seamstress'. It is so exclusively associated with females that the term 'sewing machine operator' or 'sewing worker' should be used as an immediate substitute.

"Particularly offensive are the job titles 'maid' and 'custodian.' They are both cleaners, yet a woman is a maid and a man is a custodian. Fortunately, we dug out that one. We found a wage inequity between the two in favor of the male! I'm sure nobody in this room wants us to be in violation of the law. That situation will be corrected immediately.

"Although the term 'secretary' is really a unisex job title, it has developed an unfortunate sex-linked connotation. Some of you older people present today will recall that it is only relatively recently that females were even allowed into secretarial jobs. Ironically, it is now considered a synonym for female. Let's use the neutral term 'word processor' or 'word processing technician.' It has a nice modern ring.

"Our policy manuals still carelessly use the term 'Chairman of the Board,' 'Vice Chairman,' and 'Chairman of the Executive Committee.' Let's immediately make this 'Chairperson of the Board' and follow suit with the related titles. While you are at it, please appoint only 'spokespersons' or 'representatives' for your departments. I like it better than the term 'spokeswoman' when applied to a woman.

"Another sexist term is 'design draftsman'. An atrocity is 'female draftsman' that is sometimes used to patch up the inequity. Let's get the term 'design technician' into our personnel manuals and on to our blue prints.

"Comfortware Mills is proud of its safety record with respect to fires in the facility. We operate our own Fire Department that is the envy of other companies our size. Yet we are guilty of sexist job labeling in this area. We have a job description for 'fireman.' On with it, and call these people 'fire fighters,' as recently done by the County of Los Angeles Civil Service.

"I note that we have one or two home economists on our staff to serve as liaison people with the public. Our job description refers to that person as 'she.' Maybe if we use the title 'consumer liaison specialist' there would be less danger of sex typing that position.

"Our executive dining room employs people who carry the food from the kitchen to the dining tables. Our job description here calls for 'waitresses.' Please, let us call these people 'dining room servers' as a neutral title.

"A few of you may think I'm being petty with my next one, but it's important all the same. We have to desex job titles throughout the company. Providing for the energy requirements of our mammoth organization are people who tend the boilers. One malfunctioning boiler, and we would know how important these people are. Please stop calling these people 'boilermen.' They are boiler room technicians or 'boilerpersons.'

"Because of our continuing expansion, we own our own construction company, even though its name, 'Sebastian Construction,' would suggest that it is in no way affiliated with us. We are guilty of having a job description of 'craneman' for the much more sensible 'crane operator.'

"Related to the use of sexist job titles is the use of sexist labels in our advertising program. I recognize that the outside agency created these advertisements, but somebody in our Advertising Department had to give written approval to the final copy. Several of these advertisements use the term 'housewife' to denote a person who stays at home and manages the household. The up-to-date term here is 'house spouse.' Even 'homemaker' isn't bad, but it does have a female connotation in our society.

"Allow me now to allude briefly to the sexist labels some managers, both male and female, use in our daily work. A mention of just a few of these should be sufficient to sensitize you to the nature of these practices. For one, females are frequently given affectionate terms such as 'dear,' 'honey,' or 'sweetheart,' in the context of a job. Recently one of the male members of this meeting said to me, 'Honey, when are you giving your report?' I was aghast. Does anybody here ever refer to a male clerk as 'dear,' 'honey,' or 'sweetheart?' And a female word processing technician reporting to you should no more be referred to as 'My gal' than a male at a comparable job level be referred to as 'My boy.'

"Another related suggestion I can offer is to not refer to a manager who is female as a 'woman manager,' any more than you would refer to a manager who is male as a 'man manager.' Let's desex at every job level.

"Remember, there are three very valid reasons for implementing my recommendations for desexing job titles. First, is the humanitarian consideration. A company with the stature of Comfortware Mills must do its share to stamp out sex discrimination in even its most subtle forms. It's simply humanistic to give males and females equal treatment.

"Second, it is our social responsibility to adhere to both the spirit and the letter of the state and federal government equal opportunity laws. Obeying these laws rivals in importance the laws about not polluting the atmosphere and waterways.

"Third, let's take a careful look at bottom line considerations. If we desex our job titles we may very well attract the attention of female and male consumers who favor non-sexist companies. Thinking defensively, we certainly would not want to be boycotted by a feminist group. Pickets outside the stores that market our merchandise can take a severe slice out of profits.

"I've talked enough for now. Who would like to begin the dialogue?"

Leo Kramer, a plant personnel manager, vigorously raised his arm. When he began to talk, it was apparent to the group that lengthy commentary would be forthcoming. He began:

"First of all, I, as a member of management, would like to express my appreciation to Jean Hammond and her group for having done this study. A lot of what you have found makes good sense. I'll refrain from ever again calling Jean 'Honey' unless the two of us get something going on the outside. Also, I'm quite willing to go along with desexing executive level jobs, and calling secretaries 'word processing technicians' even if word processing encompasses bringing in coffee and making airline reservations.

"But, Ms. Hammond, I must object to some of your findings that get down to the factory floor. We've experimented with some of the neutral or desexed titles with some of our operatives and they have strong objections. Surprisingly, most of the objections come from the women on the shop floor. Those unisex job titles may be okay at higher levels, but down below they seem somewhat degrading, particularly for women.

"I took an informal poll of about 15 different women and tried out some of these new job titles on them. I used some of the information Jean and her group let me see in a preliminary report. Take the term, 'seamstress.' Although it may seem mundane to many people in this room, it has some status on the shop floor. Women just don't want to be called 'sewing workers.' It comes across as a putdown job. In contrast, 'seamstress' seems to give a little more dignity to the job.

"I also asked my regular waitress what she thought of the term 'dining room server' in place of 'waitress.' Her reaction was that a dining room server sounded like the cart that gets wheeled out with the pastries in a fine restaurant. She didn't want to be thought of as a mechanical object. Besides, she pointed out, a waitress can be a very high paying job in our country. I'm sure a waiter earning $25,000 per year doesn't want to be called a 'dining room server.'

"But, back to the women who want to remain seamstresses, it's more a question of status than sexism. I would say, let's not change their job titles."

Questions

1. What should Comfortware do about desexing all company job titles?
2. How seriously should the reservations expressed by Leo Kramer, the personnel manager, be taken? Why?

3. What should the company's stance be about the use of sexist nicknames for women, such as 'sweetheart' and 'honey?'
4. Should the company discard the job title, 'secretary?' Why or why not?
5. Would you recommend that the company use neutral terms (such as sales representative) rather than terms such as salesman and saleswoman which indicate the gender of the person occupying that role?

Case 28
The Corporate Waterfall *

Marjel Corporation had tripled in size over a 10-year period both in sales volume and number of personnel. Among the problems created by the rapid company expansion were those related to both formal and informal communication. Many of the staff working for Marjel had no knowledge of where to go for the particular information needed to handle a variety of job-related emergencies. A company-wide attitude survey concluded that "communications among personnel" represented the number-one problem facing the company. Among the specific findings supporting this conclusion were the following:

- 80 percent of employees contend that they learn about organizational changes via the grapevine long before these changes are formally communicated.

- A number of write-in responses to the questionnaire indicated that the existence of changes in policy are difficult to verify. As one sales manager described it, "Quite often we hear about a change in our warranty policy, but if the customer wants verification, it's very difficult to find it anywhere. Nobody seems to know who is putting these things in writing. If somebody is putting them in writing, he seems to be keeping them a secret."

---

*A case prepared by James D. Fowler, Jr. provided the basic structure for this case and suggested the importance of collecting additional information about waterfall meetings.

- 35 percent of the employees polled agreed with the statement "Marjel has a poorer system of communication than any other company I have heard about."
- 45 percent of the managers completing the attitude survey endorsed the statement "More than once my job performance has suffered because I lacked the information I needed."

A series of small group conferences with participants in the attitude survey revealed that these people were not necessarily seeking to be privy to confidential information. What they did want was to be made aware, on a consistent basis, of where the company was headed. Also, they wanted to be kept informed on key issues. In addition to receiving information, many participants in the survey expressed an interest in providing information. Marjel employees had a well-meaning interest in sharing their thoughts, feelings, and opinions with members of top management.

One interpretation made by the consultant in charge of the attitude survey is that the communications problems at Marjel were essentially a sign of organizational *health*, not pathology. Employees at all levels were hoping for constructive, two-way communication. The problems cited by survey participants could be interpreted as an indication that Marjel personnel were not simply complaining — they were looking to improve communications for organizational efficiency.

Upper management, on the advice of the consultant and an internal organization development specialist, decided to attack the communications problem head-on by means of a series of Waterfall Meetings. Kathy Woods, the internal organization development specialist, describes the operations of the Waterfall Meeting as adapted by Marjel:

"The term *waterfall* is quite descriptive. What flows, however, is communication, not water. But the communication comes tumbling down in cascades, just like a waterfall. You might even say it's a well-organized free-for-all. Kind of a modern day takeoff on the expression 'let it all hang out.' What hangs out is useful, constructive communication designed to improve a variety of problems. Top management learns that the employees below them are real people with real problems. At the same time, the people down a few levels in the organization learn that top management is also composed of real people.

"Under our version of the Waterfall Meeting, it would begin with our Senior Vice President conducting a major conference. Next, department managers would conduct Waterfall Meetings with people under their jurisdiction. The same procedure would be followed right down to the first line supervisory level. Waterfall Meetings were to be scheduled about once a quarter. In addition to the regular kind of Waterfall Meetings I just described, there would be several 'Wide Open Waterfall Meetings,' where the Senior Vice President and his staff would meet with a cross section of about 50 to 60 employees in the division each month.

"It is easier to explain the workings of a Waterfall Meeting if I focus in on one particular meeting. I do not attend all the meetings, just an occasional one to help facilitate communications — if any facilitation is really required.

"Reggie Hunn, our Controller, scheduled the first Waterfall meeting. A two-hour session was planned, and invitations were extended to approximately 160 managers. As this was the first meeting of its kind, it was felt that some of the managers might be inhibited about speaking up with questions for discussion. To help overcome such possible hesitancy, each invitation was accompanied by an envelope and a 3 x 5 card for listing any questions he or she wanted to have discussed. The response to the request for these anonymous questions was overwhelming. Discussion questions indicated on the card were placed into about six categories.

"An agenda for the first meeting was based upon the questions. Tentative answers to these questions were formulated before the meeting. Reggie Hunn thought that he and his staff would be more effective in the meeting if some answers were prepared in advance. He and his staff pondered over such questions as:

• I read in the *Wall Street Journal* recently that an individual 'dumped' 100,000 shares of Marjel on the market all at once. Who was this person and should we be concerned that a big investor is willing to dispose of so many shares of our stock?

• What seems to be the reason we haven't come out with a successful new product in over a year? Are we losing our innovative ability?

• How come three managers in a one-month period decided to accept early retirement? Do we have an informal program of getting rid of higher salaried older employees and replacing them with lower salaried, younger employees?

• What future is there for the average middle manager in this company when all of the good jobs seem to be going to outsiders?

• What do you see as the financial future of Marjel? If your predictions are not optimistic, do you recommend that the company employees sell their Marjel stock?

"The first meeting of this type did not go off as well as expected.

With about 170 people in the room, and one person — Reggie Hunn — answering questions written on index cards, it was reminiscent of a stockholders' meeting. Reggie was candid in his answers, but there was something stilted about our first Waterfall Meeting. Another problem was that the meeting was conducted in the auditorium. Such an arrangement is not conducive to good interpersonal communications.

"The second Waterfall Meeting was divided into two sessions. At each session about half the managers in Reggie's area met with him and his staff. The meeting was held in the company cafeteria. Seats were arranged in concentric circles with Reggie right in the middle. His top managers occupied front row seats. They, too, were encouraged to respond to questions on cards or spontaneously offered by any of the other managers present at the meeting. To add to the air of informality, doughnuts, pastry, and coffee were served. As trivial as it sounds, I think that middle managers view free pastry, doughnuts and coffee as a sign of top management generosity.

"At this second meeting things got a little looser than top management would have predicted. Perhaps Reggie wasn't really ready for the kind of openness that takes place once the atmosphere proves to actually welcome wide communication. Reggie told me after the meeting that perhaps things had gotten too personal; that maybe we should control the meetings a little more. I think I can accurately reproduce a few of the incidents that prompted Reggie to make that comment.

"One younger man who raised his hand to ask a question was really more interested in making a speech than in getting information or improving communications. His diatribe went something like this: 'Mr. Hunn, I thought Marjel was founded on the idea of equal opportunity for everyone. I thought we were a good old-fashioned company that granted no special privilege to anyone because of any personal connection with top management, or hanky panky like that. Recently, I found out differently. Janet Ramsey, who was just promoted to Advertising Manager, may be qualified for her job, but I think her special tie-in with the corporate power should be brought right out into the open. Her father, Stuart Ramsey, is the largest single stockholder of Marjel aside from the founders of the company. Do you get my point Mr. Hunn? Is there a little payola at old Marjel?'

"Reggie Hunn handled that issue well. He pointed out that Stuart Ramsey did recommend his daughter Janet for a position in the Advertising Department several years ago. A man with that much money in the company would hardly recommend somebody who was an incompetent — even if it was his daughter. As things worked out, Janet Ramsey proved to be a person of superior capability. Mr. Ramsey was correct in his judgment. The promotion of Janet Ramsey was done on the basis of merit alone. Slightly perturbed, Reggie then beckoned toward another person with a question.

" 'Not so quickly,' responded the man who asked the question about Janet Ramsey, I'm not through yet.' He certainly wasn't.

" 'You, Reggie Hunn, could very well be the biggest example of hidden nepotism in this whole corporation. I found out recently that your mother is the sister of the President. When you go into the President's office on one of your frequent little confabs, do you say 'Good morning, Uncle'? No doubt, Mr. Hunn, you know what you're doing around here, but I don't think being the President's nephew has hurt your chances around here, has it?'

"I thought at this point that Reggie and this character were going to have a real corporate shoot-out, but, instead, Reggie just ended things with a mild put-down. His response was 'Okay, enough of these very personal accusations. It's about time we returned to attacking some of the real problems that this meeting was designed to resolve.'

"Following the lead of the manager who asked the questions about nepotism, another manager had some shockingly candid comments of his own. 'What I'm going to say next can't hurt me because I have landed a new job with another company. The reason I have left this fine organization is that I can no longer tolerate management's refusal to do something about a sinful problem taking place right under our noses. My boss, Larry Biggons, is not giving his full time attention to the company and I think top management knows it. He may be very creative when he's here, but he isn't here very often. I know the man has some real estate interests that amount to almost a full time job. Our department runs without any assistance from him, yet he makes about one-third more money than anybody around here. I'm leaving in protest to this situation. Half the time when I'm in Larry's office trying to get an answer to an important problem, we're interrupted by a phone call relating to his outside interests. I think we should be charging Larry rent instead of paying him a salary.'

"Reggie could only respond, 'Does anybody have a question that relates more to business problems than to personalities? I didn't think this session was supposed to be sensitivity training.' To which a woman participant responded, 'But, Mr. Hunn, all our business problems are in fact people problems.'

"The next person to comment at the Waterfall Meeting was also candid and he also made Reggie squirm. However, this time Reggie felt uncomfortable because of very positive statements. The comment was, 'Before things get out of hand and we lose perspective about what is going on here, I have some very important things to say. Call my comments false praise, apple polishing, boot licking or any other pejorative terms you want, but I speak the truth.

" 'Some of you fellow managers and employees who are moaning, groaning, and bitching about Marjel should work for some of our competitors. Our retirement and medical insurance programs are the best in the industry. Never once has management turned down a reasonable request of mine for a personal favor. When you work for Marjel, you can hold out your chest in pride. We are number one in our field. We're a first-rate outfit. Our pricing policy is the most honest in the entire field. No special unwritten deals for our best customers. No undercutting our competition to drive them out of business.

" 'As for Reggie Hunn, our leader in this department, he's the tops. I've never worked for a finer leader or a finer person. He's a man you can trust and somebody you can be proud to work for. Some people look upon Mr. Hunn as the head cop in our company, but that's because they don't understand his function. He's the man who tells if we are going wrong and why we are going wrong. If anybody doesn't like Reginald Hunn, it's his problem, not Reggie's.' "

Kathy Woods, in her capacity as organization development specialist, took it upon herself to make some tentative evaluation of the effectiveness of the Waterfall Meetings. She gives us some of her findings:

"Recognize that management didn't authorize me to conduct a far-reaching, highly scientific study of the impact of the meetings upon organization effectiveness. Yet, after six months' experience with the Waterfall Meetings (the time at which her assessment was made) I have found enough information to make a tentative evaluation. Although these meetings are not universally liked by management, I get the impression that they are beginning to accomplish their intended purpose. Here are some of the specifics of my findings:

• An informal survey of a sampling of the managers attending the meeting indicated that the Waterfall Meetings are well received. In their opinion, these meetings should be continued. I recognize that satisfaction with a program is no substitute for evidence of its effectiveness, but management has to like a program in order for it to survive. A program cannot help an organization if it is discontinued.

• One high ranking executive wrote a memo to my boss strongly recommending that the Waterfall Meetings be discontinued. His point was that these meetings can easily place management in an embarrassing position. Lower ranking managers sometimes press top management for information that cannot be divulged at the time because of its sensitive nature. Top management is then made to appear secretive when they are simply exercising prudent business judgment.

• Several middle managers have noted that the effects of the Waterfall Meeting have spilled over (pun intended) on to the job. When a subordinate has some information he or she would like to request, or share, there is much less hesitancy than in the past. One engineering manager relayed an anecdote to me that is both refreshing and amusing.

"A design engineer in his department told him at two o'clock on a Friday afternoon, 'I'm leaving the plant to go fishing. I could tell you that I have a dental emergency or that one of my children is sick, but it would be lying. It's simply that I've accomplished two-weeks' work these past four and one-half days, and I'm psychologically spent. Instead of staying here for three more hours and shuffling papers, I'm leaving. Have a nice weekend.'

• There is some evidence that managers are learning of problems earlier since the meetings began. In other words, subordinates are less timid about bringing bad news to the attention of their bosses. One sales manager phoned into the Home Office to explain that within three months his branch might be losing their biggest customer to the competition. Because of this early warning notice, the Sales Manager, the Vice President of Marketing and the Branch Manager were able to combine efforts to. bring the account back in line. This was just the type of problem that was likely to be buried until too late before the advent of our Waterfall Meetings.

• My most perplexing finding is that some of our top management people do not know how to handle some of this new openness that has come about as a result of the meetings. Top management isn't sure whether all this communication is good or bad. The Senior Vice President who began the meetings told me something like this:

"At times I wonder if I'm working in an insane asylum or a modern business organization. People stop me in the halls to tell me their job problems. A key-punch operator wrote me recently that I shouldn't wear striped ties with plaid suits. One middle manager requested a conference with me to discuss an urgent matter. The topic he wanted to discuss was my style of managing my organization. He gave me about 10 suggestions for doing a better job of managing people. I'm beginning to wonder if we are going to drown in our own waterfall."

Questions

1. From your viewpoint, should these meetings be continued? Why or why not?
2. What would you see as the most important potential benefit from such meetings?
3. Outline a systematic approach that Kathy Woods (The OD specialist) might take to determine if Waterfall Meetings are actually benefitting the organization.
4. What approaches, aside from Waterfall Meetings, might have been used to improve interpersonal communications at Marjel?
5. What are the outer limits to questions from subordinates that management should have to answer? In other words, what information can management rightfully *not* share with subordinates?

Case 29
Who Should Eat the Cost on this One? *

Ludlow Custom Builders was founded by Homer Bean in the Spring of 1973. Except for a couple of brief interludes in which he ventured into business by himself or with a partner, Homer had been in the construction business as an employee of other firms for over 25 years. Ludlow began as a corporation of five stockholders, two of whom had a direct hand in running the business with Bean. Homer was to handle the actual building; Mary Denmark was the sales representative and Richard, her husband, worked as the accountant.

This division of responsibilities lasted for about one year, when a major falling-out took place among them. One result of the altercation was the ousting of the Denmarks from Ludlow Customer Builders. Fred Morgan, the salaried Business Manager, was hired to replace them. Morgan and Bean now constitute the company management.

Ludlow grossed $1.5 million in sales in its second year of operation. At present, the company has one sales representative, a new estimator, and three field personnel. A picture of substantial growth is emerging now. Homer Bean has just confirmed a deal for the company's acquisition of a sizable subdivision in rural suburban Pottsville. A major lending institution has agreed to underwrite this

---

*Virginia Cashmore researched this case and is responsible for a substantial portion of its writing.

acquisition. Moran and Bean are ready to hire additional sales representatives, foremen, service representatives, and clerical help. Prospects are optimistic as Ludlow Custom Builders looks forward to its first big growth spurt. Morgan and Bean recognize that the success of this expansion depends on the effectiveness of their systems and procedures, and their ability to communicate vital information.

The communication networks in Ludlow have been influenced by the key figures in the company, past and present. When the Denmarks were part of Ludlow, they ran the company as if they were the true owners, and Homer reported to them. Yet their actual investment in the corporation was a ceremonial gesture of $2. Homer was willing to tolerate this domination by the Denmarks because his preference is not for the administrative workings of the firm. In his words, "I'm a builder by trade and by heart. Let me build beautiful homes, and let somebody else keep the books." As a reflection of this attitude, when the Denmarks departed, nobody knew much about the company operations, including costs, pricing, policies, and procedures.

Fred Morgan faced a business operation run in a strikingly informal manner. The first problem he encountered involved a seemingly simple one of missing kitchen drawers. According to Fred,

"After working for the company less than one week, it was obvious to me that communication was mainly by word of mouth. Even with word of mouth communication, it was only what anyone was lucky enough to pick up or pursue through various people. A good example was when a kitchen cabinet invoice arrived noting a cost for extra drawers on Lot #73. I looked for a change form and a mention of a change in the contract — the two places where custom features are noted. There was nothing about a vanity change in either place.

"Then I started the sleuthing process of asking any employee I thought might have some information on this little problem. The foreman said the location of the vanities was changed and this required more drawers; the estimator was too new on the job to know anything about the problem; the salesman said he had no knowledge of the change.

"I gave up and paid the bill because I was getting no help from the staff. Besides, it was too much trouble tracking down every person who might have information on the extra cabinets. At Ludlow they held no meetings and wrote no memos. Kind of a sidewalk business. Anyway, I felt obliged to pay because our supplier of kitchen materials wanted his money.

"A few weeks later, while checking out some pricing quotes on vanities for another lot to be sold, the question of drawers was brought up and Lot #73 was mentioned in this regard. Homer Bean insisted there had been a change because the electrician had placed the lights in a different spot and, thus, had to move the cabinets. The building plans (which you usually cannot find because they are indiscriminately passed around to subcontractors and customers) showed no change.

"The only reference to a change was a little drawing and size note in the job sheet made up by the sales representative for the production men. Homer then spent some prime time trying to track down who was at fault by speaking to the electrician, kitchen supplier, and later the sales rep. At this point the story is still not pieced together.

"When I first arrived it was like this for every detail. And nobody was available to give me any training or orientation. I couldn't even locate anything that resembled a job description. Every problem is resolved for the first time, or you spend precious construction time searching for information. It looked like a major internal rebuilding job needed to be done.

"Another example of how bad it was took place in my first month. Tom, the sales rep, told me to make up a closing statement for a house which was sold and ready to close. Yet Tom couldn't even describe such a statement. Later, I learned that nobody seemed to know exactly what a closing procedure entailed from the company's contribution. I dug through the files and made out a sheet of charges and credits for deposits and extra items as best I could. After I struggled with that, I sent the papers on to our attorneys.

"As a result of my scrambling, the closing went off all right, but Ludlow lost the cost of all the electrical fixtures normally charged to the buyer because they were not included in the original invoice. To top that, I discovered later that our attorneys do not even require a closing statement from the builders. All they require is that we phone them with the dollar amounts involved for the settlement; then they make up the statement for us, the seller. Here we were wasting our time doing an inefficient job handling part of the attorneys' job."

A significant characteristic about Ludlow's business is that a flaw in communications generally results in a direct loss. Customer selections represent a prime example of this problem. As a custom builder, Ludlow offers grades and styles of tile and slate for bathrooms and foyers. The tile subcontractor provides the selection samples in the sales office. Buyers and sales representatives are supposed to note their choices on a sales selection form and indicate their approval by signing the form. Then the tile installer must be informed of the choices in time to supply the materials and get the job completed. When the tile selections are poorly marked, or the sales representative does not oversee the choices and the signature, or the selection form cannot be located, the wrong tile may be installed, necessitating some costly retiling.

When tiles have to be torn up and replaced, the subcontractor charges Ludlow. In one month two of these tile and retile problems took place. In instance one, Morgan's first notice of a problem occurred when a buyer mentioned he left a note for the tile installer indicating that the tiles and the dots between them in his powder room were to have been the same color, not contrasting colors. Fred sympathized with the buyer's concern and dismissed the problem as lying outside of his area of concern.

Gil, the tile installer, dropped by Fred Morgan's office to ask what the note meant. Morgan told him that the buyer wanted the same color dots and tile. Without further check, Gil proceeded to rip up the entire set of newly laid tiles and install another set. Ludlow was billed for his services. Ralph, the foreman, checked out the job sheet made out by the sales representative and noted that the first way was correct according to the sheet.

Tom, the sales representative, was then asked about the problem. Apparently he allowed the buyers to mark their own selection sheet and sign it without checking the details himself. Underlying the problem is the fact that the samples are shown with a contrasting color dot and are marked poorly so that the customer has to use his or her ingenuity to indicate choices. In this case, the customer wrote "crystal gold mist tile with crystal gold dot" and then ran out of room on the paper. Everybody thought they were doing the right thing, yet Ludlow would end up paying the cost of the mistake. When the same problem reappeared two months later, Fred could only lament, "Now, who is going to eat the cost on this one?"

The same situation regarding loss is also true for changes made by buyers after construction has started. Timing, procedures, pricing, and accuracy are vital — particularly the procedure for pricing the change. The sales representative is the front person in direct contact with the buyer; he or she must quote the price for a change or addition. Lacking cost figures, the sales rep would use his or her general experience as a guide, tack on a percentage, and hope for the best. Frequently, a comparison of these changes with actual invoice costs may reveal a loss.

Homer and Tom were concerned about this problem, but neither of them ever received any feedback. Never did they receive statements of current status of the corporation or of a cost breakdown or comparison. Tom described it this way, "At Ludlow, our standard approach is to take a wild guess on a cost and hope that by the end of the year our overestimates balance out our underestimates." (This situation was alleviated to a large extent by hiring an estimator draftswoman, Martha. Her role involved keeping a check on suppliers for current prices and translating them into a form that could also be used for cost accounting.)

Service is another area of substantial potential for loss. The service function is essentially a system for handling complaints and making adjustments on house problems that occur approximately within the first year after closing. At other times service is involved with completing tasks that should have been taken care of before the time of closing, and for which the bank is holding back funds. Ludlow has earned a poor reputation in the area of after-the-sale service.

As the system existed before Fred Morgan's arrival, a home owner with a service demand would stop by the sales office or call the sales representative at night or on weekends, explaining the nature of his or her request for service. Sales representatives found requests of this nature distracting to their sales effort at the time. After receiving the call, the sales rep would write a note on legal-sized paper (or any scrap of paper available) and tape it to the front of the file cabinet for the foreman (or any other interested party) to find in the morning. The person finding the note might take appropriate action, or sometimes ignore the problem. Decisions about many problems could be left hanging; and the usual case was for the sales representative not to be informed when a required service call was completed. A court case stemmed from one request for service that was never granted. In this situation, the bathtub in a new home was improperly caulked, causing a heavy leak which badly damaged a homeowner's antique dining set. The sales rep explained that the problem would be taken care of, but nobody received the message taped to the file cabinet.

Homer Bean assumed that Fred Morgan would be able to iron out these troublesome problems at Ludlow. Fred felt that Homer's analysis of the problems at Ludlow was oversimplified — that the problems involved a lot more than a few procedures gone haywire. As Fred describes it:

"To really understand what was happening at Ludlow, you have to consider the attitude of the people involved toward dealing with their problems in a straightforward manner. Homer would prefer to be totally separated from the business aspects of the corporation in order to devote himself to building houses. Ralph, Homer's 25-year-old son-in-law dislikes memos and prefers a casual verbal exchange approach. Tom, the sales representative, writes notes and memos which he distributes haphazardly, yet he does keep a log of his daily activities. His memos can be found taped to a file, lying on the desk or copier machine, or in someone's labeled mail slot. These slots are the worst places for a message, and Tom should recognize it. These slots are used for the storage of miscellaneous material by everyone except me and Martha, our new sales estimator. As 'junk drawers,' they make poor communication vehicles.

"Whenever Ralph needed to question a feature on a particular home, he would ravage through Tom's sales files trying to find the information he needed. Since Tom retains everything, this was a time-consuming and difficult task. The collection of papers in Tom's files included contracts and all pricing and cost information, which could represent a security leak in our type of business.

"When I entered the scene, any type of formal meeting with an agenda was non-existent. It would seem like a simple thing to schedule regular staff meetings, but the key people around here work different hours. Everything is so helter-skelter around here, I wonder if I should throw in the towel or sweat it out. Something has to change. If it doesn't, Ludlow will be out of business and I'll have a coronary."

Questions

1. What course of action should Fred Morgan take to improve the communication system at Ludlow?
2. What barriers to communication are shown to exist in this case?
3. What formal role should Homer Bean occupy at Ludlow Custom Builders? Why?
4. Do you think that Fred Morgan is overreacting to a situation that merely represents the "growing pains" of a small business with growth potential? Explain your answer.
5. What role should the cost estimator/draftswoman play in improving communications?

Case 30
A Cybernetics System Feedback Blooper *

Up until two years ago, the County Public Works Authority had one of the most outdated manual accounts payable systems found anywhere in a governmental organization of its size. The department had somehow resisted computerization of its operations. Instead of automated equipment, the department relied upon manual check registers, typewriters for check preparation, and massive accounting journals.

Part of the Controller's area, the Accounts Payable Department, was staffed by 16 people — 15 women and one male. Their average age was about 40. The basic departmental task was to process about 4000 accounts payable transactions per month. Vendors were paid twice a month unless a special dispensation was granted by the Controller or his assistant. A payment processing transaction began quite simply when a bill was received from a vendor. The bill was checked for authenticity and sent to the appropriate person to initiate payment procedures. After all the necessary procedures and controls were met, the check preparation procedure began. The checks were typed and the check numbers, amounts, names, and sometimes other identifying data were entered on a check register and manually reconciled when returned from the bank. Aside from

*Roger P. Hursh prepared and wrote most of this case, except for some editorial changes.

being a tedious task, check preparation was very time-consuming.

Pete Cerone, the Controller, felt that perhaps he had waited too long to remedy this cumbersome check-writing operation. Adding to the gravity of the problem was a pending layoff of workers in all County agencies and a simultaneous increase in workload due to a planned increase in vendors. Pete called the Data Processing Manager into conference. It was decided by mutual consent to conduct a feasibility study. for a new data processing system. Lucille Watkins, an experienced and highly regarded systems analyst, was assigned as group leader to conduct the feasibility study. If the results of the study were accepted, Lucille would be asked to develop the new systems design for the Accounts Payable section.

Lucille was a college graduate accountant with over five years experience in the system design field. She had direct familiarity with new data base design concepts. Craig Williams, the other member of the systems team, held an Associate's degree in Computer Science. He backed this up with three years experience in the system design field. Craig and Lucille had worked closely on a new IMS (data base) Accounts Receivable system for another County department. Feedback from users of that system was favorable.

Lucille and Craig reported to the Controller's office at 9 a.m. the following Monday morning. After about a one and one-half hour discussion concerning current structural procedures, Lucille felt she and Craig could complete the feasibility study within a two-week time period. Management accepted the idea, and the study was under way. Lucille and Craig spent about four days discussing current procedures with the users. With this information in hand, they returned to their own department to design a new system of paying accounts. Following comprehensive discussions with supervisors and managers, their ideas were presented formally to the Controller's Department one day prior to the projected date for the completion of this feasibility study.

Strongly recommended by the report was a batch processing system, using telecommunications on IBM 3270s, data base technology using IMS, and check writing and bank reconciliaton on the IBM 370 model 155 computer. The estimated cost was $15,000 and the time estimate for completion was four months. Pete, the Controller, accepted these recommendations with enthusiasm when Lucille and Craig gave him an estimated pay-back period (all costs) of 14 months. He expressed an interest in beginning the project immediately. The Data Processing Department accepted the assignment for an immediate start.

Lucille and Craig were gleeful about the apparent smoothness of all aspects of their new assignment. Everyone in the Controller's Department gave them full cooperation. Finally, the mechanical and electronic marvel was leading the Accounts Payable Department to salvation. Both systems analysts were confident that this new system would only add to their already positive track record.

Data Processing policies and procedures called for a systems overview, detailed program specifications (including all input and output layouts), project control, adequate training of users, and, finally, supervision of the entire system. No new system installed by the County government was immune to these stringent requirements. Lucille and Craig worked diligently on their assigned task. Both were surprised at their own productivity. Lucille spent many hours patiently showing department personnel how to use the telecommunication device. Craig documented his work and carefully reviewed program specifications to the programmers. The project control reports looked impressive; everything was headed toward successful design and implementation of this vitally needed system.

Two weeks before the project completion date all parties involved expressed an air of optimism. The reports looked good, the check testing was near perfect, and a simulation of bank reconciliation worked without error. Lucille and Craig finished their documentation and testing. Everything was ready for processing.

The day of reckoning arrived. A new system was now being implemented. The reputation of the Accounts Payable and the Data Processing Departments were on the line. Two hundred and fifty claims were waiting to be processed by the new system. The batches were set up to process a maximum of 20 claims per batch. Each claim was composed of line items with edit screens for each item. In addition, each claim had an edit screen for valid vendor number, all necessary numerical and valid character recognition, batch amount input screen, type transaction code input screen, and a header screen.

Suddenly and mysteriously, a cybernetics feedback blooper crept into the system. The processing time from one screen to another was over 20 seconds and sometimes longer. Each claim could entail from three to five screens per line item. With 250 claims, the processing could take hours. Any machine down time could further inhibit processing. The woman on the remote terminal was waiting up to five minutes to process a line item. One claim could easily take an hour to process, using this sophisticated new system.

Why wasn't this embarrassing problem caught in the testing, pondered Lucille and Craig? Assiduous digging for facts indicated that the woman at the terminal knew very little about data processing. She did what she was trained to do and did it well. She made her necessary corrections, adjustments, and reinput processing. Everytime the analyst asked how she was doing, she responded "Fine." The underlying problem was that she was spending all day processing her 20 claims during test time because of the response time. She assumed that because it was a test, the process would be time-consuming. Therefore, in her perception there was no problem. She found nothing unusual to report to the systems analysts.

Lucille reports that the IBM 370 model 155 is equipped with software which provided abundant data concerning processing time of the Accounts Payable System during testing. This included log tapes, usage reports, and terminal response times. The analysts were interested in the results: (a) how the data went through the system, (b) how the reports looked, (c) how well the audit trails looked and worked, and (d) how easy the system was supposedly understood by the users. Apparently, nobody thought of searching for feedback from the people using the system.

Craig reports that things finally resolved themselves. "The system is finally running well. For a while we created a bigger mess than we cleaned up. The user department was jammed up for a couple of extra weeks while we debugged the problems in the system. We heard a few screams from people who weren't paid on time, but the biggest damage was to our psyches. Who wants to eat humble pie?"

Questions

1. How can mistakes like the one illustrated in this case be avoided in other organizations?
2. Should the woman who reported everything was working well with the system be reprimanded by management? Why or why not?
3. Does this case represent basically a technological or human error? Explain your reasoning.
4. Does "resistance to change" enter into this case? Why or why not?
5. Provide an example of your own where lack of feedback allowed an error to go undetected until after a costly mistake had been made.

REFERENCES

Athanassiades, John C. "The Distortion of Upward Communications in Hierarchical Organizations," *Academy of Management Journal*, Vol. 16, June 1973, 207-226.

Farace, Richard V. and MacDonald Donald. "New Directions in the Study of Organizational Communication," *Personnel Psychology*, Vol. 27, Spring 1974, 1-15.

Franklin, Jerome L. "Down the Organization: Influence Processes Across Levels of Hierarchy," *Administrative Science Quarterly*, Vol. 20, June 1975, 153-161.

Gibons, James L., Ivancevich, John M., and Donnelly, James H. Jr. *Organizations: Structure, Processes, Behavior*. Dallas, Texas Business Publications, 1973, See Chapter 6.

Hage, Jerald, Aiken, Michael and Marret, Cora Bagley. "Organization Structure and Communications," *American Sociological Review*, Vol. 36, October 1971, 860-871.

Hampton, David R., Summer, Charles E., and Webber, Ross. *Organizational Behavior and the Practice of Management*, revised edition. Glenview, Ill.: Scott, Foresman, 1973, See Chapter 2.

Haney, William V. *Communication and Organizational Behavior*, revised edition. Homewood, Ill.: Richard D. Irwin, 1973.

Lau, James B. *Behavior in Organizations: An Experiential Approach*. Homewood, Ill.: Richard D. Irwin, 1975. See Chapters 11 and 14.

Leavitt, Harold J. *Managerial Psychology*, third edition. Chicago: The University of Chicago Press, 1972. See Part Three.

Roberts, Karlene H. and O'Reilly, III, Charles A. "Failures in Upward Communication in Organizations: Three Possible Culprits," *Academy of Management Journal*, Vol. 17, June 1974, 205-224.

10
Intergroup Conflict

Case 31
Last Hired, First Fired, No More

Odessa Graves, a 25-year-old Black woman, received an M.B.A. from Boston University in June of 1973. Spring of that year, Odessa had been busily sorting out job offers that resulted from a series of 25 serious job interviews. As she commented to a friend, "Yes, it's gratifying to know that I can receive about 10 different job offers when many of my classmates would be happy to obtain one good offer. I pity the poor blond-haired, blue-eyed male WASP these days. In a recession economy, he is suddenly out of demand. How naive do you think I am? I know that employers perk up as soon as a Black female with appropriate qualifications approaches them for a job. Every company is trying to comply with some kind of Affirmative Action Program.

"But I don't feel that something is being handed to me that I don't deserve. If I were a loser, I would quickly be shunted over to a clerical job, or out the door. I don't consider myself to be a militant member of the Black Awareness Movement, but I do think it's about time Black people were given the benefit of the doubt. It takes a lot of 'benefits of the doubt' to compensate for over 100 years of injustices."

As Odessa proceeded through her job interviews, she searched for an employer who seemed legitimately interested in her individual qualifications. She was less interested in signing on with an employer who was desperately trying to recruit a Black female in order to alleviate pressure from the Office of Economic Opportunity. Rocky

196

Mountain Airlines seemed interested. Ms. Graves was offered the position of Market Analyst at a starting salary of $15,500. Her major assignment was to attempt to identify which groups of people were not using Rocky Mountain Airlines. Next, she was to attempt to determine what Rocky Mountain needed to do to capture some of that potential market. Odessa reflects upon why she accepted this job offer:

"One obvious consideration is that Rocky Mountain Airlines is located in Denver, which is fast becoming the world's most desirable spot for young singles. But that was just a frill. The Airline had a sense of glamour. They gave me a brightly colored, nicely appointed office. Pilots, stewardesses, and ground control personnel make interesting working companions. I've always liked travel, so this job seemed like an opportunity to apply my MBA knowledge to a hobby.

"I was given a free hand and a reasonable budget to do what had to be done to suggest leads for capturing new business. It seemed like management was behind me."

Odessa Graves started to work for the Airline in July of 1973. Her first month on the job was basically given to an orientation to the company. She talked to executives, pilots, stewardesses, ticket counter people, and ground control workers — all in an attempt to achieve a first-hand understanding of what made the airlines operate on a day-by-day basis. At the suggestion of her immediate boss, Odessa boarded about 30 Rocky Mountain flights in order to get an on-the-scene appreciation of conditions on the airline.

"I talked to loads of passengers about every aspect of the plane ride," said Odessa. "I even asked a few children how they liked our washrooms. I asked some business executives how they liked the appearance of our stewardesses in comparison to those found on the transcontinental carriers. My conversations helped me with some ideas about which people were not flying Rocky Mountain. Later, I planned to speak to some of these people."

After her orientation, Odessa confined herself to the serious and tedious work of trying to develop a demographic profile of the people who were flying Rocky Mountain. Her boss seemed content with her progress. Before giving Odessa her first assignment, he had agreed that he would not be pressing her for an immediate report. He accepted Odessa's viewpoint that if you want an immediate opinion speak to anybody who worked for the Airline. If you want a research-based answer, you have to be much more patient.

During the first four months of Odessa's employment, passenger utilization showed a steady decline. The heavy holiday volume was less heavy than in the previous three years. Coupled with a decrease in passenger volume was a 47% increase in the price of fuel. Rocky Mountain pilots began to joke that soon an additional responsibility of theirs would be to help passengers on board with their luggage.

Five months after Odessa started on her job, Maxine Husted, Vice President of Personnel, requested that she come to her office. "Odessa, we have some very unfortunate news for you," said Ms. Husted. "We are temporarily in a business crunch. The only way we can keep the airline operating for the near future is to trim expenses to the bone. Since you were the staff person most recently hired, we are going to have to sacrifice you. In most instances, it's the recently hired employees who are being asked to leave.

"We particularly dislike doing this to a potentially valuable employee. Our President and others have been favorably impressed with the fine start you have made. However, we are in business to make a profit. We just cannot afford the frill of market research right now. Again, we are awfully sorry."

Odessa did not take kindly to this unforeseen circumstance. She felt that an airline the size of Rocky Mountain should be able to weather the storm of a cyclical economy without resorting to laying off personnel. She thought that perhaps the company would not have to resort to layoffs if her function were strengthened. Perhaps market research could provide some answers to maintaining a steady volume of passenger business.

The next day, Odessa called an attorney friend of hers in Boston to determine if she had any legal rights to her job. Her friend gave her the name of a Denver attorney, L. Clayton Rivers, who knew the laws regulating employment procedures. Rivers, indeed, was interested in the Graves problem. During her first visit to his office, Rivers commented:

"As a Black man and an attorney, I am very much concerned about this sticky issue of firing on the basis of seniority. I'll take your case. I look upon it as a case of unwarranted firing on the basis of seniority. It's not so much that you were discriminated against as a person. But how many Black people has Rocky Mountain Airlines let into key jobs in its history? If they had a hidden policy against hiring Blacks, how could a Black woman have acquired enough seniority to prevent being fired? Get my point?"

Although hesitant, Odessa Graves expressed a willingness to enter into a legal battle against Rocky Mountain Airlines. She felt conflict in the sense that she liked the company and thought that they were doing the best they could under the circumstances. At the same time, she could sense that the case she was about to be involved in had ramifications for all Blacks, other minorities, and women throughout the United States. L. Clayton Rivers goaded her, stressing that she had an obligation to her sisters everywhere.

Rocky Mountain Airlines was given appropriate notification that their firing of Ms. Graves would be contested in court. Baird Gunderson, the President, Maxine Husted, and two other Airline executives pondered the problem. After much deliberation, they agreed that to make a peace offering by reinstating Odessa now would be an admission of guilt. If the seniority provision for firing people were overruled, there would be trouble ahead with the labor union representing company employees.

The labor union held steadfastly to a seniority clause whereby the most recently hired employees were the first to be released during a company layoff. Although Odessa was not a member of the bargaining unit, the union would view her reinstatement as a dangerous precedent. Rocky Mountain management believed that resorting to seniority as a criterion for layoff was a principle that most employees found acceptable. Thus, the Graves situation had serious long range implications for the Airline.

L. Clayton Rivers, Odessa's attorney, and Percy Henderson, Rocky Mountain's attorney, delivered their carefully reasoned arguments to United States District Court Judge, Lawrence Billings. Rivers and Henderson felt that circumstances had placed them in an historic case. A serious challenging of the use of seniority as a basis of laying off either union or non-union employees would violate a hallowed business tradition in the United States. On the other hand, if Black people could be laid off on the basis of seniority provision, many of the advances of civil rights in recent years would be reversed.

Several weeks later, Judge Billings delivered his decision: "In my opinion as United States District Court Judge, Rocky Mountain Airlines has violated civil rights laws by using seniority as the exclusive criterion for laying off exempt (salaried, non-union) employees at Rocky Mountain Airline. I have come to this conclusion because Blacks have been denied an opportunity to acquire seniority at the Airlines. Since Ms. Odessa Graves is the first Black person to hold an exempt position at Rocky Mountain Airlines, she could not possibly have accrued enough seniority to avoid being laid off.

"In conclusion, I rule that Odessa Graves be reinstated to her job at her previous pay. In addition, she must be compensated for any salary lost in the interim between the end of her severance pay and the day of this decision."

Percy Henderson said he objected to the judge's decision, and that he would represent Rocky Mountain Airlines in an attempt to have this decision overruled by the United States Supreme Court. He argued, "In my opinion, Blackness is not an issue. Ms. Graves was the only worker in her category and that function collapsed because of a downturn in business. We did not lay off a number of Blacks in a job category containing both Black and white workers. Despite our objection to the decision reached by Judge Billings, we will welcome Ms. Odessa Graves back to our company. She will be assigned to a position that can be justified in terms of present economic conditions." *U P Personnel   President*   *lawyer*

Later, Maxine Husted, Baird Gunderson, and Percy Henderson conferred about the implications of the judge's decision. All three were concerned also about the implications for the rest of American industry. As Ms. Husted described the consensus of their small group:

"The equal opportunity floodgates have now really been opened with respect to seniority. Seniority cannot be used as a reason, however valid, to lay off Chicanos, Puerto Ricans, Blacks, or women. Thousands of minority group members across the country will be rehired. Many high seniority whites will be bumped. We will have to be very careful that any minority group member we hire is really capable of making a contribution to Rocky Mountain Airlines."

Baird Gunderson added: "Maxine, get ready for a small war on your hands when we start to lay off senior white employees to make room for newly hired Blacks. We have got to find some workable alternatives to avoid that kind of problem in the company."

organizational climate

Questions

1. What should be the ruling of the United States Supreme Court with respect to the decision handed down by Judge Billings?
2. How might the company prevent potential conflict between high seniority whites and low seniority Blacks over layoffs?
3. What kind of job should Rocky Mountain Airlines assign Odessa Graves? Why?
4. Do you agree with the company's decision to lay off Odessa Graves? Explain.
5. What strategic error do you think that Odessa Graves might be making in relationship to Rocky Mountain Airlines?

Case 32
The Unwanted Chairman *

Lasoptic, Incorporated is engaged in the manufacture of lasers and precision optical elements. A small business, the company employs 15 fulltime people and also uses the services of subcontract specialists on an as-needed basis. The highly technical nature of its business and the heavy competition in its market place make it mandatory to have a staff of knowledgeable and innovative people. Innovation is seen as the primary force by which profitable results can be achieved. During the first six years of Lasoptic's history, the company was able to hire and retain individuals with the necessary skills and talents to manufacture products that rivaled those of its competitors.

A strategy for growth utilized by the company was to take on jobs that larger firms rejected because of the difficulties involved in production. Lasoptic management and employees prided themselves about their "quick reaction time," and "fast footwork." The specialized and intricate nature of their product line resulted in the group working on intriguing and challenging assignments requiring the coordinated efforts of all the employees. With a few small exceptions, every member of the Lasoptic team worked on every contract.

The group nature of the production tasks resulted in considerable interaction among company personnel. Virtually all employees were compatible, which effected smooth daily work relationships. Group members were asked to provide their opinions on the technical aspects of every product. A lab technician's idea might be given as

*Dennis Sigler researched this case.

much weight as one generated by a Ph.D. level physicist, provided the idea had technical merit. Rachel Merriman, an electrical engineer is employed at Lasoptic, and describes the work group this way:

"We were a hard hitting, tightly knit group. Few people outside of our company really understood what we were doing, but that didn't faze us. We had a mission to accomplish, we knew how to accomplish it. Our contracts were usually completed earlier than the targeted date of completion. We were having fun and we were getting results — a hard to beat combination."

Ralph Barker, President and founder of the company, made a distinct contribution to the spirited work atmosphere at Lasoptic. Youthful both chronologically (age 34) and psychologically, Ralph was permissive in his management of people. As Ralph describes his leadership style, "Upon founding this fledgling company, I made the decision to hire only mature, responsible people. I'm simply the man leading the charge up the hill. I'm not the warden, the cop, the staff sargeant, the dean of students, or the judge. Nor am I a scientific genius calling all the shots so my subordinates can scurry around trying to please me.

"When I'm not preoccupied with a project of my own, such as beating the bushes trying to borrow $10,000 from a bank, I shower my people with encouragement. Anyone who even obtained a "C" in introductory psychology knows that praise works more effectively with people than does punishment. If somebody needs threats, fines, or even zaps to keep going, that person should work for another employer. A company of our size can only afford to keep responsible adults on the payroll. I wouldn't want anybody on my payroll who required constant supervision."

In a strategy aimed at growth, Lasoptic acquired another, smaller laser manufacturing company, Beamatronics, principally for its two profitable, highly specialized products. Both products dealt with the application of laser technology to surgical procedures, such as removing microscopic sections of diseased tissue. Walter Helmut, Chairman of the Board of Beamatronics was the only employee retained by Lasoptic. Helmut was assigned the position of Executive Vice President (an arrangement he insisted upon before agreeing to the acquisition). Helmut's major responsibility was to develop and market new product lines and to integrate them into existing product lines. Walter Helmut was known to be both an innovative engineer and a competent marketer.

Within two weeks after Helmut's arrival, it became apparent that his new subordinates — especially those reporting directly to him —

had little regard for his attitudes toward people. Raised in an upper-class family in Germany, Helmut retained the old world philosophy, "There are gods and then there are cows." Concerned about the damage being done to the morale of the work force, two people on the staff came to Ralph Barker with their complaints. Barker was sympathetic, but felt that the situation deserved more time:

"Walter Helmut has unique selling talents that can be an asset to this company. We need growth and he is one of those rare birds who can sell sophisticated technology to sophisticated technologists. I'm happy with our company, but it looks like we need to grow in order to survive. My suggestion is to minimize your interactions with him, and I will act as an intermediary."

The group representatives were not entirely satisfied with Ralph Barker's suggestion, but they were willing to consider it at least as a temporizing measure.

Several months later, an unanticipated event (the settlement by Helmut of a lawsuit against the company) gave Helmut an opportunity to place himself in a position of even greater power than he previously had. In order to obtain the necessary financing to settle the suit, Walter Helmut utilized an outside investor. The provisions for obtaining the funds included (a) the removal of Ralph Barker and two other individuals (supportive of Barker) from the Board of Directors, (b) placement of two men acceptable to the investor on the Board and (c) the election of Helmut as Chairman of the Board and Chief Executive Officer of Lasoptic.

Despite urgent warnings by several key employees that this maneuver was the first step towards forcing Ralph Barker out of the company entirely, Ralph accepted the situation. In conference with a few of his closest associates he said, "Look, the situation isn't as bad as it sounds. I will now be able to spend more time in the technical aspects of the business and pursue expansion plans. I know that this situation still needs a lot of shaking down before things are smoothed out and that some of you are quite legitimately upset. But cool it for a while. With me acting as a buffer, I'll be able to minimize some of the bad effects this political ploy might have upon morale."

Walter Helmut quickly took advantage of his newly acquired power. He withheld important information from Barker, formulating various business plans without consulting or seeking approval from either Barker or the Board of Directors. Within three months Barker had no knowledge about the status of the company. Employee morale eroded steadily, as it appeared that the fears about the possible removal of Ralph Barker were not unfounded.

Frustration within the group emerged as Walter Helmut began to pour substantial sums of money into the laser manufacturing operation, which was losing money, while neglecting the optical operation, which was generating a profit. Sorely needed equipment and personnel were not forthcoming to the optical group. In their perception of what was happening, the staff saw the fruits of their labor after many years of dedicated work now being siphoned off into a losing operation.

Ralph Barker's role as an intermediary deteriorated as Walter Helmut began a concerted effort to bring all Lasoptic under his control. His tactics for gaining control included telling employees how to conduct their jobs, following people around the premises, demanding detailed reports (which apparently went unread). Above all, employees objected to Helmut's arrogance. Directly and indirectly he attempted to communicate the message that without him the company had little chance for survival.

As resentment toward Helmut's tactics increased, productivity decreased. More designs had to be reworked because they contained technical flaws. Normally careful technicians became less careful. Morale continued to erode. It appeared that the most dissatisfied and least productive employees were precisely those who spent the most time interacting with Helmut.

An organizational crisis was reached when Barker resigned after a heated disagreement with Helmut over questionable accounting procedures. Ralph Barker finally realized that the stress Helmut was placing upon employees was affecting morale and productivity adversely. Barker hoped that through his resignation the Board of Directors would take action regarding the accounting procedures used by Helmut. In doing so, Barker believed that Helmut would be censured so that it would be possible to begin moving Lasoptic in the right direction again.

Barker's resignation strategy proved to be ineffective. Helmut had broadened his power base to include tight control over the activities and decisions of the Board. Furthermore, Barker's resignation was accepted without any action taken against Helmut.

Ralph Barker's departure resulted in a further drop in employee morale. Frustrations increased as the group tried to work hard despite mounting job dissatisfaction. Now in complete control, Helmut created additional stress for employees simply by his increased interactions with them. The shift in leadership style was also now complete. In place of permissive Barker, employees were tightly controlled by the authoritarian Helmut. Don Wadsworth, the first engineer to resign from the group, told Helmut on his last day:

"This used to be a professional organization. Our judgment as professionals and human beings was respected. I was willing to put up with the limited money available for fancy equipment because of the excitement of contributing to something important. Since you treat me as incompetent, untrustworthy, or both, there is no percentage in my sticking around. I've accepted a position with a larger company.

Two months after Barker's resignation, the situation became critical. Worker motivation dropped to an all-time low in the history of Lasoptic. A corresponding decline in production also took place. The group still felt a close alliance with one another, but this alliance was working to the disadvantage of Helmut. As stress mounted, four more key employees left. Two others stayed just to fill contractual obligations.

At this point, production ceased, placing the company at its death stage. The Board of Directors, in a last moment, frantic maneuver, requested a meeting with the remaining employees — without the presence of Walter Helmut. With assurances of no repercussions, the employees pinpointed their grievances, pleading that the survival of the company depended upon the removal of Walter Helmut from power. Ideally, they argued, he should also be terminated.

After three days of deliberation, the Board decided to schedule another conference with the employees, again without Helmut. Frustration continues to mount. Employees feel that the Board is fearful of taking decisive action. A company insider thinks that Lasoptic will close its doors forever within two months.

Questions

1. What criticisms can you make of the appropriateness of Ralph Barker's leadership style (in relation to serving as President of a firm like Lasoptics)?
2. What action should the Board of Directors have taken after hearing the complaints offered by the Lasoptic work group?
3. What does this case tell us about the interrelationship among group cohesiveness, satisfaction, and productivity?
4. In this case Ralph Barker served as an intermediary to prevent his employees from having much direct contact with Walter Helmut. What are the disadvantages of using an intermediary to "absorb" conflict?
5. Comment upon the advisability of using an Executive Vice President in a firm with a total work force of 16 people.

Case 33
Who Needs an Interlocutor?*

Ben Weathers, Manager of Organization Planning, had an 11 a.m. interview scheduled with Sol Metzger, Manager of Manufacturing Engineering. Sol had called Ben, recommending that the latter's department should take a quick look at a situation that was getting out of hand. Arriving promptly, Sol closed the door and sat down rather hurriedly.

BEN: "How have you been Sol? I haven't seen you since my wife and I bumped into you at a duplicate bridge tournament. I like that shirt you're wearing."

SOL: "Thanks for helping me relax, Ben. But we don't have time for pleasantries. I think the company has made a severe error in organization design. We may be creating communication baffles instead of eliminating them."

BEN: "That's a pretty sophisticated criticism. I'd like to hear more about it."

SOL: "That's exactly why I'm here. I might as well tell you the story straight as I see it. Later, you may want to verify my observations by conducting some interviews of your own. Excuse me if I present you with some detail that you may already be familiar with. In your speciality, however, you should want a well developed rationale for my charges."

*David M. Knauss conducted the research for this case and contributed to its writing.

206

BEN: "What kind of charges?"

SOL: "I see a lot of conflict between the Operations Planning and Demand Analysis functions in the manufacturing organization. The paradox is that Demand Analysis was supposed to reduce conflict, not create conflict. Here is what seems to have happened."

BEN: "Please continue."

SOL: "The monthly supply/demand cycle provides the means and procedures for negotiations between Marketing's forecasted equipment demands and Manufacturing's capabilities to respond to these demands. The negotiations center around the analysis of 'what if' questions directed to Manufacturing by the Marketing representatives. Answers to 'what if' questions convey information on requested changes to production schedules. The function of Operations Planning and Demand Analysis is to analyze the impact of the 'what if' and respond to Marketing with the best case.

"Things then get complicated. The 'what if's' are received in Manufacturing by Demand Analysis which in turn directs the questions to Operations Planning.

"The analysts in Operations Planning deal directly with the manufacturing plants and evaluate the impact on material, manpower, facilities, and other resources. For instance, a 'what if' with an enormous impact would be 'What if our largest customer wants to double its order for the next six months. The reverberations would be enormous. When the analysis is complete, Operations Planning prepares a documented presentation which describes the Manufacturing position to Marketing. These presentations are in turn directed not to Marketing, but to Demand Analysis!

"Demand Analysis has the responsibility of revising and editing the responses from Operations Planning. They, in turn, present to Marketing only the information that they feel is pertinent. Operations planning complains that they are the experts on Manufacturing Operations and should have the last say on what is presented to Marketing.

"Resentment runs high when the written report prepared by Operations Planning is revised by Demand Analysis and the former are not even consulted. The way the organization is currently planned, it seems that one of the functions of Demand Analysis is to constantly criticize Operations Planning's output. Operations Planning's analysis is filtered through Demand Analysis before it reaches Marketing."

BEN: "It sounds like you are getting to the nub of the problem. Please continue."

SOL: "Oftentimes Manufacturing cannot meet the Marketing request and negotiations must take place to reach a compromise solution. For instance, Marketing might need 250 complicated machines that Manufacturing could not possibly ship in time for Marketing's request without sacrificing production on other lines. But Marketing and Manufacturing don't deal directly with each other on this gut level issue.

"The way things are set up on the organization chart, communication with Marketing is centralized in Manufacturing by Demand Analysis. According to design, Demand Analysis communicates with Marketing and Operations Planning communicates with Manufacturing. It looks clean on paper, but it doesn't make a lot of sense in practice.

"Did you realize, Ben, the way this organization has been set up, a representative from Operations Planning cannot speak to a Marketing Representative without the express consent of Demand Analysis? Equally picayune, Marketing cannot get messages across to Operations Planning without the consent of Demand Analysis. As a result, negotiations are usually ineffective, inaccurate, time-consuming and frustrating."

BEN: "Could you give me a specific? You're still talking the abstract."

SOL: "Just last month, the Southwestern region got a big order from Texas Instruments for 75 of our new Model 526 machines. Marketing's request for these machines came into Demand Analysis. Demand Analysis then sent the request for this work to Operations Planning. The people in Operations Planning worked at a hectic schedule to give Marketing some honest delivery dates. They figured they could have about half the machines by the time Marketing wanted them.

"The analysis by Operations Planning went on to Demand Analysis who edited the report, and then communicated directly to Marketing. A few Marketing executives hit the ceiling when they learned of Manufacturing's inability to respond totally to their request. They came back with a counterproposal after speaking to Texas Instruments. They would settle for 50 of the Model 526 machines. Back went the story through Demand Analysis. Operations Planning thought that 40 machines by the desired date would be the absolute maximum. Demand Analysis was acting like an information broker while the two sides fumed. We were lucky we didn't lose the order from Texas Instruments.

"As you can see instead of dealing directly with Marketing, the

Operations Planning Analyst must go to Demand Analysis and ask them to ask Marketing for information. As many of us see it, there is an annoying extra link in the communications system.

BEN: "Aside from the extra communications link you refer to, are there any other problems associated with their organizational layout?"

SOL: "For sure. Under the present system, Operations Planning complains that Demand Analysis is changing their presentations without consulting them. I overheard a woman from Operations Planning say 'Who needs an interlocutor?' Demand Analysis complains that Operations Planning is negative and hard to work with. Operations Planning is frustrated when they cannot negotiate directly with Marketing.

"Demand Analysis resents the situation because they must have complete cooperation from Operations Planning in order to get timely information about Manufacturing problems. Management has often attributed these problems to personality conflicts, inability to work with others, or immaturity. I think the problem lies in the way the organization is designed."

BEN: "Perhaps we should study this situation more carefully. It looks as if the liaison group function is not working as smoothly as planned."

SOL: "A word of advice. You had better do something besides study the situation. A lot of conflict is building up out there in Manufacturing."

Questions

1. What is the essential nature of the conflict revealed in this case? Explain your answer.
2. What changes would you suggest in organization structure to minimize some of the conflict revealed in this case?
3. What do you think was management's reasoning in establishing the Demand Analysis group?
4. Is Sol Metzger bringing the problem to the right person by going to Ben Weathers?
5. What issues might Sol be overlooking as revealed by his statement "We may be creating communication baffles instead of eliminating them?"

Case 34
A School System in Conflict *

Eight teachers agreed to participate in an analysis of some of the problems faced by 180 teachers in the school system of a district with 19,000 students. Nobody sophisticated about research methodology would argue that eight teachers constitute an adequate sampling of teacher opinion. However, all of these men and women are experienced teachers who have received some kind of formal commendation for their teaching efforts. They are living with the system and doing well by it. A logical conclusion is that if they see much conflict in their district, others who enjoy less job satisfaction will see even more conflict.

The eight participants in the study were asked questions about attitudes toward the Board of Education, the role of the Superintendent as liaison between the teachers and the Board, the functions of the principal and the immediate supervisor, and relationships with other members of the staff. Hillary Matthews, one of the teachers interviewed, commented, "I'm glad you are perceptive enough to realize that schools have problems, too. Many researchers of organizations think that the business and the military are the only institutions with problems worth analyzing."

Question 1: Do you feel the Board of Education is doing a good job?

*Robert J. Quigley researched this case and is responsible for a substantial portion of its writing.

All eight teachers had critical things to say about the Board of Education. Among the negatives expressed were that the Board was not knowledgeable enough about educational values; that the members had insulated themselves from those they were supposed to represent; that there was little consideration given to supplying teachers with information concerning the needs of the system; that the Board relied solely upon the recommendations of the Superintendent; and, lastly, that their legalistic application of the education law caused a breakdown in teacher morale.

Jeff Bannerstone, a teacher of physics, expressed his opinions: "One gets the impression that the Board's only concern with the system centers around the cost involved. Consequently, educational values are sacrificed. It appears to some of us that the Board caters to small organized pressure groups who publicly assail them. As a result, the policies coming from the Board are an appeasement to these groups. Another point of irritation is that the long range plans that should have been made were replaced with piecemeal policies which in the long run cost more than mature guidelines. I can go into specifics on this one.

"A good example of sacrificing long range goals and of showing lack of consideration for the teachers and the public is a projected building construction program. The Board had initiated a plan for redistribution of the elementary school pupils in order to provide all the students with quality education. In effect, the plan was an integrating process by which Black children were sent to various schools within the system. The plan was given approval by the majority of the public, the Superintendent, and the teachers. The cost of the program was high, but thought to be well worth the investment.

"From then on the plan came under constant pressure from other groups. Studies for new building construction brought out by the Board called for a new elementary school building. The Teachers' Association and an independent public study, working separately, called for the construction of a four-year high school. The Board summarily dismissed these recommendations. It was obvious that their decision was an appeasement of pressure groups and contradicted the Board's past decision regarding the integration plan."

Another area in which those interviewed considered the Board lacking was in its position concerning the education laws passed by the state legislature, specifically the Taylor Law and the Jerebeck bills.*

Laura Jo Bridgeman's comments about this issue come close to representing group opinion: "We felt that the Board took a strictly legalistic stand in following these laws to the letter. As a result, a chasm resulted between itself and the teachers. The first year under the Taylor Law a lawyer was hired to negotiate with the teachers. In their bargaining this year, the Board tried to do away with the salary schedule since it is a negotiable item under the Jerebeck laws. No policy concerning the probationary years of new teachers was made.

"This year the chief negotiator for the Board is the Superintendent. Using him as chief negotiator rules out his role as a liaison between the Board and the teachers in the system. This is true because he is known to represent only the Board's position through the manner in which he conducts the negotiations. It appears to us that much of the Board's position is reduced to dollar signs."

Another problem that faced the Board and was revealed in the interviews related to their concerns about "keeping quality teachers," and "professionalism of the teachers." The teachers considered this hypocritical in view of the Board's self-serving conduct during the negotiation.

Question 2: "How well is the Superintendent working out in his role?"

The teachers interviewed felt strongly that the primary duties of the school Superintendent are to advise the Board concerning implementation of policies within the system, to act as a liaison for the administrators, teachers, and the Board of Education; and to delegate the necessary authority to help principals operate their schools efficiently. When questioned about the Superintendent's record in meeting these role expectations, the teachers offered critical commentary.

Henry Hobson, a social studies teacher, offered these reservations about the Superintendent's performance: "Unfortunately, the Superintendent does not function as an advisor to the Board at all. He is the innovator of the Board's policies and its true authority. The

---

*The New York State Taylor Law grants public employees the right to organize and participate in collective negotiations with employers. It also bans strikes. Teachers who strike are fined one day's pay for every day they are out on strike. The Jerebeck legislation gives the Boards of Education in New York State the right to negotiate concerning the right of a salary schedule, the option to maximize the tenure of teachers up to five years, and the ability to give appointed administrators tenure.

Board has little knowledge of matters concerning education. One of the Board members gives me the impression he may not have graduated from high school. Most of the Board rely too heavily upon the Superintendent's own views. Besides, the Superintendent shows no regard for the teachers' knowledge of various problems within the system. Therefore, he is not equipped to bring the right problems to the attention of the Board.

"We also have to look at the personal characteristics of the Superintendent. The man is simply too authoritarian. He meets with the teaching staff only at the beginning of the school year, and he doesn't visit the schools during the year. Most teachers could not identify the Superintendent if he walked into their classrooms. He has stripped the principals of the authority they need to enforce policy. To top that, instead of reinforcing many decisions made by principals, he arbitrarily makes his own decisions about problems brought to his attention. He treats the principals like underlings. As a result, the principals lack control of their own school environments.

"Our biggest single peeve with the Superintendent is that he negotiated against the teachers at contract time, representing only the Board's position. Because of this, an unbridgeable gap exists between him and the teachers. We feel insecure with him, and we don't trust him. There seems to be some hope for the future though. The Superintendent has resigned effective the end of this school year. Perhaps this is his wisest decision since taking office."

Question 3: "How well is the principal doing in carrying out his role in your school?"

The teachers interviewed had considerable sympathy for the role of the principal. According to them, the principals were doing the best they could considering the arbitrariness of the Superintendent. Mort Olinsky, an industrial arts teacher, had these positive comments to make about his principal:

"Larry Gooch respects us as professionals. He backs us up to the fullest extent possible. He's available to help solve problems. When any of us have a personal meeting with him, we know that the contents of the meeting will be held in the strictest confidence. Gooch has a firm 'hands off policy' regarding the teachers' methods and techniques. We're all adults. He recognizes this and lets us solve our own problems.

"When the principal reprimands a teacher he shows no hostility and holds no grudge afterwards. You don't get a feeling of job insecurity under his direction.

"My only real criticism of the principal is that he has allowed himself to be stripped of authority by the Superintendent."

Question 5: "What are your feelings regarding the other teachers in the system?"

The eight teachers interviewed felt there was a spirit of cooperation and mutual respect. Interactions with each other were generally favorable. Nevertheless, some specific sources of tension and conflict were noted among teachers themselves or among teachers and other professional level workers in the system.

Max Hartley, a teacher of business, pointed to some problems he was having with the Guidance Department: "It's kind of a private joke arouund here that the Guidance Department uses us as a dumping ground for low-level students. As a result, the Business Department has been downgraded. Why don't they ever send us an alert, well motivated student? I wish there was some way we could send our poorest students to another department.

"My reasoning is that since many academic students enroll in business administration courses in two and four-year colleges, the business education courses should be emphasized more than they are. We have developed a personal way of beating the system and circumventing Guidance. On an informal basis, we recruit students ourselves for Business. Other teachers send us a few referrals.

"We've made a few futile attempts to upgrade the Department by offering a variety of business courses, but it won't work. The Administration, as usual, pleads poverty."

Another source of tension revealed in the interviews, is the literal compliance with procedures by some teachers. According to the respondents, in some instances following procedures has become more important than teaching itself. For example, one of the teachers interviewed had scheduled a field trip. Due to various reasons, he did not give the students a pass until the day before the trip. School policy called for the pass to be signed by teachers of the students three days in advance. The Department Chairman of another area would not permit students in his class to go on one day's notice, basing his reason on the importance of class and school policy. Uneasiness between the teacher and that Chairman has developed.

Other problems stemming from over-reliance on policies and procedures were also mentioned. Among them: (a) some teachers stressing the necessity of duplicate passes when one would suffice, (b) the limitation on students going to the library only for specified class projects, not simply to study, (c) the tendency of some academic teachers to transfer students of poor quality out of their classes, not for the student's sake, but in order to maintain high achievement quality on their own records. All of these problems caused stressful feelings and a lack of cooperation. Student-teacher relationships were also affected adversely by strict interpretation of policy.

Questions concerning extra-curricular activities (such as acting as a chaperone for dances or on bus trips, or serving as a counselor in activities sponsored by the students) brought out some hostile feelings. Judy Neward, a math teacher, illustrates some of these:

"The major problem is that there is so little appreciation shown by the students. On top of that, the students have very little regard for the discipline policies that must be set up for various functions. We have to insist that smoking in the gymnasium is absolutely *verboten*. Yet at every high school dance a few clowns light up cigarettes. Incidents like these have led to teachers simply not showing up to 'baby-sit.'

"Many teachers are disturbed by the fact that we do not get paid for extra-curricular activities while police officers who are off duty and work these functions do get paid. That is a classic example of injustice. Along the same line, many of the older teachers have served for years as counselors at various functions without expecting additional pay. They feel quite strongly that more of the younger teachers should be willing to do likewise. It seems only fair to share the workload."

The teachers interviewed were also concerned by the lack of interest shown by others in the Teacher's Association. Many felt that a need now exists for strong bargaining positions by teacher units — not only for salary and personal benefits, but also to make sure that the educational goals of the systems are not lost due to the recent priorities given to economy. A feeling exists that now more than ever the teachers must work as a unified group to best protect their interests. Nevertheless, cooperation among teachers is not good. Boyd Davis, an elementary school teacher, describes this lack of cooperation:

"The reasons for this less than perfect cooperation are not hard to identify. Tenured as well as non-tenured teachers are worried about job security. In this mixed up economy you never know when you have a contract for the following year. Many of the complaints about the Association come from people who never attend meetings. Some teachers are arguing about the Association when they have a limited idea of its true function.

"It makes sense that all must do their share in the activities of the Association if it is to be of value to the teachers themselves, and to the public who also share the educational concern of the community.

"Before we close this interview, let me tell you what I strongly believe is the real reason that we have so many hard feelings among the teachers. Many, if not all, of our problems seem to stem from age and time in grade. The 'Old Guard' has been teaching for a number of years and they are quite content with things as they are. In contrast, the young teachers have a newer philosophy and see the need for change within the system. Maybe it's because the newer breed of teachers recognizes they will have to live with these inequities for the rest of their working careers unless something is done now. The older teachers want us to suffer just the way they did."

Questions

1. What constructive action might be taken to reduce conflict between the Board of Education and the schools? Who should take such action?
2. How might conflict between the older and younger teachers be reduced?
3. What types of behavioral science intervention might you recommend for handling some of the problems in this case?
4. Identify three underlying causes for the conflicts between the school Superintendent and the teachers?
5. Based upon your experiences with school systems, does this school seem to have an exceptional amount of conflict?

Case 35
What Price Competition? *

The Board of Education of a high school district in Illinois believed it had a motivational problem with tenured members of the faculty. Although no teacher ever caused the district to fire him or her for bad teaching, it was the Board's opinion that the majority of the tenured faculty had little enthusiasm for their work. As an antidote to this lowered level of motivation the Board decided to institute a merit award system. Budget restrictions did not allow for school-wide awards, so a departmental award was finally decided upon. According to the system, one person in every department (excluding the department head) would be chosen as best teacher by the department head and principal. The recipient of a merit award would receive a six percent salary increase for the following year.

Six months after its implementation, the award system showed some signs of accomplishing its intended purpose. In particular, the Science Department displayed a renewed interest in experimenting with new projects and new techniques. Freshmen students built a small model of the solar system that was later displayed in a glass case in the lobby of the high school.

Team spirit seemed to have been infused into the department, and the teachers worked together as a more cohesive unit than in the past. Once into the competition for outstanding teaching, the

*This case is based upon research conducted by Sandra Colby.

217

teachers were enthused by the good results forthcoming. At the end of the year, the merit award was given to a capable teacher who seemed to be rejuvenated by the year's experiences. At the banquet commemorating the award, Ms. Alicia Perks, the winner, spoke. "It's been a great year," she said, "I never thought I would get an award for simply doing what I'm paid to do and what I love to do — work with the future leaders of our country."

A similar beneficial effect seemed to stem from the award competition in several other departments. Teachers thrived on the excitement generated by experimenting with new techniques in response to competition for the merit award. Yet in three departments, the same benefits were not achieved.

In the Industrial Arts Department — a small group of only four people, excluding the department head — it became a serious contest to win the award at all costs. Sal Conti, an industrial arts teacher had this to say about one of his colleagues:

"Bill is going too far with this competition thing. The guy is holding dinner parties for the Chairman in an effort to establish some kind of social relationship with him. He is forever in the Chairman's office feeding him ideas on new techniques that the Industrial Arts Department should try out. We know that because Tom, the Chairman, is forever feeding those suggestions back to us. We talk about some of those techniques, but we never seem to have the time or money to do much about them.

"The situation became so bad with Bill trying to curry favor with Tom, that we came to resent him. You could feel the tension when he sat next to us in the cafeteria. In the past our whole department worked together as a tightly knit little team. Now we have taken sides. It's three of us lined up against Tom and his bootlicking pal, Bill."

Three women made up the women's section of the Physical Education Department. All three teachers had received tenure. Over a five-year period they had developed a very structured physical education program. No one of the three women felt that she had made a bigger contribution than the others in establishing the program. Now when one teacher decided to try something new (like introducing elementary Yoga into one of the dance classes) the other two considered it an attempt to receive the merit award. Melissa Burke said of her colleague:

"Sara is forgetting that we have spent five years developing the P.E. Department into a team operation. Now she runs off trying things by herself without first getting our approval."

Sara became the butt of a good deal of kidding about her attempts to be innovative. Once, an anonymous telegram arrived at her office congratulating her on the fact that she had just been requested to coach the United States Olympic Women's Gymnastic Team. Sara took the kidding more seriously than perhaps her two colleagues realized. At the end of the year she handed in her resignation — two weeks before she learned that she was this year's merit award recipient.

Competition for the merit award had its least anticipated ramifications in the Social Studies Department. Eight teachers and one administrator staffed this department. Shortly after the competition for the award was announced, several members of the Social Studies Department held an informal meeting in the school cafeteria to discuss the program. Lou Dustin, one of the younger teachers, brought up the issue of the difficulty in measuring good teaching performance. All agreed that this constituted a real problem. A meeting was scheduled with all the teachers in the department to delve further into the problem of measuring good teaching performance.

It became apparent in the second meeting that defining "outstanding teaching" or "teaching effectiveness" was a complex issue that had been addressed by thousands of other educators at many levels of education and in many locations. However, one point did receive consensus. Teaching can only be outstanding if it in some way leads to increased learning. Lou Dustin then took a position that was unpopular with the group:

"Agreed that outstanding teaching must be measured in terms of outstanding learning. The only problem now is that we have no good measures of whether or not students have learned." The older teachers in the department felt that their grades were an accurate measure of whether or not outstanding learning had taken place. Lou attempted to point out the danger in that line of reasoning:

"We have gotten ourselves into an unfortunate bind on that one. If the person who claims to have done the outstanding teaching also measures the learning that comes from his or her teaching, there is a built-in conflict of interest. It's like having an art contest in which the artists who submit the paintings also judge them. We cannot accept the grades a teacher assigns to his or her own students as an objective measure of whether or not the teaching has been good."

Marie Evans, an experienced teacher, retorted: "Lou, you're being too philosophical again. That psychological mumbo-jumbo is not of concern here. We are all mature people who can assign grades fairly."

As things worked out, grades in the Social Studies Department became elevated an average of 10 percentage points over the previous semester. The grades assigned by one teacher to his social studies classes increased by 15 percentage points.

Although the merit award had less disruptive aspects in other departments of the high school, the problems experienced by these three departments became a popular topic of conversation. A faculty vote recommended to the Board that the system be dropped for the following school year. As a result of feelings expressed by the faculty, the Board chose to abandon the award system for the next year. A committee was formed of teachers, administrators, and a Board member to work on the formation of a more acceptable system.

As the Industrial Arts Department head commented, "The Board made the right decision. Why wreck good faculty team spirit for a lousy few hundred dollars per year that only one person in each department can get? What price competition?"

Questions

1. What type of award system (if any) should be implemented in this high school?
2. For what reasons do you think the teaching award system failed?
3. How might the school have prevented compeition for the award from turning into conflict?
4. If the real problem facing this school system is that tenured teachers have lost enthusiasm for teaching, what should be done about the situation?
5. What is your opinion about using student learning as one criterion of teaching effectiveness?

REFERENCES

Butler, Jr., Arthur G. "Project Management: A Study in Organizational Conflict," *Academy of Management Journal*, Vol. 16, March 1973, 84-101.

Filley, Alan C. *Interpersonal Conflict Resolution*. Glenview, Ill.: Scott, Foresman, 1975.

Keller, Robert T. "Role Conflict and Ambiguity: Correlates With Job Satisfaction and Values," *Personnel Psychology*, Vol. 28, Spring 1975, 57-64.

Kelly, Joe, *Organizational Behaviour: An Existential-Systems Approach*, revised edition, Homewood, Ill.: Richard D. Irwin, 1974. See Chapter 14.

Kochan, Thomas A., Huber, George P., and Cummings, L.L. "Determinants of Intraorganizational Conflict in Collective Bargaining in the Public Sector," *Administrative Science Quarterly*, Vol. 20, March 1975, 10-23.

Miner, John B. *The Management Process: Theory, Research, and Practice*. New York: Macmillan, 1973. See Chapter 13.

Pfeffer, Jeffrey and Salancik, Gerald R. "Organizational Decision Making as a Political Process: The Case of a University Budget," *Administrative Science Quarterly*, Vol. 19, June 1974, 135-151.

Renwick, Patricia A. "Perception and Management of Superior-Subordinate Conflict," *Organizational Behavior and Human Performance*, Vol. 13, June 1975, 444-456.

Sorensen, James E. and Sorensen, Thomas L. "The Conflict of Professionals in Bureaucratic Organizations," *Administrative Science Quarterly*, Vol. 19, March 1974, 98-106.

Zacker, Joseph and Bard, Morton. "Effects of Conflict Management Training on Police Performance," *Journal of Applied Psychology*, Vol. 58, April 1974, 202-208.

PART IV
ORGANIZATIONS

Total organizations rather than individuals or small groups are the *primary focus* of this section. The term *primary focus* is given special attention because it is difficult to draw clear-cut distinctions between organizations and the groups of people composing them. Organizations are essentially aggregates of a number of smaller groups. The cases in Chapter 13 deal essentially with bringing about changes in organizations, yet many of these changes are initiated at the individual and small-group level. To illustrate, the new president of the Chamber of Commerce described in one case represents an individual attempting to bring about organizational change of a very major sort.

Perhaps the most weakly classified case in the entire casebook is appropriately called "What Should We Do With Harry?" "Harry" is placed in the chapter about management of individual and group change because he appears to be approaching a state of managerial obsolescence. However, his case also represents an example of a manager trying to improve subordinate performance (Chapter 8). To compound the classification difficulty, Chapter 12, "Management of Individual and Group Change," could fit logically into the previous section about small groups. It represents a transitional topic between groups and organizations.

11
Organizational Climate

Case 36
The Isolation Blues
(A Simple Case of Cabin Fever, Paranoia, and Sexual Frustration)

Lieutenant Commander Roger Jensen, Captain of the Nuclear Submarine *Lancer*, was apprehensive as he sat outside his superior's office in Washington, D.C. "What a tale to tell your boss three days after returning from a heralded 75-day mission under water," he thought to himself. "But unless we find a way of coping with this problem soon, we are going to destroy the lives of a good many innocent Naval personnel. We're just not doing enough about this problem." Jensen's stream of thought was interrupted by the opening of Commander Jake Steubing's office door.

"Commander Jensen," said Steubing in a loud and positive tone, "come right in." The two men seated themselves comfortably on a sofa next to a coffee table. Steubing spoke first.

STEUBING: "Roger you called me immediately after stepping off the *Lancer* to tell me that you have a serious message. Instead of exchanging pleasantries, let's get right to the problem you have in mind. However, first let me congratulate you on a magnificent voyage. Seventy-five days is a long time to navigate a submarine without a shore break. Your voyage has done a lot for the United States Navy."

JENSEN: "Jake, I appreciate the compliment. Some of our voyage did go well. Technologically speaking, our submarine builders and designers deserve a lot of credit. The electronic circuitry was flawless, including every aspect of the computer system. Few people appreciate the complexity of a nuclear submarine. I become increasingly amazed as I learn more about the technological aspects of submarine life. If the atmosphere in submarines were fit for human beings, I think the Navy would really have something."

STEUBING: "What do you mean, 'If the atmosphere were fit for human beings?' Are you referring to a few isolated cases of cabin fever? They tell me full-time homemakers suffer from the same problem."

JENSEN: "We are not dealing with a few isolated cases. We have enormous problems aboard the submarine that go way beyond grousing, low morale, or simple cabin fever. Unchecked, these problems could snowball into an epidemic of emotional breakdowns among submarine personnel."

STEUBING: "How about a few specific examples of what you are talking about?"

JENSEN: "While on board this lengthy voyage I kept a log of my own observations and supplemented them with some detailed logs kept by two ensigns on board. Pulling it all together, we have some pretty alarming information. The ship's Medical Officer, Lt. Winsted Barat, also kept me informed of some of the more serious emotional disturbances that came to his attention during the voyage. Of course, he sees only those individuals who have overt problems. Inevitably, whenever a large group of people congregate, at least one or two percent will have some kind of emotional disturbance requiring medical attention. That could even happen on a vacation cruise ship. What worries me also are the number of cases that do not get reported to the Medical Officer aboard.

"Before I go over some of my cases with you, I want to point out that I realize the Navy has some recognition of these problems. Recently, I read some reports by Naval psychologists describing how they are trying to help submarine personnel cope better with their sexual frustrations. Some of our subs are encouraging men to satiate themselves with pornography. Later, I'll get back to that problem as it relates to the *Lancer*."

STEUBING: "Please do get on with the specifics of the problems on board the *Lancer* you have come here to discuss."

JENSEN: "About eight days after we left shore, there seemed to be a gradual increase in the number of people concerned with submarine safety. Time and time again, different crewmen could be seen scurrying about the sub looking for leaks, as if they knew that disaster was pending. One ensign reported that he thought the walls of the sub were beginning to cave in because he could detect subtle changes in the pressure upon his ears. Another crewman kept urging his superior to start a petition showing the crew's concern that the sub was running too close to the ocean floor. He contended that we were destined to hit the remains of a wrecked ship at our present depth.

"Our engineers and other technical personnel were deluged with questions about how we would surface if our power system failed. Despite constant reassurances from our officers that the *Lancer* was operating perfectly, the obsession with finding leaks or symptoms of power failure continued."

STEUBING: "A difficult problem, indeed, but not dramatically different from the concern passengers on a commercial airline have about the technical integrity of the aircraft."

JENSEN: "One concern you don't have on a commercial airliner is a massive preoccupation with mental health. I would say that about 15 percent of the submarine's personnel feel they are becoming mentally unglued by about the fourth week of the journey. Many are jumpy, irritable, and have nightmares. One man ran through the walkways screaming that an undersea culture of maggots was attacking the ship. Another man reported that he couldn't sleep because of a nightmare that his wife was chasing him with a paring knife. She wanted to kill him because he was a spy for the C.I.A. That's craziness!

"Another reason so many of our people are concerned with their mental health is that they are so depressed. After a while life on a sub is a downer to many. I'm not sure that there is any one personality type that is suited to long submarine trips. Anybody can take it, and perhaps enjoy it for up to two weeks, but after that it gives you disturbing thoughts."

STEUBING: "The picture you paint is a little more severe than other reports we have gathered about mental health aboard nuclear subs, but I'm listening. Go ahead."

JENSEN: "Another vexing problem to cope with is the rampant obsession with fresh air, or the lack thereof. People who spent most of their youth crouched in front of television sets or in smelly gyms suddenly become obsessed with the idea that they must have 'fresh' air. We tell them in eight different ways that submarine air is fresh air, but they would prefer a whiff of Los Angeles smog or a New York City inversion. They figure since there are no trees growing in a submarine, the air cannot be fresh. Men who never went fishing in their lives talk about the beauty of going trout fishing in a stream overlooking a mountain.

"One fellow raised in the most crime ridden, vandalized portion of the Bronx kept moaning about the fact that he couldn't plant a garden while on board the submarine. The only earth he ever had on his hands before joining the Navy was from sorting out ears of corn at the supermarket."

STEUBING: "I guess that kind of problem could get out of hand. Please continue."

JENSEN: "There is a rampant suspicion that things are going wrong in the world outside; particularly with the immediate family. Men think that their children have become ill or that their wives are having affairs. One man said he was convinced that his six-year-old boy was running a 105 degree fever. No reassurances seem to calm these men.

"Our program of 'family grams' was designed to alleviate morbid thoughts about the outside world. However, it occasionally works in reverse. When a crewman receives a radioed message after the ship surfaces, it sometimes means that something did go wrong at home. One crewman had to be given sedation over a long period of time when he learned that his daughter lost a hand in a lawn mower accident. First he begged us to turn the submarine around and head back for home. When he realized that this request would not be granted, he went into a rage, threatening to sue the Navy. After he threatened to mutilate the body of his officer, we had to give him heavy doses of Thorazine. Without that drug we would have needed a straightjacket."

STEUBING: "That is an unfortunate case. I hope it is atypical."

JENSEN: "One problem that is not atypical is the preoccupation with talk about sex. I think that even in remote sites in Alaska, the men believe there might be an Eskimo woman waiting for them in the wilderness. In the submarine, unless you are gay, there is no opportunity to have sexual relations. The atmosphere becomes raunchy. We show X-rated movies; our pornographic libraries would be the envy of sailors on shore; lurid sex-novels are in ample supply. Without this supply of sexually laden material things could be worse, but with it we have a preoccupation with sex that is disruptive of other activities. I suspect a submarine is worse than a prison, because in the prison many turn to homosexuality. Naval personnel probably avoid this because they know they will be returning to a heterosexual life soon. Still, something has to be done. Even the men who probably have almost no sex life on land become obsessed with talking about sexual topics while on the submarine."

STEUBING: "Can you think of any problems that are not so severe, but nevertheless require attention?"

JENSEN: "The least severe problem we have is that the crewmen sleep a lot. Over half of them must sleep between 12 and 16 hours per day. After a short while on the ship, many of the officers and enlisted men walk around as if in a stupor. Perhaps it's the absence of normal sight and sounds of the outside world that puts them into a stupor. Whatever it is, it becomes disconcerting to see so many in perpetual need of sleep. However, it's better to have somebody sleeping away time than rushing to the sonar room every spare moment in the hope of hearing the swimming noises of shrimp."

STEUBING: "Is there anything else your observations have revealed?"

JENSEN: "I guess the only other significant problem I have left out is the constant bickering that goes on after a couple of weeks into the journey. With every passing day, there are more and more picayune disputes. Some of the petty arguments are similar to the fracases children get into when playing sandlot baseball. Others are even more trivial. One crewman accused another of using his comb without permission. Two other crewmen got into a fistfight because one accused the man sleeping below him of rocking too much at night.

"One officer accused another of taking a good refill from his pen and inserting it into his own. Worse than that, people accuse each other of being paranoid, which leads to more hassling."

STEUBING: "As I listen to you Roger, I am impressed with the detailed log you've kept of some of these incidents. I'm also impressed with the fact that you are taking your responsibilities as a submarine Captain seriously. But every aspect of the service has its unique problems. The atmosphere in the infantry is hardly conducive to comfortable living. We are already doing quite a bit to compensate for the unnaturalness of the submarine life. Why are you so worried?"

JENSEN: "Jake, as I tried to tell you before, I think the submarine environment can do permanent damage to the mental health of its personnel. Human beings are not built to take long voyages on nuclear submarines. The artificial environment of the nuclear submarine may be creating a new breed of psychiatric casualties."

Questions

1. What steps should the United States Navy take to prevent or minimize the problems described by Commander Jensen?
2. Should nuclear submarines be staffed by an equal complement of

males and females? Why or why not?

3. What types of people (with respect to any relevant variables that can be measured) would be best suited for long trips on nuclear submarines?

4. Should the United States Navy disallow "familygrams"? Why or why not?

5. If Commander Roger Jensen saw all the problems that he describes, should he have headed the *Lancer* back home? Explain.

Case 37
The Drab Decor at
Steel City Nursing Home

Larry Tracy, a Regional Operations Manager for Golden Age Enterprises, (a nationwide chain of nursing homes) was packing his attache case for a field trip to steel City, one of the nursing homes in his jurisdiction.

"Is there anything else you need for the trip?" asked Jill, Tracy's secretary.

"Yes, one more thing," replied Larry, "How about a packet of Alka Seltzer? I know I'll need it when I get there. That's a first-rate physical facility with a good reputation for resident care, but we have a lot of problems at Steel City. If Shana Albert, the Administrator there doesn't see the light soon, I may have to take drastic action."

"Good luck, Mr. Tracy. I'm sure she and you can work something out. Word has gotten back to me that Mrs. Albert is a first-rate Administrator."

"I agree," replied Larry, "she's first-rate except for a bad case of tunnel vision."

Larry drove to Steel City Nursing Home, a three-hour trip from Regional Headquarters. As he approached the exit on the expressway, Larry mused to himself, "What an unlikely place to construct a nursing home! Its location is better suited for a tire factory. Many of the houses surrounding the home sold for $13,000 when they were erected 20 years ago. My boss calls this place 'Blue Collar Manor' and I can see why. You have to put up nursing homes in areas where real estate taxes are within reason. Nevertheless, we've got to do something to improve the stark prisonlike appearance of Steel City."

Larry Tracy was greeted cordially by Shana Albert. She assured Larry that they would not be interrupted during their morning conference, that she had cancelled all appointments for the morning and would be available to the staff only for emergency problems. She added that she is faced with at least one emergency on an average morning. After an exchange of pleasantries about the economic climate and the stock price of Golden Age Enterprises, Larry dove right into his agenda.

"Shana, my concern over Steel City Nursing Home has not diminished since we held our review about 30 days ago. As I size up the situation, you have a first-rate physical facility here — a 100 bed site with a well above average reputation for taking good care of people. Your place can be reached in 30 minutes on the expressway from the more affluent sections of town. That compensates to a large degree for the fact that your neighborhood is somewhat out of the way and nestled in the production worker section of town. Your location, however, is a given. There is nothing we can do about that."

"What is there something we can do about, Larry?" asked Shana.

"We have to do something about attracting a higher proportion of private pay residents. Right now you have about 25 percent private pay residents and we have to move that figure up dramatically — hopefully to 45 percent or better. We only want about one-half of our residents to be on Medicare or Medicaid. The atmosphere here is too drab to bring in more people who are spending their own money. What you have here looks more like an old-fashioned hospital or a modern prison. Everything is so stark. No natural plants, few flowers, no pictures on the wall. Every room has the same sterile looking institutional furniture. To attract the right residents you need an atmosphere that resembles a home. Old people like what-nots and bric-a-brac scattered about. They have got to be comfortable in their home away from home."

"Larry, as I tried to tell you before, we have problems at Steel City that you don't have at some of your more affluent locations. It's not uncommon for our residents to 'appropriate' paintings right off the wall. And their guests are worse than they are. Two years ago we splurged and bought a couple dozen of these low-priced original oil paintings that have flooded the United States and Canada in recent years. Within two months only three were left hanging on the wall. Our residents were giving them to their chilren and other guests as presents. When we confronted one man who was walking out with a large canvas, he told us he had brought it into the home to show to his father. When we tried to show him the Steel City imprint on the back, he threatened to take his father out of the home. Rather than create an ugly scene, we dropped the issue.

"Your idea about plants isn't a good one, either, for our clientele. More affluent people know what to do with plants. They are accustomed to having them around their homes. Most of our publicly supported residents have no concern for plants. They use the plants as a depository for gum wrappers, gum, cigarette butts, and old letters. An aide on the floor complained that one of our senile residents was caught urinating in a rubber plant. So why buy more plants?"

"Shana, you're making too much of a fuss about a few exceptions. If we want to attract the right people here, we have to have the right atmosphere."

"But, Larry, we do have the right atmosphere for the resident mix we have now. Our people come from poor homes. They would feel uncomfortable in a place that was designed for the upper-middle class. Publicly supported residents can withdraw from our facility as well as private pays. The children of some of our residents might complain that we were wasting money if we decorated the place with attractive furniture, paintings, and plants. Old people can only feel comfortable when they are in familiar surroundings.

"Shana, when you attended that marketing seminar for nursing home administrators last winter I thought you came away with some good ideas. What happened?"

"They were good ideas," replied Shana, "but not for Steel City Nursing Home. When you are in a growth situation in a prosperous section of town, the ideas espoused in the seminar will work fine. Steel City is unique. We have to take care of the residents we have now and cater to their blue collar tastes. Instead of looking for ways to add frills, maybe we should be cutting corners to add to profitability. Maybe we should put a restriction upon how many aspirins a resident can get without a doctor's prescription. Maybe some of the healthier and more mobile residents could get by with a little less attention from the aides. That could cut down a substantial amount of payroll dollars.

"Shana, you're running in the wrong direction. I'd like to see a crew of painters out here next month to begin refurbishing your facility. How about multicolored walls, and warm pastel colors in the rooms?"

"If we move in that direction, we'd simply be wasting money and paint. It's like knitting cashmere sweaters for kids in a settlement house. You might as well buy them sweat shirts at a bargain basement. They don't know the difference, and they don't care."

"Shana, I'm apparently not getting my point across to you. If you don't start getting my point soon, I may have to find myself an administrator who will understand what needs to be accomplished at Steel City Nursing Home."

Questions

1. What should Larry Tracy do about Shana Albert's unwillingness to change the physical decor at Steel City Nursing Home?
2. Do you agree with Albert's analysis that people from lower socio-economic levels feel uncomfortable surrounded by plants and multicolored walls? Why or why not?
3. Do you agree with Tracy's reasoning that the right "atmosphere" in Steel City Nursing Home will attract private pay residents from other sections of town? Why or why not?
4. How might Larry and Shana go about determining whose judgment is correct about the future of the Steel City Nursing Home?
5. Do you agree that the Steel City Nursing Home is placed in an inappropriate section of town? Explain your reasoning.

Case 38
Biting Dogs Used to be our
Worst Enemy *

Ned Langston, a college graduate with a bachelor's degree in history, has worked for several years as a United States Postal Service mailman. While attending college he worked part time for the Post Office on a regular weekly basis and full time during the Christmas rush season. Upon graduation from college he discovered that the jobs available to him in industry were in many ways less attractive than the job of a letter carrier. As Ned describes it:

"It's a pleasant feeling of independence making your daily rounds. People waiting for welfare or social security checks treat you with tremendous respect. You're almost like the happiness dispenser. The people who are expecting bad news through the mail — such as notices of past-due bills — don't take out their aggression on you. They know it's not your fault.

"The picture on the inside of the Post Office at one time seemed quite promising to me — steady pay, promotional opportunities, good retirement pay, and objective ways of determining who gets promoted. From what I hear, industry isn't nearly as fair. Recently I have detected some changes in the management philosophy of the Post Office which are giving me cause for reflection. I think the atmosphere of the Post Office has changed since it became the United States Postal Service.

*Vladimir Rudy conducted the research for this case and contributed to its writing.

"I'll give you a description of the way things are now, hitting on a few aspects about the organization that I think are the most important. Some of these aspects are favorable; some others are unfavorable. A lot depends upon whether your perspective is from the top of the organization looking down, or the bottom of the organization looking up.

"Managers and supervisors are promoted from the ranks on the basis of scores on competitive exams. Although some people claim that these tests cannot measure their true ability as supervisors, most people have come to accept these exams as a fair arbiter of who moves ahead in the Postal Service. There has been a rash of promotions lately due to expansion after a lengthy hiring freeze. Just like private business, the Postal Service gets hit with expansion and contraction due to the economic cycle.

"Supervisors serve two clients: their own management and the public postal patrons. Both have to be kept satisfied, although at times both management and the public seem to make unreasonable demands upon Postal Service employees. However, serving two groups adds challenge to our jobs. Most people in the Service realize that without our efforts the United States — and maybe the rest of the world — would come to a screeching halt.

"The Postal Service is highly decentralized geographically, with a consequent remoteness of policy from decision makers. Postal regulations, of course, do not vary from one location to another. So you have centralization of policy making in a geographically far-flung organization. In the past, the United States Post Office was the ultimate in a bureaucratic organization. Now there is an emphasis on efficiency, economy, innovation, and modernization. Most people do not realize how much the cost of postage would have increased if the Post Office had not undergone sweeping changes. Maybe a first-class letter would cost 25¢ to mail.

"The letter carriers are protected by Civil Service through a system of regulations for grievances, dismissal and similar matters. Postmen and postwomen are classified as Regulars or Substitutes (who fill in for Regulars or perform miscellaneous tasks). Age and seniority are two factors that count heavily in the Postal Service, as in the tradition of the Post Office. We have an active employees' union, but we are not authorized to strike. Most of the high seniority employees think that the no-strike provision is important considering the critical nature of the mail system. Younger employees now look at work slowdowns by doctors and garbage collectors in big cities and wonder if we aren't fooling ourselves. Why should we be exploited when we have a grievance?

"Competitive tests are used to screen people for jobs. Consequently, the average intelligence of Postal workers at every level is above the average of other workers. Despite this, there was considerable room for political payoffs under the old system. The jokes about campaign managers becoming local Postmasters are not entirely without foundation.

"The real reason for the shift from the Post Office to the Postal Service was the chronic financial deficits incurred by the Post Office. The intent was to make the Postal Service operate like a business. Even if no profits would be forthcoming, at least it could cover its costs. A gradual tightening of everything could be felt in the Postal Service.

"The original top management was highly political. Supposedly, the system is now much more of a meritocracy. Supervision has expanded, especially with increased accountability for 'time on the clock.' Carriers are routinely spied upon as they work on the streets. The purposes of these 'field audits' is to determine if letter carriers are wasting time with side trips or lengthy conversations.

"As a result of studying the working patterns of letter carriers, work loads have increased. Should an inspector decide that a given letter carrier does not have enough work, he will most likely find himself with a few more streets to cover. The standard has become busyness more than quality of service to postal patrons.

"Service, the original mail consideration of the Post Office, is now relegated to a secondary or at best equal consideration with efficiency. The public, however, does not see this happening. A good street image is to be maintained whether or not it reflects real accomplishment. A Postal Service employee is supposed to *look* competent, neat, and act polite. The inner performance is given less emphasis. Consequently, performance is declining in the Postal Service.

"The results from these sweeping changes in the postal system have been mixed. Revenues have increased, and the deficit has slightly decreased. Yet service has declined and morale, at least in our area, has been steadily eroding. Carriers don't respect or cooperate with management. A lot of bickering goes on between them. Workers are now finding ingenious ways to loaf, or at least ingenious excuses. There are frequent requests for relief (help from somebody else while performing your normal job function). Grievances through the union over relatively small issues have increased. A lot of mail gets left for later handling. It looks like absenteeism is on the increase. Substitute workers are less caring than they used to be. I believe some of them just don't care whether or not mail gets delivered on time.

"Postmen and postwomen have a lot of natural pride in their work and feel a responsibility toward the public. The dignity of the letter carrier is affronted by outdoor supervision where independence has always been a prized appeal of the job. Carriers deal directly and often quite personally with patrons. Thus, they decry the shift in focus from service to economy. You can't let an attempt at organizational efficiency destroy the very guts of the postal system.

"Letter carriers now feel that it's them versus management. Biting dogs *used* to be our worst enemy."

Questions

1. Assuming that this one postman is correct in his assessment of problems in the Postal Service, what should management do about the situation?
2. Does management have the right to audit ("spy upon") letter carriers as they make their rounds? Why or why not?
3. Specify three dimensions of organizational climate that may have changed as a result of the shift from the Post Office to the Postal Service.
4. Who should determine what constitutes a fair work load for a letter carrier?
5. Would you consider a letter carrier to be an appropriate job for a college graduate with a history major? Why or why not?

REFERENCES

Dewhirst, H. Dudley. "Impact of Organizational Climate on the Desire to Manage Among Engineers and Scientists, *Personnel Journal*, Vol. 50, March 1971, 196-203.

DuBrin, Andrew J. *Fundamentals of Organizational Behavior: An Applied Perspective.* Elmsford, N.Y.: Pergamon Press, 1974, See Chapter 11.

Friedlander, Frank and Greenberg, Stuart. "Effect of Job Attitudes, Training, and Organization Climate on Performance of the Hard-Core Unemployed," *Journal of Applied Psychology*, Vol. 55, August 1971, 187-295.

Gavin, James F. "Organizational Climate as a Function of Personal and Organizational Variables," *Journal of Applied Psychology*, Vol. 60, February 1975, 135-139.

Jurkovich, Ray. "A Core Typology of Organizational Environments," *Administrative Science Quarterly*, Vol. 19, September 1974, 380-394.

LaFollette, William. "Is Satisfaction Redundant with Organizational Climate?" *Organizational Behavior and Human Performance*, Vol. 13, April 1975, 257-278.

LaFollette, William R. "How is the Climate in Your Organization?" *Personnel Journal*, Vol. 54, July 1975, 376-379.

Schneider, Benjamin. "The Perception of Organizational Climate: The Customer's View," *Journal of Applied Psychology*, Vol. 57, June 1973, 248-256.

Wallace, Jr., Marc J., Ivancevich, John M., and Lyon, Herbert L. "Measurement Modifications for Assessing Organizational Climate in Hospitals," *Academy of Management Journal*, Vol. 18, March 1975, 82-97.

Waters, L.K., Roach, Darrell, and Batlis, Nick. "Organizational Climate Dimensions and Job-Related Attitudes," *Personnel Psychology*, Vol. 27, Autumn 1974, 465-476.

12
Management of Individual and Group Change

Case 39
The Dean Practices Participative Management

Kermit Gathers, Dean of the College of Business, Oshua State University, requested that his trusted friend and Associate Dean, Robert Hanes, meet with him about an important matter. Gathers asked that Hanes set aside all Friday afternoon for discussion. Bob then realized that Kermit had a project of major significance for him to undertake. Kermit Gathers opened the conversation in his usual straightforward, but, nevertheless, controlled manner:

GATHERS: "Bob, the reason I asked to meet with you this afternoon is that I'm somewhat concerned about the intermediate range future of our College. We have been adjusting piecemeal to the changing demands placed upon business education rather than developing a master plan to adapt to these macro-shifts that are surrounding us."

HANES: "What macro-shifts are you referring to?"

GATHERS: "I'm talking about the increased demand for the kind of training and information one typically receives in a business curriculum. People from government, particularly at the state and county level, are now looking toward colleges of business for graduate education. Equally significant, many undergraduate students who plan a career in the public sector are looking to colleges of business as a place to receive the appropriate education. Another of these macro-changes I would cite is that we are now receiving a fair number of applications from younger people who in the past would have aspired toward a career in primary or secondary education.

These people are coming to us almost by default. They hope that colleges of business will have some answers for them. They need direction and guidance."

HANES: "I wouldn't sell our College short on any of these counts. We've been talking about these problems in committees for years. A few of the faculty members now try to use cases from the public sector in their course work. Professor Wilmot regularly counsels with students about career decision making. He most often has a student in his office."

GATHERS: "I would not deny that these changes are taking place, but we have to do something on a broader scale. I'm talking about revamping the curriculum on a formal basis. Perhaps we should be establishing a career development seminar required of every student in our College of Business, graduates and undergraduates alike."

HANES: "What you are talking about is certainly far-reaching. We would need catalog changes. We might even have to change the name of the College of Business. We would defiinitely have to offer new courses and new majors. And those kinds of changes would require new budgeting. We would have to come up with some very precise estimates of the number of people who would enroll in these new programs."

GATHERS: "What you say is true. I am not talking about a few cosmetic changes. I'm saying that the College of Business should be overhauled to adapt to the changes that are taking place in society now. I suspect these changes will become more accentuated in the future. In a few years, about two out of 10 employed people in the United States will be working for the federal, state, or local government. Right now one out of six employed people in New York City works for the city, state, or federal government. It could happen in Oshua County."

HANES: "Kermit, I've known you long enough to realize you didn't call a Friday afternoon meeting just to engage in polemics. You must have something specific in mind. In other words, what action plans is the good Dean Gathers thinking about? Has my workload just been increased 50 percent with no commensurate increase in pay?"

GATHERS: "Not this time, Bob. You usually spearhead most of the big assignments around here. I want you to play a role as the coordinator of this New Directions Task Force, but I don't want you to do all the work.

HANES: Do I hear another College of Business committee being formed? That hardly deserves a Friday afternoon conference."

GATHERS: "You hear much more than a committee being formed. We are developing a New Directions Task Force that will have some teeth. Taking the lead from the management experts on my staff, I am going to be practicing participative management in its grandest tradition. The faculty members themselves, coordinated by the Associate Dean, are going to come up with a plan for making us more responsive to the times. Nothing will be sacred. You can change the name of this place, you can tell me that economics is no longer a necessary part of the College of Business curriculum, or you can recommend that I be replaced. Of course, I will still have the option to exercise my formal authority in approving or disapproving the findings of the Task Force."

HANES: "How long do you think this Task Force should be in operation?"

GATHERS: "Twelve months from Monday morning at 9 a.m. That's about the only structure I am going to give the Task Force. I would like to see monthly progress reports, written or oral. And, unbelievably, there is some money in my budget for miscellaneous expenses on this project, like travel, clerical help, and even modest entertaining. For instance, you might need to take a government official to lunch to gather some intelligence, but don't overdo it."

HANES: "Who is going to be on this Task Force?"

GATHERS: "I've selected five people who represent a good cross section of the faculty. My list is right here: Kenneth Chen, Winthrop Alexander, Darryl Hasek, John Silver, and Laura Appelwhite. Each person is from a different discipline, and they vary in rank and seniority — like a true Task Force. I would assume that each of these faculty members will in turn seek the advice and opinion of others in his or her discipline."

HANES: "Kermit, I like your approach. What should I do next?"

GATHERS: "I'll write an official memo stating the purpose of the New Directions Task Force and mentioning that you, in your official role as Coordinator, will be in touch with each of them. Let me know later what happens during the first meeting."

Two weeks later, Bob Hanes met with the other five members of the Task Force: Kenneth Chen, Assistant Professor of Decision Sciences; Winthrop Alexander, Professor of Business Policy; Darryl Hasek, Associate Professor of Behavioral Sciences; John Silver, Associate Professor of Marketing; Laura Appelwhite, Professor of Accounting. By 10 minutes after the scheduled time of the meeting all members had arrived. Appropriately, Bob Hanes made the opening comments.

HANES: "Thanks for all showing up at today's meeting. It's kind of a big moment in the history of the Oshua College of Business. We are taking some major steps in adapting to the times. Our good friend and trusted confidant, Mrs. Patricia Merriweather, will be the official scribe. She will use her judgment in screening out all profane comments by Winthrop Alexander. (The anticipated laughter was forthcoming, but in an almost forced manner.)

"Don't forget this is your show. The Dean wants you to provide all the needed input. I'll act as the Coordinator. We want your suggestions on what changes should be made in the College of Business to help us serve the needs of the public as well as the private sector. We are even open to suggestions on a name change for the school."

HASEK: "How about 'The Oshua Survival Training School?' I think what we are really doing these days is trying to help people survive in our sick, cyclical economy."

HANES: "I enjoy a good joke too, but let's get down to the core purpose of this committee. Before we do that, I think we should have an open discussion about how each of us feels he or she can best contribute to this effort. Winthrop, let's begin with you. You have a good historical perspective of our successes and failures in the past."

WINTHROP ALEXANDER: "As you all know, my speciality is Business Policy, but I'm also quite interested in Personnel and I teach courses in that area. What I would like to do is help us formulate some policy about requirements for admission to our present and proposed programs. I think we need to formulate some policies on culturally disadvantaged people who want a career in government. I think this Task Force is long overdue and I'm willing to give up a few afternoons of trout fishing to dig out some appropriate information."

HANES: "Bravo, Winthrop. We can always count on you. Ken, what preliminary thoughts do you have about your role on this Task Force?"

CHEN: "As you all know my field is quantitative methods or decision sciences. I think there is an enormous need to develop at least one course called something like "Decision Making in the Public Sector." For instance, the problems faced by our cities have a strong quantitative component. It seems to me that financial people working for most cities could do a lot of good for their organizations by estimating how long it will take them to be in a default position on their loans. Or how about developing some models to predict the financial impact of decreasing welfare fraud by one percentage point? Decision problems in business and government are not too dissimilar, but I think we should start to develop some problems more appropriate to the public sector.

"I would personally like to take on the assignment of researching the nature of the decision making skills required of government employees at different levels."

HANES: "You are hereby appointed as a one person committee in charge of that research. Go ahead, we'll even pay you 15¢ a mile plus lunch for your trips to the state capital. Darryl Hasek, what kind of a role would you like to play in this Task Force?"

HASEK: "As passive as possible. Quite frankly, do whatever you want, but don't involve me in any big way. I'm trying to develop my career, not tend to the internal problems of a College of Business that's trying to figure out how to appeal to more students. If I wanted administrative work, I would look for a department head job. Why have me participate in something I really don't care about? I will vote with approval on almost anything the Task Force wants. I would say that I'm willing to spend up to about one hour per month on the Task Force.

"It's not that I don't think our Task Force will work on a relevant problem. The conflict a college professor faces is that every minute spent on work related to internal problems takes precious time away from working on something like research that could enhance your career. Nobody ever received national recognition by serving on a Task Force appointed by his or her dean."

HANES: "Well, I guess some people have different priorities than others. Professor Silver, how might you contribute?"

SILVER: "As a marketing professor, I should be able to make a major contribution to this Task Force. After all, we are really talking about a marketing problem. We must identify the needs of the public sector for graduate education in administration and then figure out how to satisfy those needs. We must apply the marketing concept to higher education. Given a little funding, I think my students and I could do some very intelligent market research in this area. We might be able to use this problem as a class project in my advanced marketing seminar. Perhaps I'll do some planning along these lines this weekend."

HANES: "Your ideas sound quite valuable, John. It would appear necessary to conduct some research before we develop new curricula. Laura has the advantage of speaking last."

APPELWHITE: "I must say that I will be frank so long as this is an open discussion. I agree with Darryl, but perhaps for different reasons. I would not be willing to do much for this Task Force unless

I receive time off from teaching. I have about 50 students that require some individual attention. You cannot conduct an accounting course as you might conduct a liberal arts course. I have to carefully review the work of each student for mistakes and sometimes offer individual tutoring. Serving on this Task Force is incompatible with my goal of providing first-rate training in accounting to my students. It seems to me that a Task Force is a devious way to get some administrative work done without having to hire another administrator.

"Call these things commitees, task forces, or special projects. They usually culminate in a thick report that is neatly filed away and never referred to again. I will participate in this project only if ordered to. Even if my work on this Task Force should lead to some changes in the curriculum, it won't do me much good. I'll be retiring in two years. My recommendation to the Dean is to leave this assignment to the eager beavers. I have enough important work of my own without trying to tell you and the Dean how to run this school in the future."

Questions

1. What should Gathers and Hanes do about Hasek and Appelwhite?
2. What other strategies might Dean Gathers utilize to determine what future programs will be offered by the College of Business?
3. What new name (if you think a change is in order) would you recommend for the College of Business? Why?
4. How much authority should be vested in the Task Force? Why?
5. What would be the advantages and disadvantages of the Task Force members involving other faculty in their assignments?

Case 40
The Decimation of Denver Printing

Bartow, Inc., a multiproduct and multinational company, purchased Denver Printing Company, a commercial printer located in
the midwest. Denver, at the time of purchase, had an annual sales
volume of approximately $10 million. Much of their business
involves the quality printing of company publications (such as annual
reports) and hard cover popular books. Their customers include
several of the best known companies in the area and three large New
York-based publishers. Herb Bardeen, President of Denver Printing,
felt that acquisition by a large corporation would give his company
the capital necessary to purchase modern printing equipment.
Another consideration was that a parent company of the size of
Bartow — $523 million in annual sales — would provide a substantial
pool of potential customers.

Denver Printing had four company officers in addition to the
President: vice presidents of marketing, production, technical services, and finance. The average annual salary of the five officers was
$47,500 before the takeover by Bartow. The founder of Denver
Printing (and the predecessor to Bardeen) believed strongly that
"overcompensating" your management team would encourage
loyalty and decrease turnover. Bardeen reasoned that paying wages
approximately double the industry average would minimize the
chances of a Denver executive joining another company for monetary reasons. During the 12 years that Bardeen was President of
Denver Printing, no officer voluntarily left the company. Both re-

placements that did occur were due to retirement. Denver Printing is located in a town of 150,000 population. They are a well known, but not dominant employer in the city.

Six months after the acquisition, Bartow Inc. decided to make some substantial changes in the operation of Denver Printing. Bartow management felt that Denver must quickly become a more profitable investment. In order to achieve this goal, the following major changes were mandated by Bartow corporate management:

First, Bill Jackson was appointed as Executive Vice President of Denver Printing, reporting directly to Bardeen. Jackson was given immediate control of all business functions except corporate planning, a responsibility assigned Herb Bardeen. Bardeen was told that he would be offered early retirement within six months. In the interim he was instructed to work closely with Bill Jackson to smoothly bring about the transition leadership. When Bardeen retired, Jackson would be appointed President and would take personal responsibility for corporate planning.

Second, Jackson was told by Bartow management to "trim the fat from Denver Printing or take another assignment in the corporation." As a first step in trimming down the organization, Jackson was asked to give immediate notice to the four vice presidents that their jobs would be terminated in 30 days, but they would be given two months' severance pay plus whatever pension rights they had accrued.

Third, it was suggested that Jackson replace each terminated vice president with a promotion from within. The new managers in charge of each function were to be called directors instead of vice presidents (and would not be officers of the corporation). Each new director was to receive a 20 percent salary increase, effective immediately.

Fourth, Jackson was asked to suggest a few additional economies of his own. He decided to: (a) eliminate all overtime except for a legitimate emergency that would have to be approved by Jackson himself; (b) discontinue all company-sponsored memberships in clubs, professional, and trade associations; (d) issue a directive that business travel should be reduced to a minimum and that second-class accommodations be given priority over first-class; (e) temporarily freeze all new hiring.

Bill Jackson, the new President, spent an uneasy weekend contemplating the consequences of the changes he would begin to initiate on Monday morning. He planned to announce the terminations by meeting briefly with each of his vice presidents individually.

Questions

1. What do you predict will be the dysfunctional (negative) consequences to the organization of the changes Jackson will begin to initiate on Monday?
2. What are the possible functional (positive) consequences to the organization of these contemplated changes?
3. What kind of impact will these changes have on morale, productivity, customers, and the community?
4. Would you predict that the organization will emerge stronger once the shock of the initial changes has subsided? Why or why not?
5. Would you recommend that Jackson make these changes gradually over a three-month period, or suddenly, within a few days? Why?

Case 41
What Should We Do With Harry?

Harry, a 46-year-old payroll accounting supervisor, has 25 years of experience with Hinsdale Appliance Corporation, a profitable, well-managed, yet little known company. Hinsdale has specialized in the manufacture of a wide range of non-branded appliances since its meager beginnings over 50 years ago. Hinsdale is engaged in the wholesale application business. The world's third largest retail chain is one of their biggest customers. Other customers include smaller retail chains and a number of discount stores. Hinsdale currently manufactures clothes washers, dryers, refrigerators, freezers, ranges, dishwashers, and garbage compactors. All their customers put their own names on Hinsdale products.

Hinsdale's reputation for stable business, high compensation, and good promotional opportunities has helped them attract competent people at every job level. Every employee at Hinsdale participates in the company profit-sharing plan. Profits were distributed to employees in all but two of Hinsdale's 50 years of operation. Employees become eligible for this profit participation after the first year of employment. Toward the end of the first year of service, a conference is held by two members of higher management and an employee's immediate supervisor to determine whether the employee is eligible to join the profit-sharing plan. A No-response to this results in an invitation for the employee to resign. "Weeding out" of this nature has contributed to a feeling of group cohesiveness among those who become permanent members of the work force. Despite this culling out process, Hinsdale Appliance is not without its occasional sensitive personnel situation. Harry Russo is one such example.

Harry was raised in Battle Creek, Michigan, where his mother and father both worked for a large food company. An above-average student, Harry gradually became caught up in the hunting and fishing cult of people from his geographic area. His goals in high school centered around a career in industry. Harry saw industrial employment as a way of earning enough money to pursue the outdoor life without having to commit himself to expensive and time-consuming years of education beyond college. One Fall day, in his junior year in high school, Harry's plans for the future seemed to fall apart all at once.

Harry and his father had gone for a one week deer hunting trip in Northern Michigan. On the trails by seven in the morning, Harry leaned down to adjust the lace on his right hunting boot when a loud crack exploded in front of him. A bullet intended for a deer lodged into Harry's side. He screamed as his clothing instantly became drenched with blood. The next recollection Harry has of the incident was lying in a hospital bed in a small Michigan town, his mother, father, and sister standing by.

"It was unreal. I can remember lying there like I was watching a movie about a boy who gets killed in a hunting accident. But I couldn't understand why I was in the movie instead of just watching it. I kept asking what had happened and when I would be going home. The doctor told me I might be able to walk again someday. It took three days for the message to sink in. I figured the doctor was telling me that because I had been involved in an accident, they wouldn't let me out of bed for a week or two. Maybe some extra careful hospital regulations were being imposed upon me. But that wasn't the case. I was semi-paralyzed from the waist down. All my physiological functions were still working normally, but my legs were just like two heavy weights attached to me with safety pins.

"My junior and senior years of high school consisted almost entirely of studying and learning to walk without the use of my legs. It was days of physical therapy, spinning around in wheel chairs, and workouts with my set of arm braces and canes. Still intent on a career in business, I took the business program at high school. Because of all the school I missed, it took me three years to complete my junior and senior years.

"Some sensation had returned to my legs, and I wasn't nearly as bad off as some of the mangled bodies I came into contact with at the rehabilitation center. I developed powerful arms, chest and shoulders from all the special exercises my therapy program required. I met Constance, the woman I later married, at the business school. She seemed to love me as a person, and not as an object of pity."

After graduating from business school, where he received an 86 average, Harold found employment with Hinsdale Appliance Company as a bookkeeper. Working in the Billing Department, Harry was well received by his colleagues and superiors. He did not ask the company for concessions because of his disability, nor were they offered. Neither Harry nor his supervisors felt that his physical disability was a liability as a bookkeeper.

After his first year of employment, Harry was invited to join the company profit-sharing plan — a formal indication that he had successfully passed his probationary period. Harry remained in essentially the same job for his first five years of employment. His enthusiasm for having a nearly professional job with a good company, at a satisfactory salary outweighed any immediate concerns about climbing the organizational ladder. Harry's performance evaluations continued to be positive. He was considered a better than satisfactory performer, although he was not seen as a person of considerable management potential by his superiors.

Close to the beginning of his fifth year with the company, Harry was offered his first promotion and transfer. His new job title was Junior Accountant, Payroll Department. Harry and his wife Constance both felt that Harry was becoming a success in business. Here he was, a handicapped person with a two-year degree, and he was a Junior Accountant by age 25. Harry enjoyed the confidential nature of his work, learning about the salaries and profit-sharing earned by most of the company personnel.

Gradually his access to salary information about other people gave Harry some cause for concern. He began to realize that his Junior Accountant salary was still below the level of income earned by some experienced executive secretaries. Nevertheless, Harry was proud of both his job title and job responsibilities. By the fourth year in his new job (and his ninth with the company) Harry began to aspire toward supervisory and/or managerial work. However, he was told by Jim Beatty, his manager, that he was not yet supervisory material:

"Look at it this way, Harry. You really haven't been with the company that long. We think you need some breadth, some more experience. Nothing personal. You're a bright fellow, but there are many bright people in this company looking to get promoted. Why don't we discuss this problem again in another year? In the meantime, if something comes up I'll keep you in mind."

By the end of the fifth year in his new job, Harry was encouraged to take some courses in financial analysis in order to better prepare himself for future assignments in the company. Dutifully, Harry took the prescribed courses at a College of Continuing Education. And, dutifully, the company rewarded his efforts with a new position — a lateral move. Harry was now an Associate Financial Analyst in the Financial Planning Department. Although his new position was more of a lateral transfer than a promotion, Harry felt he now had more prestige than in the past. Members of the Financial Planning Department frequently moved on from those assignments to middle and upper management assignments.

But Harry did not find himself climbing toward bigger responsibilities within the company. Project after project, month after month, Harry stayed as an Associate Financial Analyst. He enjoyed the work — particularly helping other departments with their budgets — but he was not ready to accept the fact that he had reached his plateau of responsibility before age 40. Harry let it be known to the first two levels of management above him that he wanted a chance to become a supervisor.

Harry was still not thought to be an ideal candidate for supervisory work, but management felt his diligence and long service to the company should somehow be rewarded. He was called into his boss's office early one Monday morning. Because of a reshuffling of personnel in the Payroll Department, a vacancy had been created and Harry was selected as the person to fill the job. Harry was offered the position of Payroll Supervisor at an eight percent increase over his present salary. Harry looked toward the new position with the optimism of a man who had just bought his own business. To help prepare him for his new responsibilities, the company offered to sponsor Harry at a Human Relations Training Program for Supervisors offered by the local college.

Harry related well to his classmates in the same human relations course. At the end of the course, each participant was given a sheet of paper with suggestions about himself or herself offered anonymously by the other 11 members of the class. A dominant theme of the responses Harry received was that he tended to be too lenient in his relationships.

Among the response were "Harry, you're too nice a guy"; "People will take advantage of you as a boss"; "Don't let the fact that you have a handicap interfere with your making demands upon people." Harry felt that perhaps the class members misinterpreted his desire to get along well with his classmates.

During the first several years in his job, Harry performed satisfactorily as a Payroll Supervisor. For three consecutive years he received a performance rating of "satisfactory." He received a rating of "above satisfactory" for the next year, but slipped down one category the following year. After his third year on the job, two situations in Harry's life changed markedly: his relationship with his wife, and his physical health.

Constance and Harry began to drift apart in an emotional and psychological sense. As Constance herself entered her forties she began to feel confined, and married to a man who himself was physically confined. Arguments between the two frequently centered around his unwillingness to leave the house at nights and on weekends. Harry felt that his fund of energy was limited. He contended that his home (a modest home in the poorest suburb) was his place for rest and recuperation from the rigors of his job. Constance, in turn, began to find more frequent excuses for visiting relatives, friends, and running ill-defined errands. The more Constance complained about Harry's unwillingness to leave the house the more solidified Harry became in his position.

Except for an occasional close conversation, Constance and Harry were no longer a unified couple. Harry withdrew more into reading about the stock market and executive life. Constance, now an administrative assistant, found more reasons to work late at the office. Often two or three days went by without conversation between them.

At about the same time as his marriage was beginning to deteriorate, Harry also developed a few physical problems. He suffered severe headaches periodically that would respond only to heavy medication prescribed by a physician. At least once or twice a month Harry would stay home from work or leave the job early because of these headaches. Colds and influenza-like symptoms also began to plague him. The muscular weekness, sneezing, and fever he experienced at the height of these attacks caused more absences from work.

Harry's small department seemed to function well even in his absence. The eight employees reporting to him rarely asked him for advice on routine matters. At least half the department did not regard Harry as the real boss, but as merely a figure head carrying the title "Supervisor." Management, also, began to question Harry's capabilities as a Payroll Supervisor. Comments from his last three performance appraisals suggest that Harry was considered a marginal employee for at least three years:

1974— Harry is performing satisfactorily, but I notice a decrease in his capacity to function effectively as a Supervisor. His employees still regard Harry as a kind and good-natured person, but he offers them very little advice and/or guidance. They tend to come to me on any matters of importance. Harry is rarely mentioned in their conversations. Yet the Payroll Department is still functioning effectively as far as the rest of the company is concerned. His attendance must improve. He is absent from work about 12 percent of the time.

1975— Harry's problems at home are beginning to have a negative impact upon his job performance. He now requests frequent time off from the job to attend conferences with his lawyer about a contemplated legal separation from his wife. One day he asked to be excused from a management conference, offering the explanation that he was unable to concentrate upon company problems that day. Nevertheless, Harry is performing the routine aspects of his job well. He is not able to innovate, but he responds well to the pressures of a peak work load. He gives some indication of being better suited for work as an individual contributor than as a supervisor.

1976— Harry's performance has shown another decline since the previous year. He is now a minimum satisfactory performer in his present position. He has contributed no new ideas to the department in the last year. He tends to agree with every comment I have about the payroll function and offers no suggestions of his own. Since his recent divorce, he has become somewhat sullen instead of good-natured. He keeps to himself and has almost no interaction with his employees unless requested by one of them.

Harry has requested that he be considered for a promotion to a more responsible job because he feels he has become "stale" in his present job. I would not recommend such a course of action be taken. My recommendation, as his immediate superior, is that a conference be held rather immediately to discuss what we should do with Harry.

Questions

1. What should management do about the situation of Harry Russo?
2. What relationship do you think exists between Harry's physical disabilities and his job performance?
3. Would management be justified in firing Harry? Why or why not?
4. What are some potential disadvantages to the organization resulting from Harry remaining in the Payroll Supervisor position?
5. Identify two mistakes you believe Harry has made in relation to his job.

REFERENCES

Benne, Kenneth, Bradford, LeLand, Gibb, Jack, and Lippitt, Ronald. *The Laboratory Method of Learning and Changing: Theory and Applications.* Fairfax, Virginia: NTL Learning Resources Corporation, 1975.

DuBrin, Andrew J. *The Practice of Managerial Psychology: Concepts and Methods for Manager and Organization Development.* Elmsford, N.Y.: Pergamon Press, 1972. See Chapter 6.

Johnson, Doyle P. "Social Organization of an Industrial Work Group: Emergence and Adaptation to Environmental Change," *The Sociological Quarterly,* Vol. 15, Winter 1974, 109-126.

Kaufman, H.G. *Obsolescence and Professional Career Development.* New York: Amacom, a division of American Management Associations, 1974.

Kelly, Joe. *Organizational Behaviour: An Existential Systems Approach.* Homewood, Ill.: Richard D. Irwin, 1974. See Chapter 16.

Luthans, Fred, and White, Jr., Donald D. "Behavior Modification: Application to Manpower Management," *Personnel Administration,* Vol. 72, July-August 1971, 41-47.

Shearer, Richard L. and Steger, Joseph A. "Manpower Obsolescence: A New Definition and Empirical Investigation of Personal Variables," *Academy of Management Journal,* Vol. 18, June 1975, 263-275.

Taylor, James C. *Technology and Planned Organizational Change.* Ann Arbor, Michigan: Institute for Social Research, 1971.

Vroom, Victor H. and Yetton, Phillip W. *Leadership and Decision Making.* Pittsburg, Pa.: University of Pittsburgh Press, 1973.

White, J. Kenneth and Ruh, Robert A. "Effects of Personal Values on the Relationship Between Participation and Job Attitudes," *Administrative Science Quarterly,* Vol. 18, December 1973, 506-514.

13
Organizational Change

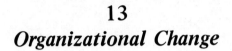

Case 42
The Superhonest Politician

"Alstair M. McIntosh a candidate for United States Senator on the Party ticket?" said a Party worker, "I cannot believe it. He's too much of a cornball. His ideas, his policies are too far from mainstream Party thinking. The Party is a pretty big umbrella, but Alstair is kind of at our lunatic fringe. I mean, I respect what the man has done, but allowing him to run for the senatorial slot is going too far. Are we trying to make jokes, or are we trying to win an election? If we wanted entertainment, we could have hired a comedian to run for Senator."

In contrast to this Party worker's pronouncements, Alstair McIntosh considered himself a very serious candidate for United States Senator. McIntosh looked upon this challenge as the most serious mission of his life, despite his apparent nonchalance. Many times during his life Alstair has been accused of being lethargic, or plain bored, simply because of his casual mannerisms. In actual behavior, he is a fierce competitor, revealed by the highlights of his personal history.

As a law school graduate, young McIntosh went directly into public service. He struggled along in minor jobs for several years until he became a prosecuting attorney for the State. He quickly developed a reputation for objectivity and firmness in his courtroom behavior. Eventually he became a District Attorney at the State level. His penchant for objective investigation led to the conviction of a number of State officials accused of accepting kickbacks from major contractors to the Highway Construction Department.

McIntosh became a controversial figure because of these kickback scandals involving the State. Two of the people he helped get convicted were former superiors who had been helpful in his receiving a promotion to District Attorney. When asked how he could turn in a former boss — one who had helped him in his career — Alstair replied in his just-plain-folks manner, "Heck, when I was a boy working the family store, I caught my brother with his hand in the till and turned him in to my father. My brother proceeded to whup me, but, after he realized that I was really helping him, we became good friends."

McIntosh and his handful of Party workers are launching a modest, rather simple campaign. His opponent is a distinguished Senator, an incumbent who has successfully straddled the middle of the road for six years. The McIntosh campaign headquarters are located in the oldest office building in the State Capitol. Befitting the McIntosh image, the furniture is stark and battered. Ten plain black telephones are constantly ringing and callers are intermittently disconnected. Alstair has refused to install an adequate telephone communication system, despite the pleas of the communication specialists from the telephone company. In his words, "No sense in spending too much time yapping on the phone. Frittering away time on the phone has become a disease in this country."

Contributing to Alstair McIntosh's reputation for uniqueness are several other aspects of his campaign strategy. Originally, Alstair unilaterally decided that he would not accept campaign gifts in excess of $25. As it became apparent that the inflow of money could hardly pay postage and transportation, he upped the figure to $75, and as campaign expenses mounted despite McIntosh's fiscal conservatism, he grudgingly settled for a $100 maximum campaign gift from an individual.

To the glee of Trailways, Greyhound, and other public transporters, McIntosh insists upon taking a non-chartered bus for campaign trips. He reasons, "Why waste money on frills like a chartered bus or airplane? The people I'm trying to impress are more likely to be found on a Greyhound bus than at an airport, anyway." When a bus ride is not feasible, McIntosh packs himself and one or two political aides into his seven-year old black Checker Cab. "Never was a better car built in the United States," says Alstair, to the chagrin of Big Three automakers. An official of the United Auto Workers claims McIntosh drives a Checker Cab because of his basic dislike for big business and organized labor, the "very heart of our country."

A third campaign strategy (or lack thereof) is Alstair McIntosh's manner of relating to people he meets during his public appearances. He refuses to smile unless somebody says something that he thinks is amusing. Although a minor aspect of total behavior, his deadpan mannerisms do alienate some people. A beauty contest winner proclaimed that "Mr. McIntosh is downright mean. He's the only person I've ever met who did not smile when he saw me." A production worker outside a factory was quoted on television as saying, "I wouldn't vote for a man who looks so unhappy. I figure he has so many problems of his own that he won't be able to help other people with their problems. And that's the reason we elect a person Senator."

To his critics along these lines, McIntosh replies, "I'll smile more when I'm elected and we get some of the country's problems under control."

Even more vexing to conservative members of the Party are some of McIntosh's more radical policies. Although many of his aides and top Party officials agree with some of McIntosh's more controversial policies, they believe that the country is not ready for his innovative suggestions. A strongly held opinion is that McIntosh should wait until (or, if) he is elected, and then work toward incorporating into law some of his more radical ideas.

One policy advocated by Alstair is to reduce the defense budget by $50 billion per year. "My firm conviction is that after we reduce our defense budget about half, we will wonder why we ever spent so much money for defense in the first place. Some of my other policies on improving society will create jobs for the dislocated people, but why in God's name are we pouring billions into playing war? It's a great big hoax that is self-perpetuating. My plan is to divert defense funds into urban renewal of a kind that works. If Lockheed can build supersonic jet fighters, they can learn how to refurbish old frame houses. I would like to see the Chairman of Lockheed Aircraft with a paint brush in his hands painting the hallways of a slum building. You can put those thousands of engineers into some crash training for plumbers or electricians.

"After a while we could reduce the defense budget another $25 billion per year. I would put a permanent freeze on hiring on any defense-related business. Every year we could reduce their appropriations another $10 billion until anybody who wanted to be in the defense business would have to work for free."

Another radical, but straightforward suggestion offered by McIntosh for improving life in the United States is to decentralize

Health, Education, and Welfare. HEW offices would be moved into areas of the United States plagued by chronic unemployment. For instance, McIntosh has urged that the entire Welfare work force be moved to Buffalo, New York. He says, "This way any bureaucrat who did not want to leave Washington, D.C. would be without a job, and an unemployed auto or steel worker would get a job in his or her place. Think of all the hundreds of inner-city children who could be trained to become clerks for the Welfare Department. We could set up day care centers and give mothers receiving Aid to Dependent Children a chance to earn a living. Creating jobs for people who are currently unemployed might be the best thing the Welfare Department could do for people."

With equal candor, Alstair comments upon the Pentagon: "I would immediately move the Pentagon to the middle of Maine. It would create a number of jobs, at least for a temporary period. All defense business would be operated from the Maine headquarters. If one of the officials wanted to leave town, he would only be given expenses to cover a bus ride. I suspect we will always have some kind of defense operation in the United States, but I would keep it in Maine. When a potato farmer in the area felt that he or she was too old and tired to keep farming, I would give that person a defense job and fire a colonel who had already been riding the gravy train for too many years. When a Russian official wanted to talk about a defense dispute, I would refer him to that old potato farmer."

McIntosh's taxation policies are even more straightforward and iconoclastic: "Our tax system, as everybody recognizes, has become a monstrosity. Something that nobody is really satisfied with, but that is being repaired on a quiltlike basis. You patch up one part, and then you find that another is out of whack. Let's tax everybody and every corporation at a flat 20 percent of their gross income. The rich people who make out a little better on this basis will undoubtedly spend more money that will create more jobs for more people. Instead of the government lopping off a big chunk of successful people's money, little people like maids, tailors, artists, and housepainters will be getting the money. If we stop all these crazy deductions, we'll be able to cut down income tax cheating by 90 percent. Our present tax structure encourages cheating by individuals and tax preparation specialists."

McIntosh also has a plan to help insure that people are reporting their income accurately: "I would immediately convert the Central Intelligence Agency to the Tax Intelligence Agency. Nobody would be out of a job, but they would be doing something worthwhile. I would make sure everybody who used dirty tricks such as electronic bugs would be fired. The remaining honest members of the former C.I.A. would keep the rest of us honest about our taxes."

Alstair's plan for rebuilding our cities goes beyond turning defense workers into city renewal workers: "I would immediately call back every soldier, sailor, or marine located off our shores and give him or her a chance to work for the Corps of Engineers. Their task would be to fix up old buildings and build new ones where reconstruction was not economically feasible. Until the military person learned an appropriate trade, he or she would be simply a construction aide.

"We'd take about one quarter of these soldiers, sailors, and marines and make rat control specialists out of them. It's going to do a lot more good for the United States to have a soldier killing rats than sitting in an office in South Korea typing out requisitions for supplies we wouldn't need if he wasn't there."

Surprising to his other Party workers, the public, and the media representatives, Alstair McIntosh is as open and candid in his present dealings with people as hinted at by his sweeping proposals. On many occasions, his openness has shocked people. A party official believes that each "shock" is worth 5000 lost votes. Seven of his more shocking comments made directly to people or on talk show appearances are presented next.

• Asked how he differs as a person from his opponent, McIntosh replied, "My opponent is a nice guy, which I am not. He is also not as bright as I am. In fact, I believe the man is on the dull side. When he is asked a spontaneous question, even by his chauffeur, he fumbles like a kid in a freshman speech class. If he were brighter, I think he could do a better job."

• Asked by the Dean of a College of Criminal Justice what he thought is the most important lesson he learned in his many years of exposure to the criminal justice system, he replied: "I think the jury system is a waste of time. You pull a lot of ordinary people together to decide the fate of a life. If we eliminated the jury system, we would automatically lay the groundwork for revamping our criminal justice system into something more than the farce that presently exists."

• In an encounter with a Catholic Cardinal at an airport, McIntosh asked him, "Cardinal, what does the Catholic Church do with all its wealth? If elected, I'm going to sponsor a bill to tax churches on their revenue in excess of expenses."

• While visiting a federal prison, McIntosh said on a platform set up for the occasion, "It's hard to tell who the real criminals are around here. I think many of the prison administrators should exchange places with the prisoners."

• In chatting with a reporter about internal changes he would make in the Party, McIntosh stated: "I don't like those $100-a-plate fund raising dinners where we twist the arm of people to attend. We tell them that if they don't attend, or at least pay the $100, their names will be put on a special list. I think that is rotten."

• During a Columbus Day rally, he told the Chief of Police that politicians didn't deserve public protection any more than the ordinary citizen deserves protection against muggers. "If I'm damn fool enough to run for office, that's my problem. Besides, my life is no more valuable than that of anybody else in this city."

• On a street corner, he saw a woman stepping out of an expensive car with her adolescent daughter. McIntosh approached her and said, "Excuse me, Madame, I'm Alstair McIntosh and I'm running for Senator. May I make a suggestion? Please sell that fancy car of yours and get your daughter's teeth fixed. She needs orthodontia more than you need a $10,000 car."

Toward the middle of his campaign, Alstair was asked to confer with the Party National Chairperson. She begged for an explanation of what he was trying to accomplish by some of his tactics. "Simple," he replied, "I think that both a political party and a politician must be honest. Only by being candid can we prove to the world that we are honest. Beyond that, unless we are candid, we never will *be* honest. Just saying we are an honest Party won't bring about any real change."

Questions

1. What should the Party do with Alstair McIntosh?
2. What impact will Alstair McIntosh's behavior have upon the voting behavior of people in his Party and the opposition Party?
3. Does Alstair McIntosh seem sincere in his position on popular issues?
4. What strategic errors might Alstair McIntosh be making?
5. What other strategies would you suggest for making the Party more credible to the electorate?

Case 43
Centralization will Ruin Us

Lucy Minsky considered herself fortunate to find a position as Planning Manager with the Community Chest of Belleville County — a position that would undoubtedly provide good experience for development of her career in human services administration. After four years as an administrative assistant in the Motor Vehicle Department, Lucy was looking for job experience outside of the State government and more specifically in the field of human services. An important appeal of the Planning Manager assignment was that the job included helping the Community Chest develop a more efficient form of organization.

After several weeks of orientation, Lucy's immediate superior, Dave Olin, went into more detail about the nature of her first big assignment — an assignment that could take up to one year to plan and implement. Dave spoke with considerable conviction:

"Lucy, as you know, we hired you because of a real need to make the Community Chest and its affiliated agencies a more efficient, more modern organization. The rest of the staff and I have been convinced for several years that there is too much duplication of function among our 20 participating agencies. The organizations we provide funds to are sometimes in competition among themselves.

"There simply isn't enough money in our budget for so many of the agencies to duplicate the same functions. We have already taken a careful look into some aspects of the problem. For instance, we discovered two years ago that there were way too many social workers for the client population we serve. Two small agencies not five miles from each other had a full staff of social workers. We reassigned a few of the workers and put a three-year freeze on new hiring. By these measures we have cut down the social work staff by 10 people so that, including salaries, benefits and miscellaneous charges, we are now saving about $200 thousand per year in payroll costs.

"Despite our preliminary inroads into the problem of becoming more efficient, I don't think we have approached the true magnitude of the problem. We could operate a lot more efficiently if we were more centralized."

Lucy responded, "But, Dave, we are kind of centralized. The 20 agencies more or less report to us, the Community Chest of Belleville."

"You put your finger on the right problem when you said 'more or less,' Lucy. In many cases the only reporting to us we have is the fact that the agencies get money from us. That's a weak excuse for centralization. We need to figure out what services we can provide for the agencies under our jurisdiction and what services they can best provide for themselves.

"There is no doubt we are moving toward centralization. We want your analysis of how we should best go about it, and what functions we should centralize. You're the person to recommend to us what should be done. Maybe you'll tell us we should lease a modern office in the suburbs and move all the agencies under one roof. Maybe you'll recommend a more moderate form of centralization. A wide number of choices is conceivable. We are making no commitment at this time that we will buy all your recommendations, but we will listen carefully to them. Our goal is to become a lean, efficient operation within two years. Right now the community chest and its affilliated agencies are operating at a low level of efficiency."

"Dave, I have a suggestion," replied Lucy. "Before I sit here drawing up the grand organization plan for the Social Agencies of Belleville County, let me visit the agencies and find out the thinking of their officials on this matter of centralization. I'll get their opinions and recommendations before I even begin to suggest some tentative changes."

"Good idea," replied Dave Olin, "but why not draw up a questionnaire and mail it out to all of the agencies. That would probably be much more efficient."

"Dave, I would say that would seem to be more efficient. It's too early to start mailing out questionnaires. Collecting data by a questionnaire might be better suited at the formal stages of my study. Right now I'm just trying to capture the flavor of people's thinking. Also, there is a political factor here. I think I'm better off getting to know the people by conducting discussions with them about their agencies and their problems. If I come on strong by sending out a questionnaire on centralization, and they don't even know me, I may be in for trouble later on. An organization planner has to move in gradually, not hit people on the head with a survey and then announce some sweeping organizational changes."

Lucy Minsky then arranged to visit all 20 of the affiliated agencies over a two-month period. She spent about two hours at each agency discussing the issue of the centralization of certain aspects of community services. Despite frequent questions by her boss on the status of the project, Lucy did not want to divulge any of her findings until her initial discussions with all the agency heads were completed. Two and one-half months after the planning project had begun, Lucy scheduled a long conference with Dave to give a verbal report of her preliminary findings. She spoke partially from memory and partially from notes taken during the interviews.

"Dave, it looks like the agency executives are not accepting the inevitable. They are more opposed to centralization than you and I might have guessed. They look upon our plan to streamline operations as simply another tightening of the budget, something they have lived with periodically for a long time. So far they haven't taken seriously a real move toward centralization of services. From their standpoint, our master blooper was laying off social workers and putting the freeze on new hiring. One agency head said the kindest adjective he could muster to describe that action was 'reprehensible.'

"It might be premature for me to draw a lot of conclusions from the preliminary information I have. Instead, I'll go over the highlights with you of some of the raw data I've collected. What I have in mind specifically is to give you the gist of some of the agency heads' thinking about the value of centralization for him or her. This information will help you appreciate the task ahead of us.

"Shirley McNamara, the Director of Eastside Child Center, believes that the Community Service would be doing them a disservice by trying to establish policy, rules, or regulations for them. She points out that their neighborhood is highly unique. The socioeconomic level of the families they serve is much higher than that served by the usual day care center. McNamara points out that the average family income of the families served by Eastside Child Center is $17,500. Also, many of the parents are college graduates. In her evaluation, policies established for other day care centers would be inapplicable to them.

"One major difference between Ms. McNamara's center and many others assisted by Community Chest is that Eastside is heavily committed to the cognitive and emotional learning of its children. As Shirley points out, 'We are not simply a baby sitting service. We are essentially a child development center that supplements the efforts of the school system and the home.'

"May Maxwell, the Director of Downtown Day Care Center, is another person who has very strong feelings about our inability to provide services to all other agencies that would also be helpful to her organization. Ms. Maxwell feels she needs more supervisors or teachers than the other centers. In her 'shop' she deals with such problems as children suffering from parental neglect, many cases of toddlers requiring diapering, and discipline problems. May points out that centralized policy about the funding of day care centers could well put her out of business. Almost none of the families she serves pays the full share of the services they require. Many of the families make token payments that only cover 10 percent of the cost of services.

"In her evaluation, some day care centers in the city are essentially nursery schools, while Downtown Day Care is a parental substitute for many children who receive a minimum of interest or attention from their natural parents. Therefore, her day care center would have to continue to formulate its own policy on almost all matters affecting its operation.

"Whirlwind is a unique organization, perhaps one of the few of its kind in the United States. It is located right in the heart of downtown, across the street from one of the largest office buildings in the city. Whirlwind is geared to handling almost any drop-in problem of a non-medical emergency. Clients just drop in without an appointment or without a referral from another agency.

"People — mostly young adults — walk in off the street with almost any kind of problem. In a given week, a Whirlwind counselor might speak to people who want to talk about a drug addiction problem, an impending abortion, venereal disease, incest, poverty, alcoholism, fear of physical abuse by parents, or a threat made upon their life by a spouse. Whirlwind listens to these problems and sometimes makes recommendations or further referrals. However, the basic point of Whirlwind is that anybody with any kind of a problem can just drop in without having to cope with the bureaucratic obsession with forms and waiting lines. They are almost the converse of a clinic run by the city.

"Billie Barnes, the Director of Whirlwind, said centralization will ruin us. He believes once Community Chest begins to dictate policy, or lend administrative support (other than send them money) Whirlwind will lose its uniqueness. As he told me during our interveiw, 'What Community Chest knows about our operation could be fit into one of the hypodermic needles discarded by one of our clients. Once you begin to lay your bureaucratic hands upon our operation — even if you have our welfare 100 percent in mind — you will have planted the seeds of our destruction.'

"Barry Stremmick at Belleville Family Services has some pointed concerns about increasing centralization. He told me, 'If you centralize our services any more, you may put us out of business. Before Community Chest began its move toward making social agencies more efficient, we had a staff of six overworked social workers. Now we have only two social workers who work for us full time. We share five other social workers with two other agencies. In the past our social workers felt they could conduct some marriage counseling that was actually doing some good. Now all our depleted social worker staff can do is to listen to problems very briefly and make some recommendations. They feel they are losing their professional function.

" 'Of course, I wouldn't mind your centralizing a few of the non-professional functions. If you could get us volume discounts on paper clips, typing paper, office furniture (if we can ever afford to buy new furniture) and provide less expensive janitorial services, we'll jump at the opportunity. We accept legitimate help with open arms. You might also help us by doing our bookkeeping for us. It's not fun trying to collect fees or keep straight who has or has not paid for their services. Sometimes I think the amount of money we actually collect in fees is less than the cost of collecting them. We would appreciate help with that problem.'

"Gertrude Steingut at the Bayside Settlement House reinforces the reservations most of the other agencies have about centralization of services. She points out that a settlement house is a fading, yet a much needed institution. Most people just don't understand the vital role a settlement house plays in keeping marginal families glued together. Adults drop in to speak to the settlement house staff on a mixed bag of problems. Bayside has been nested in a dilapidated building for 30 years. Gertrude points out that if they redecorated or modernized they would probably lose most of their clientele.

"She may be irrational, but she believes that further centralization will lead to a modernization and upgrading of her settlement house that could be self-defeating. People in her neighborhood have come to trust the present broken-down establishment to some extent because it resembles home to them. Steingut points out that Bayside policies (or the lack thereof) are tied to the specific problems of its neighborhood. Centralizing policy would result in a list of policies and procedures that would not make sense for them and that would therefore be violated.

"She pointed to an example of a settlement house in Philadelphia that imposed a new policy of charging clients $2 for spending the night on the premises. In the month following the imposition of this policy the number of people accepting hostel for the night decreased from 60 to three. One of the people who was refused a night's refuge because she didn't have the $2 returned home to be murdered by her husband that night. She had sought shelter because of a threat of violence by her husband.

"Dave, do you see the point I'm making?" asked Lucy. "We have to move cautiously in our attempts to both study the problem of centralization and in doing something about it. Change is not going to be easy."

Questions

1. What should Lucy Minsky and Dave Olin do next in their attempts at organization change?
2. What constructive suggestions can you find among the commentary provided by the social agency heads?
3. What type of organization development program might you recommend for the social agencies? Why?
4. What errors in strategy do you think Dave Olin has made up to this point in this case?
5. If the goal of the Community Chest is truly to create a "more efficient, more modern organization," what steps should be taken (recognizing that the Community Chest probably has a tight budget)?

Case 44
The Disappointed OD Practitioner

Brent Garwood, a behavioral science consultant and college professor, was contracted by the Plastics Division of a manufacturing corporation to analyze the problems the manufacturing supervision seemd to be experiencing. Division management wanted Brent to make some recommendations about the type of training the forepersons should receive in order to be more effective in their work. Professor Garwood noted that an analysis of training needs alone would not represent a valid prescription for any organization's problems. Usually other problems underlie training needs.

Brent conducted a series of organization analysis sessions with all the Plastic Division forepersons (about 50 foremen and 10 forewomen) to obtain a clear perspective about company problems. The 60 forepersons were divided into five groups. The sessions were loosely structured. Brent acted as notetaker and discussion leader, while group members talked about company problems. Participants were told that (a) top management would receive a general report of the finding, (b) no foreperson would be identified in the report, (c) some form of feedback on the sessions would be provided to participants. Toward the conclusion of the second session, with each group, Brent summarized the main problems and concerns he felt the group had identified. Group members were encouraged to critique any of the consultant's perceptions of their comments.

At least one member in every group cautioned Brent that the company would probably not use whatever findings he uncovered.

Several foremen commented that attitude surveys had been conducted twice in the last several years. In both instances, nothing constructive was done with the findings. Brent reassured the forepersons that the company seemed serious about using the results of this organization analysis. He promised them that he would strongly recommend to management that participants be provided feedback on the results of the organizational analysis. Furthermore, he would urge management to take immediate corrective action on some of the more pressing problems.

Brent conducted his organization analysis sessions on Friday mornings for several months, each meeting lasting about three hours. Two sessions were held with each group. Group participation in the meetings was widespread and intensive. Brent was optimistic that these organization development sessions would be a force for constructive change in the Plastic Division. Two weeks after the last OD session was conducted Brent submitted a written report to management (as they had requested). A copy of the report is presented next.

To: Martin Griffin and John H. Baldwin
From: Brent Garwood
Subject: Report on Organization Analysis Sessions With
          Plastic Division Production Foremen and Forewomen

BACKGROUND

Summarized in this report are findings gathered in 18 organization analysis sessions conducted by me with approximately 60 Plastic Division forepersons and superintendents. (Statements made in this report about forepersons also apply to superintendents.) Fifteen categories are used to summarize the findings. Some overlap exists among many of the categories. Not every problem cited in the report occurs in every department; however, there was high consistency among the nine foreperson groups about the nature of problems facing them. None of the problems cited have been verified by an objective investigation of my own. I base my conclusions upon the perceptions and attitudes of the program participants. One exception is that I received a thorough plant tour.

Recommendations to management made by me later in the report are based upon my interpretation of the opinions expressed, and my own opinion about what is feasible and practicable. Management may be aware of an underlying problem on a given issue that would make a recommendation by a consultant (or foreperson) unfeasible.

PROBLEM AREAS

Turnover and Absenteeism

A major problem facing foremen and forewomen is the high rate of turnover and absenteeism among low seniority hourly personnel. One foreman noted, for example, that "110 employees in the coating department left in one year." Forepersons seem to have a feeling of futility in coping with these problems. Often factors beyond their control — such as modest wages, difficult working conditions, and high welfare and unemployment benefits — encourage turnover. Even government regulations, it was noted, such as OSHA standards about wearing masks and heavy clothing, have a negative influence upon longevity and coming to work regularly.

Communications to Forepersons

Almost unanimously, forepersons felt that communications about important matters are too infrequent to allow them to perform their best. Some specific examples include: (a) operating instructions for new products are given at the last moment, causing confusion, (b) often four different people or groups elicit information from the foreman or forewoman on the same problem, such as an order inquiry, (c) some departments receive master scheduling forms with almost no explanation, (d) communications between forepersons on different shifts are impoverished, (e) quality specifications are infrequently communicated to forepersons, resulting in needless rejects of finished parts. On the positive side, several experienced forepersons noted that communications have improved in the last year.

Demands Placed Upon Forepersons

In general, foremen and forewomen feel they are spread too thin (too many responsibilities in terms of the time available). Various problems cited include receiving insufficient recognition, having no formal job description, too many forms to complete, no time for proper training of subordinates, and very tight schedules. One foreman reported humorously: "Management treats us like mushrooms. We're kept in the dark and fed horse manure."

Wages

No other problem area received as much attention in the team building sessions. Forepersons felt that their wages are low in comparison to foremen and forewomen in comparable companies and also in comparison to their own subordinates. Many forepersons noted that a competent hourly employee on incentive and overtime earns more than most foremen or forewomen. Secretiveness about salary ranges is an area of high concern, including how one might qualify for the maximum pay. Asked about what would be a fair wage for company forepersons, some opinion was expressed that $1 more per hour would be adequate. A major complaint expressed was that forepersons should receive time and one-half rather than time and one-quarter for overtime work.

Benefits

A number of minor irritations were expressed in this area. In general, forepersons think that their benefits should be better than those of their subordinates. Forepersons believe that their benefits exceed hourly workers only in the areas of sick pay and life insurance. Two specific complaints were: (a) employees who work four out of eight Saturdays prior to shut down receive one day of bonus pay while forepersons do not, (b) forepersons, unlike hourly employees, are told when to take a floating holiday.

Prestige

A variety of factors appear to be responsible for the low prestige of forepersons, including issues covered at other points in this report. Comments such as these illustrate the feelings of low prestige observed: "Very few people would take a foreman's or forewoman's job." "A foreman or forewoman is the 'whipping boy' around here."

A foreman or forewoman is a fire hydrant." "The workers feel we are messengers." "Face it, life is better as a setup man." "Maintenance personnel have more power than we do."

Job Security

An important underlying theme is that the job security of Plastic Division forepersons is threatened. They wonder if the local division will continue to operate much longer. They react strongly to the early retirement of other salaried employees, feeling that some people are released because of chronological age and not poor job performance. Concern is also evident about the possibility of being replaced by younger employees with more formal education.

Manufacturing Service Personnel

Considerable intergroup conflict exists between manufacturing service personnel and line forepersons. From the foreman's or forewoman's viewpoint, many of these people are inexperienced about production and therefore they establish unrealistic standards and procedures. It is thought that engineers take foreperson's ideas and later receive credit for them. Foremen and forewomen note that one of the reasons Master Scheduling has not yet lived up to expectations is that inexperienced people are providing the basic input.

Budgeting

Forepersons, in general, feel that the type of budgets they are preparing are of limited value. According to their perception, unstable marketing forecasts necessitate frequent changes, budgets are imposed upon them from above with little real input of their own, and they are prepared haphazardly. Also noted was that proper instruction in budget preparation was missing.

Caliber of Newly Hired Hourly Employees

A root cause of many of the foreperson's problems — in their analysis — is the low caliber of newly hired hourly employees.

Opinion was expressed that the more qualified members of the labor pool gravitate to higher paying companies. The "youth culture," and "decline of the work ethic" undoubtedly contribute heavily to the problems of hiring well motivated, dependable people. A genuine concern was expressed that the prospect of replacing competent, dedicated, senior employees as they retire appears remote. Superintendents note that the new work force contains very few prospects for foreperson positions.

Machinery

With few exceptions, the opinion was expressed that much of the Plastic Division equipment is antiquated. Case examples were cited of purchasing equipment that was already obsolete, and the impossibility of purchasing parts to repair some of the equipment. "We're expected to perform miracles with scrap iron" is a typical sentiment. It was noted that forepersons and perhaps operators would be involved in decisions about new equipment purchases. The lack of preventive maintenance was cited as a major reason for many equipment problems.

General Working Conditions

A variety of general working conditions were cited as substandard. Included among these are a building that was last painted in 1927, leaky faucets, leaky roofs, cramped and crowded working areas and aisles, an incentive system that encourages high scrap rates, and a poor security system that is unable to cope with vandalism in the parking lot. Many forepersons said that the reluctance to erect new buildings combined with the growth in business created the space problem. Among poor working conditions mentioned were poor ventilation and excessive temperatures in a few areas.

Training of Employees

The high turnover rate combined with the heavy demands of the foreperson's job contribute to inadequate training of hourly employees (which in turn creates even more problems for the forepersons). Few experienced employees are available to train newer employees, and forepersons are so busy with paper work, projects with engineering, etc. that not enough time is left to work with employees.

Worker Morale

A variety of factors, such as low wage rates and poor physical working conditions, contribute to low morale among many members of the work force. A low morale work force, in turn, creates more pressures upon the foreperson. Some opinion was expressed that older workers would like to see a return of the "division newsletter" and the suggestion system. A system of profit sharing was cited as an important way of raising morale for all levels of manufacturing personnel.

Miscellaneous Problem Areas

Various concerns were expressed that perhaps do not deserve the status of a separate category. These are: (a) Too much competition rather than cooperation among departments. An instance was cited of some people shipping their scrap to other departments. (b) The corporation makes public statements of prosperity while internally manufacturing is pressed for cost cutting measures. (c) The difficulty in getting constructive suggestions implemented. (d) The complex order entry system that results in delays, creating pressures on forepersons to rush production schedules. (e) Minor areas of neglect such as providing shoes and protective clothing for "dirty" jobs.

RECOMMENDATIONS FOR TRAINING

Several program topics will be suggested here for training for forepersons and superintendents. All courses should be workshop-seminar in format. Details about the conduct and content of these programs can be worked out between representatives of the Plastic Division and the Center for Management Studies. All of the suggestions focus upon job-related issues, and, from my observations, would be well received by manufacturing personnel.

Motivating Younger Employees

A program of this nature must receive top priority. It should emphasize coping with the "new breed" of young people in terms of their value system and work motivation. A major emphasis would be placed upon the problems of absenteeism, turnover, and lack of concern for company objectives.

Budgeting

Some emphasis should be given to both budget preparation and interpretation. Brief information about budgets in general combined with an explanation of company budgeting is recommended. A representative of company management should conduct most of this program.

Team Building Sessions

Group discussions should be held by forepersons and superintendents on the one hand and manufacturing service personnel on the other. These meetings will bring to the surface some of the conflicts between the two groups and also lead to a resolution of some differences and to improved communications. I, or any other organization development specialist, might conduct these sessions.

Safety

A brief reminder and perhaps some new information on this perennial topic will be well received by forepersons. The current safety manager would be the seminar leader of choice. (He is well liked by your people.)

Interpretation of Company Policy

Forepersons need some clarification about their job responsibilities, the extent of their authority, interpretation of plant regulations, and the union contract. Only a member of company management is qualified to conduct this program. A union official should be invited to the contract interpretation session.

New Foreperson Orientation

Training for new forepersons should include a more extensive on-the-job orientation. Perhaps visits to work areas other than their own would be helpful. An orientation "refresher," about six months to one year after assuming foreperson responsibilities is also recommended.

Industrial Broadening

Many forepersons suggested they would welcome visits to vendor and customer plants. Among its many values, this will help forepersons explain the proper function (end use) of many of the Plastic Division products.

RECOMMENDATIONS FOR MANAGEMENT ACTION

1.   Immediately review the wage and benefit schedules for forepersons and superintendents. Without improvement in this area, very little else management might do can improve morale.

2.   Provide forepersons more lead time (if possible) on new instructions and make a concentrated effort to increase the flow of communications to forepersons and superintendents.

3.   Provide a frank discussion of the future of the Plastic Division to forepersons and superintendents.

4.   Provide more verbal encouragement and praise for good performance.

5.   Hire as many four-year and two-year college students as the union contract allows for hourly production work during summers and throughout the year. Forepersons seem to agree that the motivation and output of these workers is better than that of full-time, permanent employees. College students are often available for part-time shift work throughout the year.

6.   Conduct periodic "Executive Rap Sessions" with forepersons, superintendents, and hourly employees. In these sessions a

member of top management holds an informal discussion with a few people down the line about problem areas and concerns. Such sessions are vastly superior to "tours of the ship" in obtaining upward communication.

7.   Immediately make several urgently needed repairs, such as to leaky roofs or peeling paint. Investigate the true status of the widely perceived "obsolete equipment."

8.   Review the training program for manufacturing service personnel. Perhaps they in fact need more "hands on" production experience.

9.   In general, take appropriate action on problems cited in this report.

10.   Conduct a group feedback session on this report. Ideally, I should meet with about one half of the group at a time, accompanied by a member of top management. He could then discuss with forepersons what plans management might have to remedy some of the valid problem areas uncovered by this report. (The group feedback will be conducted in such a manner as to reflect favorably upon Plastic Division top management.)

EFFECTIVENESS OF THE PROGRAM

Without the group feedback session mentioned above, and without some constructive action on management's part in regard to a few valid problem areas, this program will fail to achieve its most important objective — improvement of organizational effectiveness. However, the objectives of providing an interesting experience for participants, improving communications among plant supervision, and the identification of training needs, have all been met (in my opinion).

Brent Garwood describes the follow-up action taken to this report in these words: "Two, three, four weeks, and still no reaction from the company. I phoned them and was informed by the Division President's secretary that Mr. Baldwin (the Coordinator of the program) would be sending me a written reply shortly. The letter did arrive three days later and it was a shocking disappointment. John Baldwin wrote me a curt note stating that the company found my observations interesting and that they would be in touch with me should the need arise. They completely ignored my comments about the importance of feedback and management action. The basic purpose of organization development was perverted. Instead of using my findings to bring about constructive change, the company was just collecting information. My program was aborted and my professional integrity was sacrificed. I felt I owed something more than a company-sponsored rap session and some free doughnuts and coffee to the participants. OD work can be very frustrating."

Questions

1. To what extent do you think the consultant's efforts were wasted?
2. What strategic errors do you think were committed by Brent Garwood in handling this consulting assignment?
3. Once the consultant recognized that the company was probably not going to make further use of his report, what action (if any) should he have taken?
4. How do you think top management probably reacted to the contents of the report?
5. Is there a danger in being too frank when telling management about its problems? What are some of the probably consequences of being entirely frank in presenting the results of an organization analysis?
6. Should the consultant have determined the validity of the problems cited by the foremen and forewomen before telling management of the problem?

REFERENCES

Argyris, Chris. *Management and Organizational Development: The Path from xa to yb.* New York: McGraw-Hill, 1971.

Argyris, Chris. *Behind the Front Page: Organizational Self-Renewal in a Metropolitan Newspaper.* San Francisco: Jossey Bass, 1974.

Armenakis, Achilles and Field, Hubert S. "Evaluation of Organizational Change Using Nonindependent Criterion Measures," *Personnel Psychology*, Vol. 28, Spring 1975, 39-44.

Baldridge, J. Victor and Burnham, Robert A. "Organizational Innovation: Individual, Organizational, and Environmental Impacts," *Administrative Science Quarterly*, Vol. 20, June 1975, 165-176.

Benne, Kenneth, Bradford, LeLand, Gibb, Jack, and Lippitt, Ronald. *The Laboratory Method of Learning and Changing: Theory and Applications.* Fairfax, Virginia: NTL Learning Resources Corporation, 1975.

French, Wendell L. and Bell, Jr., Cecil H. *Organization Development: Behavioral Science Interventions for Organization Improvement.* Englewood Cliffs, N.J.: Prentice-Hall, 1973.

Marguilies, Newton and Wallace, John. *Organization Change: Techniques and Applications.* Glenview, Ill.: Scott, Foresman, 1973.

Schon, Donald A. "Deutero-Learning in Organizations: Learning for Increased Effectiveness," *Organizational Dynamics*, Vol. 4, Summer 1975, 2-16.

Smith, Peter B. "Controlled Studies of the Outcome of Sensitivity Training," *Psychological Bulletin*, Vol. 82, July 1975, 597-622.

Steele, Fred I. *Physical Setting and Organizational Development.* Reading, Mass.: Addison-Wesley, 1973.

PART V
APPENDIX

ANNOTATED BIBLIOGRAPHY OF ORGANIZATIONAL BEHAVIOR

ARTICLES

Achilles A. Armenakis and Hubert S. Field, "Evaluation of Organizational Change Using Nonindependent Criterion Measures," *Personnel Psychology*, Vol. 28, Spring 1975, 39-44.

The authors propose one means for coping with nonindependent criterion measures in evaluating organizational change. It is shown that a productivity index cannot be treated as a series of independent measures because of the fact that adjacent points have a higher correlation than do nonadjacent points. In a situation where productivity is on the increase, conventional statistical procedures are inappropriate.

John C. Athanassiades, "The Distortion of Upward Communication in Hierarchical Organizations," *Academy of Management Journal*, Vol. 16, June 1973, 207-226.

A school and a police department were studied to investigate relationships between distortion of upward communication, needs of subordinates, and aspects of organizational climate. Distortion of upward communication is (1) negatively related to level of security, (2) positively related to achievement needs, (3) positively related to a "heteronomous" organizational climate, and (4) negatively related to an "autonomous" climate.

J. Victor Baldridge and Robert A. Burnham, "Organizational Innovation: Individual, Organizational, and Environmental Impacts," *Administrative Science Quarterly*, Vol. 20, June 1975, 165-176.

Based upon two large-scale studies in school systems, this article contends that research on the diffusion of innovation and organizational change has too frequently focused on the wrong cluster of variables. A productive analysis of the change process should concentrate on the diffusion of complex technologies with unclear evaluations, would shift focus from individualistic variables to roles and organizational structure, and would examine closely environmental factors.

Richard W. Beatty and Craig Eric Schneider, "A Case for Positive Reinforcement," *Business Horizons*, Vol. 28, April 1975, 57-66.

An enthusiastic essay about positive reinforcement (PR), which focuses on actual behavior rather than on measures of effectiveness by emphasizing positive rewards rather than punishment. Simultaneously, it recognizes the power of immediate feedback and different reinforcement schedules. An analysis of PR often reveals the current ineffective and illogical use of rewards presently offered in organizations.

David E. Berlew, "Leadership and Organizational Excitement," *California Management Review*, Vol. 27, Winter 1974, 21-30.

The author espouses Stage 3 Leadership which is charismatic rather than custodial or managerial. It involves three key elements — (1) the development of a common vision for the organization related to values shared by the organization's members, (2) the discovery or creation of value-related opportunities and activities within the framework of the mission and goals of the organization, (3) making organization members feel stronger and more in control of their own destinies, both individually and collectively.

Thomas J. Bouchard, Jr., "A Comparison of Two Brainstorming Procedures," *Journal of Applied Psychology*, Vol. 56, October 1972, 418-421.

A modified brainstorming procedure that required people to identify psychologically with significant components of the task (synectics) was compared to standard brainstorming over three sessions and nine different problems. The synectics groups were superior to the brainstorming groups on all nine problems, leading to the conclusion that synectics was a more effective group-problem-solving strategy than brainstorming.

Bruce Buchanan II, "Building Organizational Commitment: The Socialization of Managers in Work Organizations," *Administrative Science Quarterly*, Vol. 19, December 1974, 533-546.

Based on a questionnaire survey of 279 business and government managers, this study examines two questions: (1) which organizational experiences have the greatest impact on commitment attitudes, and (2) how does the significance of such experience vary with organizational tenure, particularly at early career stages? Among the commitment related variables found were years of organizational service, job achievement, and hierarchical advancement.

Arthur G. Butler, Jr., "Project Management: A Study in Organizational Conflict," *Academy of Management Journal*, Vol. 16, March 1973, 84-101.

The author reasons that project management in functional organizations provides a fertile field for much-needed reexamination of the presumption of dysfunctional conflict when managers and employed professionals interact in organizations. Systematic analysis must identify the foundation of human conflict and determine the extent to which the implications of such conflict for organizational behavior are functional or dysfunctional.

Patrick E. Connor and Boris W. Becker, "Values and the Organization, Suggestions for Research," *Academy of Management Journal*, Vol. 18, September 1975, 550-561.

It is noted that, despite long interest in human values, few investigators have focused on values and organizational process. Questions regarding how values relate to reward structure, upward mobility, goal commitment, and control are unresolved. An organizational paradigm to identify reciprocal effects of values and organizational factors is presented and hypotheses for research are offered, but no conclusions are reached.

Robert C. Cummins, "Leader-Member Relations As A Moderator of the Effects of Leader Behavior and Attitude," *Personnel Psychology*, Vol. 25, Winter 1972, 655-660.

One hundred and thirty-three formen were administered questionnaires to investigate the interaction between leader-member relations and leader behavior and attitudes. It was concluded that (1) Leader-member relations, as measured by superiors, moderates the relation between leader's attitudes toward leadership and work group performance; (2) Group atmosphere, as measured by the foremen, moderates the relation between leadership behavior and work group performance. Foremen who are able to remain involved despite apathy and hostility, and who do not attempt to coerce or direct uncooperative workers, have a better chance of being successful.

David R. Day and Ralph M. Stogdill, "Leader Behavior of Male and Female Supervisors: A Comparative Study," *Personnel Psychology*, Vol. 25, Summer 1972, 353-360.

Matched pairs of 36 male and female civil service supervisors completed the Leadership Behavior Description Questionnaire and were also evaluated by their subordinates. Biographical data about these supervisors were also obtained. It was concluded that male and female supervisors who occupy similar positions and perform similar functions exhibit similar patterns of leader behavior and levels of effectiveness (when evaluated by subordinates).

H. Dudley Dewhirst, "Impact of Organizational Climate on the Desire to Manage Among Engineers and Scientists," *Personnel Journal*, Vol. 50, March 1971, 196-203.

Two hundred and fifty engineers and scientists from two non-profit organizations with different climates were administered questionnaires about the desire to manage. Results showed that members of one organization changed their desire to manage in response to the organizational climate that places a high value on management. A comparative analysis suggested tha young professionals do not automatically become interested in managerial careers — encouragement by the organization is a vital factor.

John Dowling and Jeffrey Pfeffer, "Organizational Legitimacy: Social Values and Organizational Behavior," *Pacific Sociological Review*, Vol. 18, January 1975, 122-136.

This paper presents a conceptual framework in which organizational legitimacy is defined as the congruence between the values associated with the organization and the values of its environment. Corporate philanthropic contributions, the composition and size of Boards of Directors, and the content of annual reports and other organizational communications are presented as efforts on the part of organizations to achieve legitimacy.

Douglas E. Durand, "Effects of Achievement Motivation and Skill Training on the Entrepreneurial Behavior of Black Businessmen,"

Organizational Behavior and Human Performance, Vol. 13, August 1975, 76-90.

An 18-month study was made of a training program designed to increase entrepreneurial activity among Blacks. A group that received both achievement motivation training and management development training became significantly more active (hours worked, new investments, employees hired, etc.) than a group receiving only management development training or a control group. The data suggested that an "internal" perception might be a prior condition to increased business activity.

Dov Eden, "Organizational Membership vs Self-Employment: Another Blow to the American Dream," *Organizational Behavior and Human Performance*, Vol. 13, February 1975, 79-94.

The hypothesis that membership in work organizations has ill effects upon individual well-being was tested by comparing national survey data for 1902 members and 183 self-employed workers. Mental health and job satisfaction were about the same for the two groups. It is concluded that self-employment, despite its numerous other advantages, does not provide workers with the greater psychological benefits promised by the American dream.

Richard V. Farace and Donald MacDonald, "New Directions in the Study of Organizational Communication," *Personnel Psychology*, Vol. 27, Spring 1974, 1-15.

The authors synthesize some of the literature on organizational communications in order to clarify new research directions required in this field. Among the research questions generated were (1) What is the effect of growth of an organization on its communication structure? (2) What are the alternative messages available to accomplish a task? (3) What are the appropriate communication behaviors for middle and lower management?

Mitchell Fein, "Job Enrichment: A Reevaluation," *Sloan Management Review*, Vol. 15, Fall 1973, 69-88.

Based on an extensive review of the job enrichment literature, the author concludes that there are few, if any, genuine cases where job enrichment has been applied successfully to a large, heterogeneous work force. Most applications of job enrichment either have been common sense job redesign or have occurred among such a select group of workers that the success of the program was independent of its content. Furthermore, the intrinsic nature of the job is of secondary concern to production workers.

Fred E. Fiedler, "Validation and Extension of the Contingency Model of Leadership Effectiveness: A review of Empirical Findings," *Psychological Bulletin*, Vol. 76, March 1971, 128-148.

A review of studies of the contingency model suggest (1) The model predicts leadership performance better in field than laboratory situations. (2) The situational favorableness dimension does moderate the relationship between leadership style and group performance. (3) Coaching task groups appear to follow the predictions of the contingency model.

B.D. Fine (now Dov Eden), "Comparison of Work Groups with Stable and Unstable Membership," *Journal of Applied Psychology*, Vol. 55, April 1971, 170-174.

Work groups with unstable membership are compared to similar groups with stable membership. Employees in unstable work groups reported less within-group peer leadership, but more favorable organizational context. Increased lateral linkage among work groups of unstable membership is suggested as the mechanism that appears to compensate for the decreased peer leadership evident in unstable work groups.

R.H. Finn and Sang M. Lee, "Salary Equity: Its Determination, Analysis, and Correlates," *Journal of Applied Psychology*, Vol. 56, August 1972, 283-292.

Professional employees in the Federal Public Health Service were divided into an equity subsample (n = 96) and an inequity subsample (n = 74) based on their perceived fairness of salary treatment. Questionnaires were completed by the professionals and their immediate superiors. People in the equity subsample demonstrated less dissonance, more favorable attitudes toward their work and the organization, and a lower propensity to terminate voluntarily than did people in the inequity subsample.

Jerome L. Franklin, "Down the Organization: Influence Processes Across Levels of Hierarchy," *Administrative Science Quarterly*, Vol. 20, June 1975, 153-161.

The direction and form of influence processes across levels of hierarchy were empirically examined using two waves of data from 1770 individuals in 246 groups from 10 sites. Results indicated the primacy of downward over upward influence and support a basic pattern of relations including the flow of major influence from indicators of group functioning — group process — reported by members of superior-level groups to situational conditions — organizational climate — reported by members of subordinate-level groups.

Jerome L. Franklin, "Relations among Four Social-Psychological Aspects of Organizations," *Administrative Science Quarterly*, Vol. 20, September 1975, 422-433.

A model describing causal relations among four social-psychological factors — organizational climate, managerial leadership, peer leadership, group process — in organizational functioning is empirically examined. Data from 30,000 individuals in 37 industrial sites were examined. The relations suggested by the theory were generally supported. Specifically, the major links are from organizational climate to managerial leadership, from managerial leadership to peer leadership, and from peer leadership to group process.

David R. Frew, "Transcendental Meditation and Productivity," *Academy of Management Journal*, Vol. 17, June 1974, 362-368.

Forty-two people (meditators) completed questionnaires about their work experiences. Coworkers also completed questionnaires about the meditators. Three conclusions were reached: (1) T.M. appears to be positively related to productivity, (2) productivity gains are an increasing function of structural level, (3) gains in productivity are more apparent in a democratic than an autocratic organization structure.

Frank Friedlander and Stuart Greenberg, "Effect of Job Attitudes, Training, and Organizational Climate on Performance of the Hard-Core Unemployed," *Journal of Applied Psychology*, Vol. 55, August 1971, 287-295.

Several potential contributors toward the job performance and retention of 478 hard-core unemployed were explored. The sole correlate of the HCU's work effectiveness and behavior was the degree of supportiveness of the organizational climate in which he was placed. In addition, the HCU saw this climate as far less supportive than did his supervisor.

James F. Gavin, "Organizational Climate as a Function of Personal and Organizational Variables," *Journal of Applied Psychology*, Vol. 60, February 1976, 135-139.

Employee perceptions of organizational climate were believed to be influenced by organizational and individual difference factors and their interaction. One hundred and forty managerial workers in a medium-sized bank served as subjects. The findings failed to support the expected interaction of personal and organizational measures, but did indicate that personal and organizational variables alone accounted for significant amounts of variance in climate perceptions.

Edwin E. Ghiselli and Douglas A. Johnson, "Need Satisfaction, Managerial Success, and Organizational Structure," *Personnel Psychology*, Vol. 23, Winter 1970, 569-576.

A need satisfaction questionnaire was administered to 413 managers in a wide variety of firms. Approximately an equal number of managers worked in tall and flat organizations. A correlational analysis indicated that for managers in tall organizations there is little relationship between the degree of need satisfaction and success. For managers in flat organizations the relationship between satisfaction and success is negligible for the lower order needs, but more substantial for the higher order needs. Thus, flat organizations are superior to tall ones in encouraging individuality.

Edwin E. Ghiselli and Jacob P. Siegel, "Leadership and Managerial Success in Tall and Flat Organization Structures," *Personnel Psychology*, Vol. 25, Winter 1972, 617-624.

A questionnaire pertaining to views about authoritarian versus democratic leadership was administered to 442 middle managers from a variety of business firms. The sample was divided into members of tall versus flat organizations. A major finding was that neither in flat nor tall organizations is either authoritarian or democratic leadership given complete and uniform support. Also, firms with flat structures reward more with rapid advancement than those whose managers favor sharing information and objectives with their subordinates.

William F. Glueck, "Decision Making: Organization Choice," *Personnel Psychology*, Vol. 27, Spring 1974, 77-93.

Thirty-one male students majoring in business and engineering were studied with respect to how they chose and were chosen by an employer. Fourteen followed a decision pattern called maximizer; nine followed the validator pattern; seven the satisficer pattern. In general, it appeared that the students made decisions in a way congruent with their preconceived perceptions of the business world. For example, satisficers took the first acceptable offer because they believed that little differences existed among companies.

Charles N. Greene, "Causal Connections Among Managers' Merit Pay, Job Satisfaction, and Performance," *Journal of Applied Psychology*, Vol. 58, June 1974, 95-100.

Using advanced statistical techniques, this study investigated the source and direction of causal influence in the relationships among merit pay, satisfaction, and performance. The results indicated that merit pay caused satisfaction and, further, that merit pay increased the correlation between these two variables. Satisfaction was found to be an effect and not a cause of performance. The influence of performance was to increase the correlation between performance and satisfaction.

Charles N. Greene, "The Reciprocal Nature of Influence Between Leader and Subordinate," *Journal of Applied Psychology*, Vol. 60, April 1976, 187-193.

A study with 103 first-line managers with three organizations suggests that consideration causes subordinate satisfaction and, conversely, that subordinate performance causes both leader consideration and structure across conditions. However, when the relationship between initiating structure and subordinate performance was moderated by consideration, there was evidence of reciprocal causation. The results indicate how a leader might positively affect subordinate performance by increased emphasis on both consideration and structure.

Leopold Gruenfeld and Saleen Kassum, "Supervisory Style and Organizational Effectiveness in a Pediatric Hospital," *Personnel Psychology*, Vol. 26, Winter 1973, 531-544.

Eighty-three female supervisors were studied, using the Leader Behavior Description Questionnaire to measure style and criterion measures of patient care and coordination. It was concluded that in a pediatric hospital, nursing supervisors who combine high levels of structure and consideration are more likely (than those with opposite styles) to provide higher levels of satisfaction among their subordinates and better patient care as perceived by other nurses.

J. Richard Hackman, "Is Job Enrichment Just a Fad?" *Harvard Business Review*, Vol. 53, September-October 1975, 129-138.

The author cautions that if work redesign projects continue to be implemented the way they are today, there may be no tomorrow for job enrichment. Among his positive suggestions are (1) key individuals responsible for the work redesign project should attack the especially difficult problems right from the start, (2) management should insure that a diagnosis of the changes needed in the target jobs, based on some articulated theory of work redesign, is conducted before implementation.

Jerald Hage, Michael Aiken, and Cora Bagley Marrett, "Organization Structure and Communications," *American Sociological Review*, Vol. 36, October 1971, 860-871.

Using 16 health and welfare organizations as the research setting, hypotheses were developed relating the variables of complexity, formalization, and centralization to communication rates. In general, interdepartmental communications, both scheduled and unscheduled, are found to be affected most by these structural characteristics.

H.L. Hearn and Patricia Stoll, "Continuance Commitment in Low-Status Occupations: The Cocktail Waitress," *The Sociological Quarterly*, Vol. 16, Winter 1975, 105-114.

A description and analysis of the work of the cocktail waitress as an example of low-status occupations are reported using an interactionist framework. A processual view of continuance commitment is employed to account for persons remaining in occupations with few, if any, intrinsic rewards. It is pointed out that the Playboy Bunny is considerably different from the "regular" waitress.

Frederick Herzberg, "Motivation-Hygiene Profiles: Pinpointing What Ails the Organization," *Organizational Dynamics*, Vol. 3, Autumn 1974, 18-29.

The author points to the most common problems in employee attitudes encountered in organizations. Problems revealed by deviations from these "normal" profiles are real problems, reflecting an empirically tested theory of human behavior. Each problem is singular and requires its own solution. Managements that are not prepared to provide whatever motivators are possible in the job are not prepared to meet the challenge of managing adults.

Paul M. Hirsch, "Organizational Effectiveness and the Institutional Environment," *Administrative Science Quarterly*, Vol. 20, September 1975, 327-344.

Despite similarities in technology and other aspects of their operation, the typical pharmaceutical manufacturing firm is far more profitable than the typical phonograph record company. Strong differences in organizational effectiveness regarding their ability to control three aspects of the environment — pricing and distribution, patent and copyright law, and external opinion-leaders — are suggested to help account for the differential performance.

John A. Hornaday and John Aboud, "Characteristics of Successful Entrepreneurs," *Personnel Psychology*, Vol. 24, Summer 1971, 141-153.

Sixty male and female, white and Black entrepreneurs were interviewed and administered value and personality tests to explore the major hypothesis that a number of personal characteristics differentiate successful entrepreneurs from people in general. Both the Edwards Personal Preference Schedule and the Survey of Interpersonal Values yielded scales that discriminated between entrepreneurs and people in the standardization group for these tests. Differences were found in achievement, support, and leadership.

Robert J. House, "A Path Goal Theory of Leader Effectiveness," *Administrative Science Quarterly*, Vol. 16, September 1971, 321-338.

According to path goal theory the motivational functions of the leader consist of increasing personal payoffs to subordinates for work-goal attainment, and making the path to these payoffs easier by clarifying it, reducing road blocks and pitfalls, and increasing the opportunities for personal satisfaction en route. A test of eight hypotheses generated from propositions contained in the theory provided general support for the theory.

Lawrence G. Hrebiniak, "Job Technology, Supervision, and Work-Group Structure," *Administrative Science Quarterly*, Vol. 19, September 1974, 395-410.

A general hospital was studied in reaching the conclusion that the relationship between technology and structure at the individual level was found too weak to indicate a technological imperative. At the group level of analysis, variables such as the perceived hierarchical independence and decisional participation of the supervisor were significantly related to structure, independent of job technology. Both technology and supervision were found to be important for work-group structure.

John M. Ivancevich, "Changes in Performance in a Management by Objectives Program," *Administrative Science Quarterly*, Vol. 19, December 1974, 563-574.

A multiple-time-series quasi-experimental research design was used to study the effects of MBO. The performance of the subordinates of 181 MBO involved supervisors in production and marketing departments was analyzed. Results included (1) improvements in the production units occurred earlier than in the marketing units, (2) the reinforcement schedule chosen may influence performance.

John M. Ivancevich and James H. Donnelly, Jr., "A Study of Role Clarity and the Need for Clarity for Three Occupational Groups," *Academy of Management Journal*, Vol. 17, March 1974, 28-36.
Role clarity and the need for role clarity are investigated empirically as interpreted by a total of 261 salesmen, supervisors, and operating employees in a medium-size electronic manufacturing plant. It was found that a high need for clarity moderates the relationship between role clarity and a number of variables for the three groups.

John M. Ivancevich and James H. Donnelly, Jr., "Relation of Organizational Structure to Job Satisfaction, Anxiety-Stress, and Performance," *Administrative Science Quarterly*, Vol. 20, June 1975, 272-280.
A study of 295 trade sales representatives in three organizations examined the relationship between organization shape or structure (tall, medium, and flat) to job satisfaction, anxiety-stress, and performance. The findings indicated that sales representatives in flat organizations (1) perceive more satisfaction with respect to self-actualization and autonomy, (2) perceive lower amounts of anxiety-stress, and (3) perform more efficiently than sales representatives in medium and tall organizations.

Bruce D. Jamieson, "Behavioral Problems with Management by Objectives," *Academy of Management Journal*, Vol. 16, September 1973, 496-505.
This paper rationally analyzes some of the behavioral problems associated with the practice of management-by-objectives. Among them are problems relating to managerial style, relating to change, interpersonal skills, setting objectives, measurement, and management-by-objectives quality control.

Doyle P. Johnson, "Social Organization of an Industrial Work Group: Emergence and Adaptation to Environmental Change,"

The Sociological Quarterly, Vol. 15, Winter 1974, 109-126.

The author was a participant observer in a small work group on the night shift in a food processing plant. The analysis is guided by the small group theory of George C. Homans. Clear support was found for the general proposition that commitment to formal organizational goals, group morale, and individual satisfaction is positively related to a lenient work style and high autonomy.

Ray Jurkovich, "A Core Typology of Organizational Environments," *Administrative Science Quarterly*, Vol. 19, September 1974, 380-394.

This article presents a core typology of 64 types which can be expanded, depending on the user's interests and problems. Different types of environment have consequences for the planning of strategies, operations, and tactics, coalition behavior, and decision making. Among the variables covered in the typology are change rate, level of complexity, stability, and degree of organization.

Robert T. Keller, "Role Conflict and Ambiguity: Correlates with Job Satisfaction and Values," *Personnel Psychology*, Vol. 28, Spring 1975, 57-64.

Fifty-one professional employees of a research and development organization participated in a study to test the general hypothesis that employees are more satisfied with their job when expectations for performance are well defined and non-conflicting. Two sets of findings supported the hypothesis: (1) Role conflict was negatively correlated with job satisfaction, dimensions of supervision, pay, and opportunities for promotion. (2) Role ambiguity was negatively correlated with satisfaction with the work itself. Values were not appreciably related to the variables studied.

Gerald A. Kesselman, Eileen L. Hagen, and Robert J. Wherr, Sr., "A Factor Analytic Test of the Porter-Lawler Expectancy Model of Work Motivation," *Personnel Psychology*, Vol. 27, Winter 1974, 569-579.

Seventy-six draftswomen and toll operators completed questionnaires containing measures of job satisfaction, effort expended on the job, and expectancy relationships between behavior and pay. Supervisory ratings were used for criterion data. The general outline of expectancy theory was supported, along with the contention that this theory can be applied by managers only if they can identify, clarify, and facilitate the expectancies, outcomes, and satisfactions of their subordinates.

David Knights, "A Classificatory Scheme for Occupations," *The British Journal of Sociology*, Vol. 26, September 1975, 294-308.

The author develops a three-dimensional model to classify occupations that bears some relationship to the occupational studies available. It also contributes to theory and integrates seemingly disparate sets of occupational studies. The dimensions are Action (individualistic versus collective), Community (fragmented versus integrated), and Ideology (working class versus middle class).

Thomas A. Kochan, George P. Huber, and L.L. Cummings, "Determinants of Intraorganizational Conflict in Collective Bargaining in the Public Sector," *Administrative Science Quarterly*, Vol. 20, March 1975, 10-23.

This study examines conflicts among city management officials in 228 cities. Results indicated that goal incompatibility and factors that provide the ability to interfere with goal attainment of others are significantly correlated with conflict. However, the form of the relationship suggested in the original formulation of a model of intraorganizational conflict was not supported.

William R. LaFollette, "Is Satisfaction Redundant with Organizational Climate?" *Organizational Behavior and Human Performance*, Vol. 13, April 1975, 257-278.

This research investigated whether organization climate is redundant with job satisfaction. For a sample of employees in a major medical center, organizational climate and organization practices related to performance in a different manner than the satisfaction/performance relationship, which did not tend to support the redundancy hypothesis. In addition, other research was evaluated which tended to support the climate-causes-satisfaction hypothesis as opposed to the redundancy hypothesis.

William R. LaFollette, "How is the Climate in Your Organization?" *Personnel Journal*, Vol. 54, July 1975, 376-379.

The author reviews the literature to show that the psychological atmosphere of an organization is a significant factor affecting organizational behavior. Organizational climate affects an organization and can be potentially devastating to the survival of an organizational atmospheric climate. A diagnosis of climate can help managers increase the performance potential of their organizations and the satisfaction of their employees.

Ervin Laszlo, "The Meaning and Significance of General System Theory," *Behavioral Science*, Vol. 20, January 1975, 9-33.

In this essay about general systems theory, the author indicates that the theory holds promise of being able to draw on emerging parallelisms in different scientific fields and provides the basis for an integrated science of complex organizations. The combined factors of the valuation of integrated general theories and the support for interdisciplinary research point toward the emergence of such a theory.

Edward E. Lawler, III, "Job Attitudes and Employee Motivation: Theory, Research, and Practice." *Personnel Psychology*, Vol. 23, Summer 1970, 223-237.

Among the key conclusions reached by this intensive analysis are (1) ability combines multiplicatively with motivation to determine performance, (2) superiors should be aware of what type of outcomes their subordinates value so that these outcomes can be tied to performance, (3) organizations using pay or other rewards as motivators should select people on the basis of how important these rewards are to them.

Harry Levinson, "On Executive Suicide," *Harvard Business Review*, Vol. 53, July-August 1975, 118-122.

Levinson reasons, on the basis of his clinical experience, that the conscientious person with high aspirations which he pursues intently is especially vulnerable to setbacks that may lead to depression and even self-destruction.

Robert A. Luke, Jr., "Matching the Individual and the Organization," *Harvard Business Review*, Vol. 53, May-June 1975, 17-34, 165.

According to Luke, many social scientists agree that there is no one correct design that fits all organizations or even all departments of functions within an organization: each design ought to be tailored to the particular situation. Managers should assume the role of the behavioral scientist in bringing about change (i.e. become OD practitioners themselves).

Craig C. Lundberg, "Patterns of Acquaintanceship in Society and Complex Organization: A Comparative Study of the Small World Problem," *Pacific Sociological Review*, Vol. 18, April 1975, 206-222.

This study investigates the elementary features of social nets in two business firms which differ in their degree of bureaucratization and in the nature of their technology, and in a sample of society-at-large. The data show differences among rates of acquaintance chain completion, the length of chains, and the number of final links in chains which not only reflect organizational structure and technology, but also, line, staff, and hierarchical level factors.

Fred Luthans and Donald D. White, Jr., "Behavior Modification: Application to Manpower Management," *Personnel Administration*, Vol. 72, July-August 1971, 41-47.

An essay about behavior modification describing it as a technique which may enable human resource specialists to modify or eliminate undesirable employee behavior and replace it with behavior that is more compatible with goal attainment. The process allows the individual whose behavior is being modified to elicit an environmental stimulus as a result of a prior response. Behavior modification differs from the usual dispensing of rewards in organization because of its systematic nature.

Roger Mansfield, "Bureaucracy and Centralization : An Examination of Organizational Structure," *Administrative Science Quarterly*, Vol. 18, December 1973, 477-488.

A reanalysis of data reveals that the concept of bureaucracy still holds merit. In reviewing the methodology of the Aston group (who contended that Weber's concept of the bureaucratic type is no longer useful) Mansfield concludes that the main variables in their research are scalar quantities, not vector quantities as they suggest.

Philip M. Marcus and James S. House, "Exchange Between Superiors and Subordinates in Large Organizations," *Administrative Science Quarterly*, Vol. 18, June 1973, 209-222.

A hypothesis was advanced that both expressive and instrumental behavior of superiors increase the subordinate's social profit, resulting in increased loyalty to the superior, greater compliance with his demands, and reduced conflict between the two organizational levels. However, the intermediary exchange process differs in both: (1) Expressive behavior reduces subordinate's cost of interaction on the job, and (2) Instrumental behavior provides rewards to subordinates. Self-administered data from 180 workers in a utility provided support for this three part hypothesis.

David C. McClelland, Stephen Rhinesmith, and Richard Kristensen, The Effects of Power Training on Community Action Agencies," *Applied Behavioral Science*, Vol. 11, January-February-March 1975, 92-115.

Power motivation training workshops were designed for Community Action Agency staff members in one state and their effects on individuals were measured six months later. It was concluded that the training was successful. Four to six months after training 115 out of 167 staff members interviewed said they felt stronger as a result of training, and 87 were judged by the research interviewers to have shown signs of improvement. Control measures were used to help evaluate the results.

Herbert H. Meyer, "The Pay-for-Performance Dilemma," *Organizational Dynamics*, Vol. 3, Winter 1975, 39-50.

According to the author, to the extent pay is attached directly to performance of the task, intrinsic interest in the task itself decreases. When pay becomes the important goal, the individual's interest tends to focus on that goal rather than on the performance of the task itself.

Vance F. Mitchell, "Need Satisfaction of Military Commanders and Staff," *Journal of Applied Psychology*, Vol. 54, June 1970, 282-287.

Compares the need fulfillment and dissatisfaction perceived by commissioned officers at three levels of military grade who were serving in command, and five different types of staff assignment. A questionnaire provided data from 675 officers serving in an overseas Air Force Command. The findings showed that commanders at all grades were more fulfilled and less dissatisfied than officers in most types of staff assignments.

Robert J. Mockler, "Situational Theory of Management," *Harvard Business Review*, Vol. 49, May-June, 1971, 146-155.

According to Mockler, the situational approach to management is affecting all major areas of management theory including organization, leadership, staffing, control, and planning. Furthermore, few management principles exist that are hard and fast guidelines. At best, one can develop conditional or situational principles that are useful in specific kinds of business situations.

Richard A. Morano, "Managerial Counseling for Organizational
  Effectiveness," *Personnel Journal*, Vol. 54, September 1975,
  494-495, 500-501.

According to the author, managers who are well trained in
assessing the achievement needs of employees and who can provide
genuine counseling can contribute enormously to the attainment of
an organization's goal. The point is not to crush or suppress
employees' motives, but to provide alternative goals which are
attractive and more readily attainable than the original ones.

Greg R. Oldham, "The Impact of Supervisory Characteristics on Goal
  Acceptance," *Academy of Management Journal*, Vol. 18, September 1975, 461-475.

Employing a laboratory setting with paid undergraduate volunteers, this study found that supervisory characteristics affect subordinates' stated acceptance of supervisor-assigned goals, but not
the quantity or quality of subordinates' task performance, nor do
subordinates who accept the assigned goals perform at a higher level
than those who reject them. Perceptions of the instrumentality of
the supervisor most strongly influenced goal acceptance.

D.A. Ondrack, "Defense Mechanisms and the Herzberg Theory: An
  Alternate Test," *Academy of Management Journal*, Vol. 17,
  March 1974, 79-89.

A constructive replication of Herzberg's findings using the semi-
structured Occupational Values Scale to elicit projective response
about satisfying and dissatisfying job situations failed to yield the
two-factor pattern. Subjects were 70 MBA students. Results from
the use of the author's methodology appear to support Vroom's
ego-defense criticism of the recall methodology.

Richard N. Osborn and James G. Hunt, "Environment and Organizational Effectiveness," *Administrative Science Quarterly*, Vol. 19,
  June 1974, 231-246.

Environmental complexity is viewed as the interaction among
environmental risk, dependency, and interorganizational relationships. Research questions concerning complexity in the task environment are investigated in 26 small, rigidly structured social service
organizations in a populous mid-western state. Both task environmental dependency and interorganizational interaction alone and in
combination are positively correlated with effectiveness.

Jeffrey Pfeffer and Gerald R. Salancik, "Organizational Decision Making as a Political Process: The Case of a University Budget," *Administrative Science Quarterly*, Vol. 19, June 1974, 135-151.

Measures of departmental power in a university are found to be significantly related to the proportion of budget received, even after controlling for such universalistic bases of allocation as work load of the department, national rank, and number of faculty. The more powerful the department, the less the allocated resources are a function of departmental work load and student demand for courses. Precise measures of subunit power were taken.

Lee E. Preston and James E. Post, "The Third Managerial Revolution," *Academy of Management Journal*, Vol. 17, September 1974, 476-485.

The authors observe that the appearance of professional management as the dominant means of organizational control in society is referred to as the managerial revolution. This required, however, a prior revolution — the appearance of specialized management within hierarchical organizations. A third revolution, based on participation both internal and external, is now in progress. Hence, participative organizations should be a primary focus of management study.

William E. Reif, Robert M. Monczka, and John W. Newstrom, "Perceptions of the Formal and Informal Organizations: Objective Measurement Through the Semantic Differential Technique," *Academy of Management Journal*, Vol. 16, September 1973, 389-403.

A sample of 341 managers and the semantic differential technique was used to examine the assumption made by many behavioral scientists that the informal organization has a greater impact on organizational effectiveness than the formal organization. The research demonstrated that employees perceived the formal organization to be more valuable in satisfying individual needs and more influential in affecting behavior than the informal organization.

Leon Reinharth and Mahmoud A. Wahba, "Expectancy Theory as a Predictor of Work Motivation, Effort Expenditure, and Job Performance," *Academy of Management Journal*, Vol. 18, September 1975, 520-537.

The predictive power of expectancy theory with respect to work motivation, effort expenditure, and job performance was tested in four homogenous samples of industrial sales personnel (n = 348). The base of behavioral alternatives is expanded to include both approach and avoidance acts. Findings did not support the classical expectancy model or its components.

Patricia A. Renwick, "Perception and Management of Superior-Subordinate Conflict," *Organizational Behavior and Human Performance*, Vol. 13, June 1975, 444-456.

This study investigated interpersonal conflict that occurred on the job. Members of 36 superior-subordinate dyads representing 10 organization subunits completed the Employee Conflict Inventory. An independent sample of 169 employees from the same subunits completed the Profile of Organizational Characteristics. Results indicated that dyad members held similar perceptions concerning the topics and sources of superior-subordinate conflict. Technical and administrative issue were the most frequent topics, and differences in perception and knowledge were the primary reasons.

Karlene H. Roberts and Charles A. O'Reilly, III, "Failures in Upward Communication in Organizations: Three Possible Culprits," *Academy of Management Journal*, Vol. 17, June 1974, 205-224.

Using 388 respondents from diverse organizations, the impact of trust in the superior, perceived influence of the superior, and mobility aspirations of subordinates on upward communication behavior were examined. While the importance of trust as a facilitator of open information exchange was supported, this was less true of influence of the superior and mobility aspirations.

Betty Boyd Roe and James R. Wood, "Adaptive Innovation and Organizational Security," *Pacific Sociological Review*, Vol. 18, July 1975, 310-326.

This paper treats the propensity of organizations to adapt appropriately to social changes in their environment. A study of 50 sororities (on three campuses) provides data for examining the relationship between "adaptive innovation" and organizational security (indexed by financial solvency, prestige, and recruitment success). It is concluded that secure sororities are more likely to adjust to their environment in ways appropriate to their organizational character.

W.W. Ronan, "Individual and Situational Variables Relating to Job Satisfaction," *Journal of Applied Psychology Monograph*, Vol. 54, February 1970, (Whole).

For a sample of 1310 managerial-supervisory, 3641 salaried, and 6212 hourly employees, data were collected concerning job satisfaction using 32 items from a questionnaire. In the same organization, data descriptive of work units and behaviors in the units (such as tardiness) were collected. In general, little relationship was found. Where such a relationship is found, the link appeared to be direct supervision. Ronan suggests that future studies concentrate upon individuals.

Benson Rosen and Thomas H. Jerdee, "Influence of Sex Role Stereotypes on Personnel Decisions," *Journal of Applied Psychology*, Vol. 54, February 1970, 9-14.

An in-basket exercise was used to investigate the influence of sex role stereotypes on the personnel decisions of 95 male, bank supervisor. The design consisted of four separate experiments (in-basket items) in which an employee's sex and other situational attributes were manipulated. Results confirmed the hypothesis that male administrators tend to discriminate against female employees in personnel decision involving promotion, development, and supervision.

Benson Rosen and Thomas J. Jerdee, "Sex Stereotyping in the Executive Suite," *Harvard Business Review*, Vol. 52, March-April 1974, 45-58.

Using male and female versions of identical hypothetical situations, 1500 HBR subscribers were asked to idicate what decisions they would reach about the situations. The responses revealed two general patterns of sex discrimination: (1) there is a greater organizational concern for the careers of men than of women, and (2) there is a degree of skepticism about women's abilities to balance work and family demands.

Benjamin Schneider, "The Perception of Organizational Climate: The Customer's View," *Journal of Applied Psychology*, Vol. 57, June 1973, 248-256.

Climate was defined as the summary perception that bank customers have of their banks. Perceived climate was conceptualized as an intervening variable — a summary perception based on specific service-related events but preceding customer account switching. Questionnaire data obtained from 674 present and 87 former bank account holders indicated that (1) present customer intentions to switch accounts are more strongly related to summary perceptions and (2) former customers have significantly more negative perceptions of the bank than do present customers.

Donald A. Schon, "Deutero-Learning in Organizations: Learning for Increased Effectiveness," *Organizational Dynamics*, Vol. 4, Summer 1975, 2-16.

The author reasons that the effective business firm is one that has a high capacity for organizational learning. The effective business manager, in turn, is one who has developed the capacity to foster organizational learning. A goal to move toward is a behavioral world conducive to shared inquiry ("Model II").

Richard L. Shearer and Joseph A. Steger, "Manpower Obsolescence: A New Definition and Empirical Investigation of Personal Variables," *Academy of Management Journal*, Vol. 18, June 1975, 263-275.

Of 12 major determinants of managerial and technical job obsolescence, high need achievement and high levels of organizational participation were found to be the major contributors to nonobsolescence. Managerial obsolescence, as opposed to professional obsolescence, tended to depend more on experience and less on education. Data were obtained from the self-reports of 451 United States Air Force officers and civilians working on weapon systems development.

Henry P. Sims, Jr. and Andrew D. Szilagyi, "Leader Structure and Subordinate Satisfaction for Two Hospital Administrative Levels: A Path Analysis Approach," *Journal of Applied Psychology*, Vol. 60, April 1976, 194-197.

The path-goal theory of leadership was examined by investigating relationships between leader initiating structure and subordinate satisfaction at two hospital administrative levels. Two hypotheses were substantiated; (1) At the higher occupational level (20 female associate directors) initiating structure would be negatively related to role ambiguity, and positively related to expectancy II and subordinate satisfaction. (2) At the lower occupational level (20 female head nurses) initiating structure would be negatively related to subordinate satisfaction and unrelated to expectancy II.

David Sirota and Alan D. Wolfson, "Pragmatic Approach to People Problems," *Harvard Business Review*, Vol. 51, January-February 1973, 120-128.

The authors contend that companies confronted with employee discontent need to find out what the problems are before they set out to solve them. A recommended program is to begin with diagnosis, effectively implement solutions, and use honest evaluations. The result may be a permanent industrial relations tool for revealing trouble in the company long before it erupts.

John W. Slocum, Jr., "Motivation in Managerial Levels: Relationship of Need Satisfaction to Job Performance," *Journal of Applied Psychology*, Vol. 55, August 1971, 312-316.
This study compares the need satisfaction of first-line supervisors with top and middle managers and relates need satisfaction to job performance (in a steel mill setting). The findings support Porter and Lawler's model relating need satisfaction to performance, but only partially support the hypothesis that satisfaction of higher order needs is more closely related to top managers' performance than to lower managers' performance.

E. Allen Slusher, "A Systems Look at Performance Appraisal," *Personnel Journal,* Vol. 54, February 1975, 114-117.
The author reasons that results of goal achievement measurements of a manager's performance are used by most organizations with varying degrees of sophistication. Too often, however, the systems view of the performance appraisal process is overlooked. It is from such a viewpoint that a broader perspective on the management of human resources can be developed.

Peter B. Smith, "Controlled Studies of the Outcome of Sensitivity Training," *Psychological Bulletin*, Vol. 82, July 1975, 597-622.
The studies included in this review had control groups and a repeated measures design, and training lasted not less than 20 hours. Of 100 studies using measurement immediately after training, 78 detected changes significantly greater than those shown by controls. Of 31 studies using measures completed one month or more after training, 21 also found significant change. The changes most frequently found included more favorable self-concept, reduced prejudice, changed behavior as perceived by others not present during training, and a variety of ways in which groups are conducted within an organization.

James E. Sorensen and Thomas L. Sorensen, "The Conflict of Professionals in Bureaucratic Organizations," *Administrative*

Science Quarterly, Vol. 19, March 1974, 98-106.

A study of 264 certified public accountants in large public accounting firms showed that when professionals work in a professional-bureaucratic organization, conflict and deprivation result with predictable consequences such as job dissatisfaction and job migration. Scales for bureaucratic and professional orientations were developed for the study.

Matt M. Starcevich, "Job Factor Importance for Job Satisfaction Across Different Occupational Levels," *Journal of Applied Psychology*, Vol. 56, December 1972, 467-471.

Three occupational levels of employees, first-line managers (n = 155), middle managers (n = 182), and professional employees (n = 181) judged the importance of 18 job factors as contributing separately to job satisfaction and job dissatisfaction. Occupational level did not significantly affect the judged order of importance of the job factors for either job satisfaction or job dissatisfaction.

John E. Stinson and Thomas W. Johnson, "The Path-Goal Theory of Leadership: A Partial Test and Suggested Refinement," *Academy of Management Journal*, Vol. 18, June 1975, 242-252.

Hypotheses derived from the path-goal theory of leadership were tested, using 90 persons employed as military officers, Civil Service personnel, and project engineers. Results supported the theory with respect to the leadership dimension of consideration, but tended to counter the theory regarding the dimension of initiating structure. An extension of path-goal theory is suggested.

Ross M. Stolzenberg, "Education, Occupation, and Wage Difference between White and Black Men," *American Journal of Sociology*, Vol. 81, September 1975, 299-323.

An analysis of available data suggests that racial differences in quality of schooling are largely irrelevant to within-occupation race differences in earnings. To arrive at this conclusion, a hypothesis suggesting that years of schooling and years of labor-force participation have joint nonadditive effects on earnings was formulated, tested, and supported by several regression analyses. A measure of race differences in wage returns to schooling was computed for 62 different occupations.

John O. Todd, " 'Cafeteria Compensation': Making Management Motivators Meaningful," *Personnel Journal*, Vol. 54, May 1975, 275-276, 281.

Executives usually do not reap the full benefits of cash bonuses, according to the author. In order to maximize the yield of these hard-earned rewards, consideration should be given to a more flexible compensation plan in which the emphasis is on individual selection based on individual situations.

John F. Veiga, "The Mobile Manager at Mid-Career," *Harvard Business Review*, Vol. 51, January-February 1973, 115-119.

The author contends that very little is known about the forces that influence job mobility despite the familiarity of this phenomenon. A mobility matrix is presented that was developed from an extensive study of the job moves of nearly 1300 managers. It depicts mobility phases throughout the average manager's career and the major influences on these phases.

Marc J. Wallace, Jr., John M. Ivancevich, and Herbert L. Lyon, "Measurement Modifications for Assessing Organizational Climate in Hospitals," *Academy of Management Journal*, Vol. 18, March 1975, 82-97.

The degree to which the Halpin and Croft Organizational Climate Description Questionnaire generalizes from business and educational settings to hospital settings was investigated. Two criteria were established for the instrument: (1) reliability, and (2) factor structure replication from previously investigated settings to hospital settings. After cross-validation in two hospitals, the results appeared promising.

Richard E. Walton, "Quality of Working Life: What Is It?" *Sloan Management Review*, Vol. 15, Fall 1973, 11-21.

Walton notes that dissatisfaction with working life is a problem which affects almost all workers at one time or another, regardless of position or status. Intense job dissatisfaction can be costly to both the individual and the organization. The author defines the major criteria for the quality of work life and examines the interrelationships and conflict among them. Two such criteria are future opportunity for continued growth and security, and the social relevance of work life.

L.K. Waters, Darrell Roach, and Nick Batlis, "Organizational Climate Dimensions and Job-Related Attitudes," *Personnel Psychology*, Vol. 27, Autumn 1974, 465-476.

The purpose of this study was to factor analyze 22 organization climate scales and to relate these dimensions found in the factor analysis to subjective reports of satisfaction, involvement, intrinsic motivation, effort, and performance. Respondents were 105 employees of seven radio and TV stations. The most pronounced finding was that Factor V (Management and Peer Support or Employee Centered Orientation) was important to almost all of the job-related attitude areas.

Peter Weissenberg and Michael J. Kavanaugh, "The Independence of Initiating Structure and Consideration: A Review of the Evidence," *Personnel Psychology*, Vol. 25, Spring 1972, 119-130.

A review of 72 studies exploring the relationship between Consideration and Initiating Structure casts doubt on the notion that these two dimensions of leadership behavior are in fact independent: "The most important conclusion of this review is that the two leadership dimensions of C and S are not always empirically independent as stated and implied in various research studies and management training programs."

Paul F. Wernimount and Susan Fitzpatrick, "The Meaning of Money," *Journal of Applied Psychology*, Vol. 56, June 1972, 218-226.

An explanatory study to determine whether groups of persons who are distinguishable on the basis of biography differ in the meaning they attach to money. Values about money were measured via a modified semantic differential in 11 different groups, including hard-core trainees, employed persons, and college students. Results indicate that there are a variety of such differences and that these differences may be modified by work experience, sex, and socioeconomic level.

J. Kenneth White and Robert A. Ruh, "Effects of Personal Values on the Relationship Between Participation and Job Attitudes," *Administrative Science Quarterly*, Vol. 18, December 1973, 506-514.

The moderating effects of individual values on the relationships between participation in decision making and job attitudes were investigated for a sample of 2755 employees from six manufacturing organizations. Correlations found between participation in decision making and job attitudes were consistently positive for both the total sample and the subgroups. No support was obtained for the hypothesized moderating effects of values.

J.C. Wofford, "The Motivational Bases of Job Satisfaction and Job Performance," *Personnel Psychology*, Vol. 24, Autumn 1971, 501-518.

Nine hypotheses were tested relating to the general formulation that job satisfaction is a function of the strength of a person's needs and the extent to which these needs are fulfilled. Approximately 200 non-managerial personnel responded to questionnaires about job satisfaction, need satisfaction, and expectation (does employee expect job performance to result in need fulfillment?). Support was found for the expectancy theory of job satisfaction and job performance.

Joseph Zacker and Morton Bard, "Effects of Conflict Management Training on Police Performance," *Journal of Applied Psychology*, Vol. 58, April 1974, 202-208.

The performance of patrolmen in three matched public housing projects was compared on a number of different criteria. Patrolmen in one project received special affective-experiential training; patrolmen in the second project received special cognitive training; the patrolmen in the third project received no special training. Affective-experientially trained officers performed significantly best of the three groups.

BOOKS

Chris Argyris, *Management and Organizational Development: The Path from xa to yb.* New York: McGraw-Hill, 1971.

Several case histories are presented illustrating the difficulties and frustrations found in moving a company from a Theory X (Pattern A) style of management to one of Theory Y (Pattern B). Argyris indicates that the role of the behavioral science interventionist is difficult because of the slowness in which a work organization is able to make the transition toward the democratic-participative-consultative (Pattern B) style of management.

Chris Argyris, *Behind the Front Page: Organizational Self-Renewal in a Metropolitan Newspaper.* San Francisco: Jossey Bass, 1974.

A first-hand descriptive report of a three-year organization development (OD) program in a large newspaper that was skeptical about the program at the outset. Argyris carefully details the purposes of the program, the diagnostic and treatment stages, and the successes and failures of the program. Two data-filled appendices are provided for the research scholar. A final section of the book presents the author's insights into evaluating organizational self-renewal.

Frank Baker (Ed.), *Organizational Systems: General Systems Approach to Complex Organizations.* Homewood, Ill.: Richard D. Irwin, 1974.

A sociologically oriented anthology including: (1) overview of general systems theory, (2) general systems models of organizational structure and process, (3) environmental influence upon the differentiation and integration of organizational system, (4) systems theory and organizational effectiveness, and (5) evaluation of organizational systems.

Kenneth Benne, LeLand Bradford, Jack Gibb, and Ronald Lippitt, *The Laboratory Method of Learning and Changing: Theory and Applications.* Fairfax, Virginia: NTL Learning Resources Corporation, 1975.

In addition to the authors' own writings, other specialists in the field contribute to this volume attempting to answer the question: what is laboratory method? Its five-part organization is (1) Laboratory Method: Definition and Review, (2) Conceptual and Methodological Perspectives, (3) Applications to Persons and Groups, (4) Applications to Larger Social Systems, (5) Issues of Professionalization and Quality Control.

Elmer H. Burack, *Organization Analysis: Theory and Applications.* Hinsdale, Ill.: The Dryden Press 1975.

A research oriented, theory laden text that attempts to point the reader toward application of the material presented. Part I examines environmental, structural and systems factors as the causal variables and suggests their impact on organizations. Part II analyzes behavioral variables such as motivation and leadership as major determinants of organizational activity and performance. Part III brings to bear the influence of environmental and individual factors upon applications such as human resource planning and organizational change.

Edward L. Deci, *Intrinsic Motivation.* New York: Plenum, 1975.

An important reference source for researchers and advanced practitioners, Deci's book maps the genesis, structure, and functions of intrinsically motivated behavior. Among the major issues addressed are (1) How are behaviors motivated intrinsically? (2) How are they affected by rewards and punishments? (3) How do changes in intrinsic motivation relate to changes in attitude? (4) How do people attribute motivation to each other?

Andrew J. DuBrin, *The Practice of Managerial Psychology: Concepts and Methods for Manager and Organization Development.* Elmsford, N.Y.: Pergamon Press, 1972.

An overview of the methods and techniques used by managerial psychologists in attempting to improve individual and organizational effectiveness. Among the interventions described are psychological evaluation, approaches to conflict resolution, and dealing with managerial obsolescence. A central theme of the book is that interventions by managerial psychologists can have helpful, harmful, or neutral consequences depending upon the conditions under which they are applied.

Andrew J. DuBrin, *Fundamentals of Organizational Behavior: An Applied Perspective.* Elmsford, N.Y.: Pergamon Press, 1974.

Emphasizes the application of behavioral science information to improve individual and organizational effectiveness. Presents for the first time in a management text entire chapters on political maneuvering ("office politics") and the stresses faced by managerial and professional personnel. Another major emphasis is information about human behavior as it applies to the "knowledge worker" — managerial, professional, technical, and sales personnel.

Andrew J. DuBrin, *Managerial Deviance: How to Deal With Problem People in Key Jobs.* New York: Mason/Charter Publishers, 1976.

A descriptive and prescriptive approach to deviant behavior in management, defined as "maladaptive behavior in a managerial level worker stemming from a personality, character, or value defect that has an adverse impact upon the organization, both in terms of job performance and/or morale." A behavior modification, coaching oriented approach is prescribed for deviants, including alcoholics, drug abusers, pathological liars, con men and women, compulsive gamblers, and abdicators of authority.

Alan C. Filley, *Interpersonal Conflict Resolution.* Glenview, Ill.: Scott, Foresman, 1975.

The author deals with the sources of interpersonal conflict and the ways in which such conflict may be resolved so that the parties involved achieve a mutually beneficial solution. Particular emphasis is placed on the problem-solving techniques of consensus and the Integrative Decision Method as an alternative to more conventional methods of conflict resolution. The methods are said to be applicable to interpersonal conflict in work and family units.

Edwin A. Fleishman and Alan R. Bass (Eds.), *Studies in Personnel and Industrial Psychology*, Third edition. Homewood, Ill.: The Dorsey Press, 1973.
　　A collection of important articles in its field, they comprise a balanced coverage of topics in industrial and organizational psychology. Among these are organization development, work motivation, employing the hard-core culturally disadvantaged, performance appraisal, engineering psychology, and consumer psychology.

Wendell L. French and Cecil H. Bell, Jr., *Organization Development: Behavioral Science Interventions for Organization Improvement.* Englewood Cliffs, N.J.: Prentice-Hall, 1973.
　　A brief text devoted exclusively to organization development, this book presents some basic facts for the practitioner. Among its features are (1) tables for making diagnoses of organization problems, (2) a classification of team building activities and, (3) a chapter on organic-systems models and contingency theory. Very little supporting research is presented and most topics are briefly treated.

James L. Gibson, John M. Ivancevich, and James H. Donnelly, Jr., *Organizations: Structure, Processes, Behavior.* Dallas, Texas: Business Publications, Inc., 1973.
　　A heavily research oriented, detailed and comprehensive review of the literature style text on organization theory. Two relatively unique features of the book are complete chapters on organizational effectiveness and situational organization design. A five-part presentation includes Structure of Organizations, Processes Within Organizations, Behavior Within Organizations, The Climate and Development of Organizations, and Application of Concepts.

Robert T. Golembiewski and Arthur Blumberg (Eds.), *Sensitivity Training and the Laboratory Approach: Readings about Concepts and Applications.* Itasca, Ill.: F.E. Peacock Publishers, 1970.
　　A book of readings about the T-group integrated under the

following headings: (1) What is a T-group? (2) What happens in a T-group? (3) What concerns are there about T-groups? (4) Where can T-group dynamics be used? (5) How can T-group dynamics be studied? Four to 10 classical articles are found under each section. A précis of each article is presented along with commentary by the authors.

Robert T. Golembiewski, *Renewing Organizations: The Laboratory Approach to Planned Change.* Itasca, Ill.: F.E. Peacock Publishers, 1972.

A widely quoted book about the laboratory (basically T-group) approach to planned organizational change, yet some of its information requires updating. The author observes that the success of the laboratory approach depends upon the acceptance of values such as a collaborative concept of authority, mutual belonging relationships, and authenticity in interpersonal relationships.

David R. Hampton, Charles E. Summer, and Ross Webber, *Organizational Behavior and the Practice of Management* (revised). Glenview, Ill.: Scott, Foresman, 1973.

A 939-page combination of text, cases, and mostly readings, this book is a standard reference work in its field. Conventional topics in organizational behavior are included along with material on group decision making, and methods for using and containing conflict in organizations.

Frank A. Heller, *Managerial Decision Making: A Study of Leadership Styles and Power Sharing Among Senior Managers.* New York: Harper & Row (A Tavistock Title), 1972.

A study of various styles of decision making and factors affecting them, it is geared toward the specialist in organizational behavior. Styles studied are: (1) unilateral, (2) leader makes independent decision but communicates details to subordinates, (3) leader consults subordinates first, but makes final decision on own, (4) decision emerges on the basis of joint discussion with subordinates, (5) decision is delegated to subordinates. A conclusion is reached that senior managers do not use any single style indiscriminately.

James G. Hunt and Lars L. Larson (Eds.), *Contingency Approaches to Leadership.* Carbondale, Ill.: Southern Illinois Press, 1974.

Six papers are presented stemming from a leadership symposium at Southern Illinois University. "Contingency approach" is a term used to include a wide range of studies, all designed to specify operationally the specific conditions under which a given kind of leadership will be preferable to another. Careful evaluations are provided of the path-goal theory of leadership effectiveness, and Fiedler's Contingency model.

Eugene E. Jennings, *Routes to the Executive Suite.* New York: McGraw-Hill, 1971.

Geared toward the person intent upon climbing the organizational ladder, the book presents a number of success strategies. Among them: (1) maintain the widest set of options, (2) observe the penalty of loss of career time, (3) become a crucial subordinate to a mobile superior, (4) look for increased exposure and visibility, (5) leave the company when it fits into your plans, (6) think of the corporation as a market. The author's underlying thesis is that the career-centered period has replaced the loyalty era.

Robert D. Joyce, *Encounters in Organizational Behavior: Problem Situations*, Elmsford, N.Y.: Pergamon Press, 1972.

A book of 54 cases and problem situations, with a high reader interest value, organized in sections: Communication and Productivity, Leadership Styles and Techniques, Problem Analysis and Decision Making, Acquiring and Keeping Talent, Achievement Growth and Recognition, Problems in Motivation, Personal Problems and Job Effectiveness, Individual Identity, Values and Ethics, Group Conflict and Team Development, and Technology and the Future.

H.G. Kaufman, *Obsolescence and Professional Career Development.* New York: Amacom, a division of American Management Association, 1974.

In a text directed primarily toward the practicing manager, the author has combined empirical research with job experience to write a first book devoted exclusively to the problems of managerial and professional obsolescence. The principal causes of obsolescence are cited as the knowledge revolution, inappropriate personal characteristics, and factors related to the work environment and organizational climate. Among the prescriptions offered for obsolescence are stimulating entry jobs, increasing decision-making responsibility, and periodic changes in job assignments.

Emanuel Kay, *The Crisis in Middle Management.* New York: Amacom, a division of the American Management Association, 1974.

A non-technical presentation by the author identifies the stresses faced by middle managers and suggests some coping mechanisms. Stresses include inequitable salary, job insecurity, lack of authority, career inflexibility, and obsolescence. In addition to a loss in status in recent years, these forces have lowered the job satisfaction of middle managers. Coping mechanisms include stagnation (no solution), changing jobs, changing careers, finding fulfillment off-the-job, and education.

Shigeru Kobayashi, *Creative Management.* New York: American Management Association, 1971.

A successful Japanese industrialist (now Managing Director of Sony Corporation) took steps to revitalize an ailing plant. Personal and autobiographical rather than research oriented in tone, this book emphasizes the point that people work better when they feel they are important. Among his innovations was to eliminate cafeteria attendants and time clocks. Although a loose informal arrangement, the organizational design used in the revitalized plant was a combination of interlocking cells and work teams. The book supports the behavioral humanist point of view popular in the United States.

David A. Kolb, Irwin M. Rubin, and James M. McIntyre, *Organizational Psychology: An Experiential Approach.* Englewood Cliffs, N.J.: Prentice-Hall, 1971.

A first in its field, this text both describes key concepts in organizational psychology and provides a number of experience based learning exercises. Representative units include learning and problem solving, decision making, dynamics of achievement motivation, leadership, and interpersonal communication. A companion book of readings helps provide necessary underlying information.

Elliott A. Krause, *The Sociology of Occupations.* Boston: Little, Brown, 1971.

A scholarly, comprehensive text which examines the world of work from a variety of perspectives — historical, biological, division of labor by structure and function, and conflicts of interest that arise from a division of labor. Krause examines a number of fields from these four perspectives including the health field, the legal profession, the military, business and industry, education and public service.

James B. Lau, *Behavior in Organizations: An Experiential Approach.*
   Homewood, Ill.: Richard D. Irwin, 1975.

A learning by doing approach, this book features involvement
exercises ("experiential learning") which emphasize the process of
interaction and thinking rather than conventional content learning.
The goal of the text is to help to improve human understanding and
to learn ways to change the behavior of oneself and others. Students
are prepared for involvement by beginning with more structured, less
personal exercises that are readily recognized as relevant to human
effectiveness in a work environment. As the course progresses, the
material becomes more personal. A sampling of organizational theory
is integrated into the text.

D.J.   Lawler, *Effective Management: A Social Psychological
   Approach.* Englewood Cliffs, N.J.: Prentice-Hall, 1972.

A systematic attempt to apply social psychological research to
the daily problems of supervision and management. Its five parts are
Social Behavior, Harmony Among Groups, Group Dynamics, Leadership, and the Science of Organizational Behavior. Included in the
book is a discussion of the author's personal opinions on effective
management.

Edward E. Lawler, III, *Pay and Organizational Effectiveness: A
   Psychological View.* New York: McGraw-Hill, 1971.

A major contribution to understanding the subtle and complex
relationships between pay and performance, the author concludes
". . . under certain conditions pay can be used to motivate good
performance . . . but is easier said than done." Lawler exhaustively
reviews the research literature (most of it conducted by himself and
his associates) that would help bridge the gap between management
information about wage and salary administration and industrial
psychology. Lawler advocates more participative methods and less
secrecy about pay.

Edward E. Lawler, III, *Motivation in Work Organizations.* Monterey,
   California: Brooks/Cole, 1973.

A synthesis of the current status in the field of work motivation
and satisfaction with an emphasis upon the integration of expectancy
theory with other contemporary approaches. The author carefully
evaluates the evidence for the various theories presented and points
to gaps in the literature. Topics given extensive coverage include
Lawler's own expectancy model, a review of the research history and

theories of job satisfaction, attempts by organizations to control turnover, and the relationship between extrinsic rewards and job performance. A central thesis to Lawler's thinking is that incentives should be tied directly to performance.

Harold J. Leavitt, *Managerial Psychology*, Third edition. Chicago: The University of Chicago Press, 1972.

A standard in its field, this book translates psychological research and theory into an informal and useable package for managers and students. Part One deals with the psychology of individuals, including motivation, perception, problem solving, and individual differences. Part Two deals with superior-subordinate-relationships with an emphasis upon the influence process. Part Three deals with small group behavior including information flow and manager development. Part Four is about total organizations, including structure, decision making and technology, and relationship with the external environment.

Harold J. Leavitt and Louis R. Pondy (Eds.), *Readings in Managerial Psychology*, *Second edition*. Chicago: University of Chicago Press, 1974.

A collection of 46 leading articles in organizational behavior, this book samples literature from a variety of disciplines including sociology, political science, and economics as well as psychology. To achieve balance, the authors have in several places selected articles which present opposing points of view, such as the need for authenticity in communications versus political maneuvering.

Harry Levinson, Janice Molinari, and Andrew G. Spohn. *Organizational Diagnosis*. Cambridge, Massachusetts: Harvard University Press, 1972.

The authors contend that adequate diagnosis must precede treatment efforts in organization development intervention. As such, a manual for the practitioner of organizational diagnosis is presented. Detailed instructions are presented on how to proceed in general, followed by a business case. Following his professional orientation, the author gives a psychoanalytic interpretation to a number of organizational situations.

Alan McLean (Ed.), *Occupational Stress*. Springfield, Ill.: Charles C Thomas, 1974.

Psychiatrist McLean, along with eight contributors, presents a range of concepts about occupational stress. Based upon the Occupational Mental Health Conference — whose purpose was to gain a greater understanding of occupational stress — this book offers theoretical concepts, research results, and various specific suggestions for coping with stress-related problems. Much of the information presented is not available in other sources.

John R. Maher (Ed.), *New Perspectives in Job Enrichment.* New York: Van Nostrand Reinhold, 1971.

An anthology, this book works toward giving operational meaning to concepts of job enrichment — which is shown to have multiple meanings. Articles included range from the scientific and tentative to popular and dogmatic. Charles L. Hulin, one of the contributors, notes ". . . either positive or negative results may be expected from a program of job enrichment and the type of results depends to a great extent on the motivations of the work force involved (among other things)."

Norman R.F. Maier, *Problem Solving and Creativity in Individuals and Groups.* Belmont, California: Brooks/Cole, 1970.

A valuable collection of studies on problem solving and creativity conducted by Maier and his associates, this book presents an underlying theory of problem solving and a group leader's guide to facilitate the problem solving process. An optimistic viewpoint is expressed about group problem solving and research buttressed findings are offered such as "Success in problem solving requires that effort be directed to overcoming *surmountable* obstacles."

Newton Marguilies and John Wallace, *Organization Change: Techniques and Applications.* Glenview, Ill.: Scott, Foresman, 1973.

Third in a series of OD paperbacks published by Scott, Foresman, this book provides a first-hand look at the theory and practice of a number of techniques. Among the many topics covered in the 10 chapters are a theory of organizational change, and specific OD techniques, including team building, behavior modification and T-groups. A separate discussion of role playing as an organization change technique is also included.

Alfred J. Marrow (Ed.), *The Failure of Success.* New York: American Management Association, 1972.

A major thesis of this collection of readings is that American industry faces many problems despite its enviable record of success.

It is anticipated that the application of behavioral science knowledge will alleviate such problems. Among the potential areas of contribution by behavioral scientists described are assessment centers, action research, job enrichment, participative management, and the study of job related stress.

Lyman W. Porter, Edward E. Lawler, III, and Richard J. Hackman, *Behavior in Organizations.* New York: McGraw-Hill, 1975.

An advanced, research oriented text that is much more descriptive than prescriptive. The authors use a five part organization: (1) Individuals and organizations are considered separately and then in terms of their interaction, (2) Individual-organizational relationships in terms of problems such as training and development, (3) Job design and its effect upon behavior, (4) Consequences of evaluating and rewarding work effectiveness, (5) Methods of organization change.

William J. Reddin, *Effective Management by Objectives: The 3-D Method of MBO.* New York: McGraw-Hill, 1971.

An important book about the implementation of an MBO system with an emphasis upon the manager achieving the output requirements of his or her position. Reddin's objective is ". . . to teach in a way that is hoped to be interesting how to develop job effectiveness descriptions, how to obtain commitment to them, and how to breathe life into them so a true effective MBO is produced." His objectives are well met.

Edgar J. Schein, *Organizational Psychology*, Second edition. Englewood Cliffs, New Jersey: Prentice-Hall, 1972.

A minor updating of this classic, brief, primer of organizational psychology. The author concentrates upon basic processes, rather than presenting extensive reviews of empirical research. Among the basic topics covered are the nature of organizations, training, group relationships, and the organization and its environment.

Fremont A. Shull, Jr., Andrew L. Delbecq, and L.L. Cummings, *Organizational Decision Making.* New York: Mc-Graw Hill, 1970.

A text intended for the social or behavioral scientist, it explores the complex process of choosing among alternatives in field settings. A variety of psychological, sociological, statistical, and structural concepts are used to explore decision making. Key aspects of the book include a decision making model, a comprehensive bibliography, and a multidisciplinary analysis of most issues. Decision making is shown to be influenced by variables of the past, present, and future.

Fred I. Steele, *Physical Setting and Organizational Development.* Reading, Mass.: Addison-Wesley, 1973.

An analysis of the relationship of the organization to its physical environment, that uses a "socio-physical approach to organizational development." The author provides a framework for analyzing the transactions that go on between a person and the environment. Six dimensions are used for this purpose: Security and Shelter, Social Contact, Symbolic Identification (messages in settings which tell what a person, group, or organization is like), Task Instrumentality, Pleasure, and Growth. In addition, the author provides a means whereby individuals and organizations can optimize the full potential of their physical settings.

Arthur L. Stinchcombe, *Creating Efficient Industrial Administration.* New York and London: Academic Press, 1974.

Challenging some of the most widely held theories of economic development — particularly those of David McClelland — the author develops his own theory which considers the social conditions for efficient administration. Cross cultural studies of steel plants are used to help arrive at a major conclusion that conditions of organizational structure are infinitely more important than cultural values or personal motivations.

Ralph M. Stogdill, *Handbook of Leadership: A Survey of Theory and Research.* New York: The Free Press, a division of Macmillan Publishing Company, 1974.

A compendious volume reflecting six years of research by the author of all known empirical studies on leadership behavior and its effects. Information in the volume is organized into 41 chapters and eight sections: Leadership Theory; Leader Personality and Behavior; Leadership Stability and Change; Emergence of the Leadership Role; Leadership and Social Power; Leader-Follower Interactions; Leadership and Group Performance; Conclusions. Stogdill's major conclusion is that structuring expectations is the central factor in leadership and this fact should be integrated into training approaches.

James C. Taylor, *Technology and Planned Organizational Change,* Ann Arbor, Michigan: Institute for Social Research, 1971.

A study testing several hypotheses about the effects of automation on job-related behaviors in work groups. It describes findings in support of the hypothesis that the state of automation is associated with a more autonomous work group structure at lower levels in industrial organizations. The monograph includes a literature review, a model of technological effects, a measure of sophistication of technology, and some longitudinal survey data from two organizations.

Linda King Taylor, *Not For Bread Alone: An Appreciation of Job Enrichment.* London: Business Books Limited, 1972.

Consisting of two theoretical sections on motivation, eight case studies, followed by five brief examples, and a wide ranging bibliography, this book contains information not seen elsewhere. A unifying theme is that job enrichment leads to increased job satisfaction, job motivation, and productivity. A variety of jobs are used for enrichment examples, including secretaries, refinery operators, and skilled toolmakers. Situations described include the Swedish State Power Board and Volkswagen.

Victor H. Vroom and Phillip W. Yetton, *Leadership and Decision Making.* Pittsburg, Pa.: University of Pittsburgh Press, 1973.

An advanced book which presents the results of a program of research begun in 1968 and still in process at the time of its writing. Central to the research is a normative model including these features: (1) The central dimension of leadership is participative decision making (PDM), (2) Situational determinants of leadership processes are crucial, (3) Increased PDM will not inevitably lead to increased organizational effectiveness — a mediator is the nature of the decision problem and the characteristics of the subordinates. Although esoteric, this book has been proclaimed as a major contribution to the study of leadership.

Robert E.C. Wegner and Leonard Sayles, *Cases in Organizational and Administrative Behavior.* Englewood Cliffs, N.J.: Prentice-Hall, 1972.

A book of 32 cases illustrative of a wide range of human behavior relevant to many concepts in organizational behavior, including leadership and supervision, small group behavior, role prescription, integration, and organizational change. The cases presented vary in complexity and locale — only nine of the cases are from manufacturing settings. Wegner and Sayles present a seven-paragraph guide to the analysis of cases.

Work in America: Report of a Special Task Force to the Secretary of Health, Education and Welfare. Cambridge, Massachusetts: The MIT Press, 1973.

A report prepared at the request of then HEW Secretary Elliot L. Richardson, for a wide ranging study of the institution of work and its implication for health, education, and welfare. In summary, "The redesign of jobs is the keystone of this report. Not only does it hold out some promise to decrease mental and physical health costs, increase productivity and improve the quality of life for millions of Americans at all occupational levels, it would give, for the first time, a voice to many workers in an important decision-making process."

Sheldon Zedeck and Milton Blood, *Foundations of Behavioral Science Research in Organizations.* Monterey, California: Brooks/Cole, 1974.

An advanced treatment, the book focuses upon the techniques and strategies by which information about people at work is sought. Among the diverse topics covered are scientific method, laboratory and field studies, measures of organizational effectiveness, job design and analysis, a statistical discussion of criteria, selection and place-ment, training, and maintaining the organization. In general, the book is a methods oriented approach to industrial and organizational psychology.